# Harvests Under Fire

# Harvests Under Fire

## Regional Co-operation
## for Food Security in
## Southern Africa

### CAROL B. THOMPSON

**Zed Books**
London and New Jersey

*Harvests Under Fire* was first published by
Zed Books Ltd, 57 Caledonian Road, London, N1 9BU, UK, and
165 First Avenue, Atlantic Highlands, New Jersey 07716, USA.

Cover design by Andrew Corbett.
Typeset by Opus 43, Cumbria.
Printed and bound in the United Kingdom
at Biddles Ltd, Guildford and King's Lynn.

A catalogue record for this book
is available from the British Library

ISBN 1-85649-016-5 (hb)
ISBN 1-85649-017-3 (pb)

The author and publishers would like to acknowledge the kindess of
Penguin Books in allowing them to make use of a map prepared for
*Apartheid's Second Front* by Joseph Hanlon (Penguin, 1986).

*To Bud, who has shared every struggle:*
*Crying in anger over the killings by apartheid*
*Organising to end US support of apartheid aggression*
*Learning more from villagers than in academe*
*Loving and laughing with Southern Africans as they turn*
*their visions into reality.*

# Contents

# Tables

# Acknowledgements

This book would not have been possible without the insight, generosity, and patience of many Southern Africans. Having studied SADCC (Southern African Development Coordination Conference) since its inception in 1980, I have benefited greatly from long discussions and interviews with SADCC officials, from technicians to government ministers. They patiently answered fumbling questions, pointed out new areas for enquiry and explained apparent contradictions. Those in the government of Zimbabwe, the coordinator for food security for SADCC, were particularly helpful, even while fully involved in new regional coordination of such details as growing new hybrids, to major policy changes, such as public-private relations for agricultural marketing.

Colleagues at the University of Zimbabwe, the Zimbabwe Institute for Development Studies, the University of Eduardo Mondlane, Mozambique, the University of Dar es Salaam, Tanzania and the University of Zambia criticised tentative hypotheses and first explanations. Their incisive analyses raised new questions and corrected conclusions. Investigative reporters in Zimbabwe and Mozambique (AIM, the Herald, ZIANA, AFP and AfriqueAsie) shared data, interviews and understanding as we followed SADCC from conference to conference, debating the latest innovation or hesitation of this new regional entity.

Financial support for over a year came from the Fulbright Senior Research programme; we disagree about attempts by the Reagan Administration to curtail freedom of speech of grant recipients, and this book demonstrates the importance of the first amendment right. The University of Zimbabwe extended generous hospitality to me as a research associate, offering support for all phases of the study, without which this work could not have been completed.

ZIMOFA (Zimbabwe-Mozambique Friendship Association) officials, who have expanded the family support from Zimbabwean villages to Mozambican displaced persons into a nation-wide organisation, also took time to help this North American understand the suffering and the hope. They made it possible for me to visit camps for displaced persons within Mozambique, to see first-hand the devastation wrecked on human life by apartheid aggression. Oxfam America facilitated visits to many Zimbabwean villages over two years. Such grass-roots understanding is vital to putting such a 'macro' project as SADCC in perspective.

Colleagues in the Association of Concerned Africa Scholars not only critically reviewed the analysis of relations between the United States and SADCC, but also shared the goal of activist scholarship. One of the major burdens on Southern Africa in the 1980s was the US policy of 'constructive engagement' with apartheid; only a 'people's divestment' by churches, universities and labour unions of funds from US corporations in South Africa induced the US Congress to pass the 1986 (partial) sanctions bill over a presidential veto. This study is the result of lessons learned from ACAS colleagues in trying to change US foreign policy towards Southern Africa. On a grand scale, activist scholars have failed miserably, but if we can reduce by one day US support of apartheid – either in its present or future forms – we will have succeeded in lessening some of the burden on Southern Africa.

It is impossible to investigate such a dynamic interaction as SADCC without making errors, and they remain fully mine. Neither SADCC itself, nor Southern African colleagues, will agree fully with the critique or conclusions. As the region moves tentatively towards post-apartheid, the debates will correct the errors and complete the omissions.

Bud Day has been very much part of this book – from intense intellectual discussions to full-time encouragement. As a sanitary engineer working with rural latrine and water supply projects, he was invaluable in raising basic issues – how the individual peasant is aided or ignored by SADCC. As important, he was out there organising against US patronage of apartheid, linking it with racism at home and aggression abroad (from Angola to Iraq), while I was often buried in notes and drafts.

My only hope is that in the not-so-distant future Southern Africans will send foreign assistance to the US to teach us how to overcome racism and to cooperate with, not dominate, our neighbours.

# Abbreviations

| | |
|---|---|
| AAC | Anglo-American Corporation |
| ACP | African-Caribbean-Pacific |
| ADMARC | Agricultural Development and Marketing Corporation |
| AECI | African Explosives and Chemical Industries |
| ALDEP | Arable Land Development Programme |
| ANC | African National Congress |
| ARDA | Agricultural Rural Development Authority |
| Armscor | Armaments Corporation of South Africa |
| ASEAN | Association of South East Asian Nations |
| CACM | Central American Common Market |
| CAIL | Limpopo Agro-Industrial Complex |
| CIA | Central Intelligence Agency |
| CIS | Council for Inter-American Studies |
| CMEA | Council for Mutual Economic Assistance |
| COMECON | *see* CMEA |
| CONSAS | Constellation of Southern African States |
| CTC | Consultative Technical Committee |
| DMI | Directorate of Military Intelligence |
| ECA | Economic Commission for Africa |
| ECF | Export Credit Facility |
| ECOWAS | Economic Community of West African States |
| EEC | European Economic Community |
| ESCOM | Electricity Supply Commission |
| FAO | Food and Agriculture Organisation |
| FSTAU | Food Security Technical and Administrative Unit |
| GATT | General Agreement on Trade and Tariffs |
| GDP | Gross Domestic Product |
| GDR | German Democratic Republic |
| GMB | Grain Marketing Board |
| GNP | Gross National Product |
| IBPGR | International Board for Plant Genetics Research |
| ICRISAT | International Centre for Research on Agriculture in Semi-Arid Tropics |

| IFF | International Freedom Foundation |
|---|---|
| IITA | International Institute for Tropical Agriculture |
| IMF | International Monetary Fund |
| JMC | Joint Military Command |
| LAFTA | Latin American Free Trade Area |
| LDC | Less Developed Country |
| MPLA | Popular Movement for the Liberation of Mozambique |
| NAM | Non-Aligned Movement |
| NGO | Non-Governmental Organisation |
| NIS | National Intelligence Service |
| NMC | National Maize Corporation |
| NSDD | National Security Decision Directive |
| NSMS | National Security Management System |
| OAU | Organisation for African Unity |
| OECD | Organisation for Economic Co-operation and Development |
| PAC | Pan Africanist Congress |
| PFIAU | Post Production Food Industry Advisory Unit |
| PLO | Palestine Liberation Organisation |
| PTA | Preferential Trade Agreement |
| SACCAR | Southern African Centre for Co-operation in Agriculture |
| SACU | Southern African Customs Union |
| SADCC | Southern African Development Coordination Conference |
| SARCUSS | Southern African Regional Commission for the Conservation of Soil |
| SATCC | Southern African Transport and Communications Commission |
| SSC | State Security Council |
| SWAPO | South West Africa People's Organisation |
| TNC | Transnational Corporation |
| UN | United Nations |
| UNCTAD | United Nations Conference for Trade and Development |
| UNICEF | United Nations Children's Fund |
| UNIDO | United Nations Industrial Development Organisation |
| US | United States |
| USAID | United States Agency for International Development |
| USDA | United States Department of Agriculture |
| WACL | World Anti-Communist League |
| WNLA | Witwatersrand Native Labour Association |
| ZACPRO2 | Regional Legislation for Management of the Zambezi |
| ZACPRO5 | Integrated Water Management Plan for the Zambezi Basin |
| Zimphos | Zimbabwe Phosphate Industries |

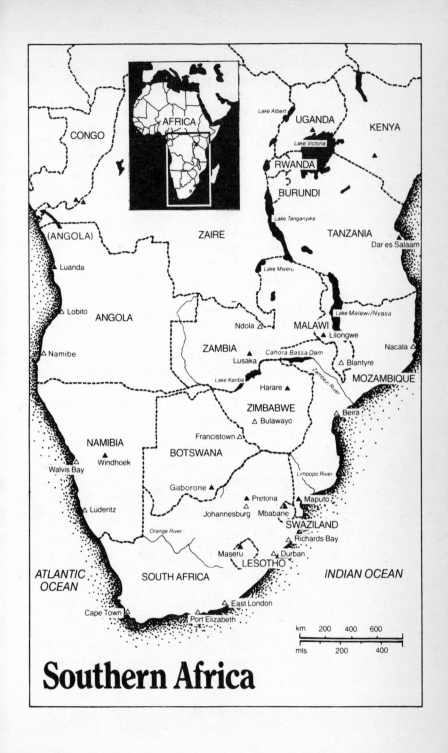

# Southern Africa

# Preface

When we were in charge during the riots, we pulled down the national flag
outside the supermarket. In its place we hoisted our own flag. It symbolised
victory. Do you know what it was? It was an empty polythene bag of
maize meal.
Unemployed Youth in Zambia
April, 1986

By raising their own new flag, the youth in Zambia ardently displayed
the fundamental correlation between economic and political viability.
They were protesting against the 120 percent increase in the price of
maize meal, a measure imposed by the International Monetary Fund's
requirement to cut subsidies. With the protesters' 'victory,' the government reinstated the food subsidies, acknowledging the people's appeal
for their right to basic subsistence.

At the same time, in war-torn areas of the region in Angola and Mozambique, a child was dying of malnutrition every four minutes. Such
innocent and frequent casualties stress the urgency to analyse and
understand the forces which produced this human tragedy–and may
continue to cause suffering for years to come. By beginning with the
unemployed youth who cannot afford food and with the starving child,
this study is not so much about agriculture or economics as it is about
the politics of food production and distribution. We live in a food surplus
world; no one needs to starve. The reason they do is not necessarily by
neglect of governments or ignorance of the best technologies, but more
the result of overt policies, of long-range planning.

According to the United Nations Children's Fund (UNICEF), the most
serious danger to the children of Southern Africa has been apartheid
South Africa. In addition to the detention, torture and murder of children
inside South Africa, aggression by that regime against its neighbours has
perpetuated several wars for well over a decade.

A longer-term danger to the children is the policies of those extending
aid and finance to the region. Obviously, international donors are vital
in the short run, but much documentation now demonstrates they are a
menace in the long run, advocating policies for agricultural production

1

which are inappropriate to the climate – natural or political – of Southern Africa. The abolition of apartheid is indeed a necessary step to put out the fires burning the crops in the fields. However, many international agencies providing aid and loans are already pursuing policies to cultivate production to serve their own interests, minimising the priorities of Southern Africans. This fire, though figurative, is unrelenting, and perhaps more devastating.

The bright side of the future lies with the people of Southern Africa who are working together to reduce the suffering, to implement programmes which produce more food and ensure its more equitable distribution. Collectively and individually, they are finding answers to the crises, sometimes in spite of government negligence, but often with government support. Forming a regional economic organisation to discuss common problems and to co-ordinate research, the governments are training men and women alike in agriculture and removing barriers – such as poor roads, inadequate seeds and water – to increased agricultural production. This study analyses the objectives and performance of the Southern African Development Coordination Conference (SADCC)[1] from the perspective of agricultural production. Unique on the African continent and only eleven years old, it has already offered lessons for both developed and developing countries in regional co-ordination and planned agricultural production.

Not a descriptive overview of all SADCC sectors,[2] this analysis explicitly focuses on the food and agriculture sector to address four main themes. As an economic necessity, food – its pattern of production and distribution – reveals much about economic and political power relations. First, in Southern Africa, food has been used as a weapon. Why? Agricultural extension workers and food aid trucks have been attacked more than the army. What are the goals in a war that targets unarmed civilians, not enemy forces?

Second, increasing food production has also become the major impetus for regional co-ordination, and more successfully than anywhere else in the developing world. Why? What has food to do with regional co-operation? Southern African nations have acted on the principle that together they can realise more of the region's potential to be a major food producer than they can separately. The efforts for regional co-operation are small, but serious, steps beyond the confines of narrow nationalism. The region was defined economically and politically by European powers under colonialism; now Southern Africans are redefining it in their own terms.

Third, food security, for the individual and the nation, is a basic issue of development. (In SADCC, food security is defined as regional self-sufficiency in grain production and availability of food for each household.[3]) How do the agricultural policies of the region promote development?

What kind of development and for whom? Even tentative answers to these questions bring the region directly in conflict with conventional development strategies, for they are challenging dominant theories of the market, of production for food security, and most important, of the role of the state.

SADCC argues that an input here (chemical pesticides) or a policy change there (privatisation of marketing boards) will not alleviate agricultural crises, for the shortfalls and starvation are endemic to a system established by colonialism and perpetuated by powerful interests inside and outside the region. Nothing short of restructuring their economies in regional cooperation will prevent the raising of more 'maize bag flags' by hungry people who have been pushed to the limit.

Fourth, food is a major trading commodity, made available to, or withheld from, food deficit countries according to the political preferences of the donors. This study will focus on the United States (US), the major food aid donor to the region, analysing the results and assessing the future of US policy. The US programme for 'post-apartheid' Southern Africa is already operative, and many Southern Africans do not like the field plans. One SADCC goal is to restructure the regional economy away from South African dominance, even of a free South Africa. For over 100 years Southern Africans worked for the benefit of colonial powers, with African natural resources provisioning the industries and homes in Europe and more recently, North America and Japan. They will not wait another 100 years to restructure their economies for their own benefit, in spite of the current repeated sabotage by apartheid South Africa and the more subtle dislocation by the donors. The peoples of Southern Africa are putting out the fires – actual and figurative – which are destroying their crops; they are beginning to bring in the harvests.

# Notes

1   SADCC members are Angola, Botswana, Lesotho, Malawi, Mozambique, Namibia, Swaziland, Tanzania, Zambia, Zimbabwe. Because this analysis centres on SADCC agriculture in the 1980s, it does not include Namibia, which joined after independence in 1990.

2   For excellent overviews, refer to : Arne Tostensen *Dependence and Collective Self-Reliance in Southern Africa.* Research Report No. 62. Uppsala: The Scandinavian Institute for African Studies, 1982; Jens Haarlov. *Regional Cooperation in Southern Africa: Central Elements of the SADCC Venture.* CDR Research Report No. 14. Copenhagen: Centre for Development Research, 1988; Margaret C. Lee. *SADCC—The Political Economy of Development in*

*Southern Africa*. Nashville: Winston-Derek Publishers, 1989; Joseph Hanlon. *SADCC in the 1990s – Development on the Frontline*. Special Report No. 1158. London: The Economist Intelligence Unit, 1989.
3 Food security was defined by the Committee on World Food Security of the Food and Agriculture Organisation (FAO) in 1983: "Food security should have three specific aims, namely ensuring production of adequate food supplies; maximising stability in the flow of supplies; and securing access to available supplies on the part of those who need them." Food and Agriculture Organisation, Council. *Report of the Eighth Session of the Committee on World Food Security,* CL 83/10, Rome (13-20 April 1983): 6.

# 1.

# From Harvests to Hunger in Southern Africa

After a decade, the Southern African Development Co-ordination Conference (SADCC) is celebrating its survival. At its inception in 1980, apartheid South Africa had other plans for the region: economic co-ordination for production and wealth in South Africa. The more crude expression of that plan, the Constellation of Southern African States (CONSAS), is defunct, but the idea continues to re-emerge under new guises as discussions about a free South Africa most often speak of reform, not transformation. In the meantime, SADCC, not South Africa, has written and implemented 20-year plans for co-ordination of transport and for other diverse projects such as a genebank for germ plasm and research for hybrid food crops. SADCC has opened new markets for its exports, while some have closed to South Africa: from apples to passion fruit and mangoes, Europeans became averse to eating politically questionable fruit from South Africa. Reversing 100 years of South African supervision, it is now SADCC which co-ordinates agricultural research for the region, providing, for example, improved strains of sorghum and millet to peasant farmers whom colonial regimes ignored or constrained.

By organising and hosting its own annual conferences to which interested overseas agencies and governments are invited, SADCC has attracted new attention to the tremendous potential of the region – from the East, the West and the non-aligned. More important, SADCC officials have spent a decade arguing with and adapting to each other over development methods and priorities. Still learning to think regionally, the lessons for the sovereign governments in fighting drought, world recession, and apartheid aggression have been poignant reminders of the goal.

SADCC's goals are at once modest and ambitious. As evident in the name, Southern Africans are not talking of regional integration, either on a Western or Eastern model, but of regional co-ordination which will evolve an African model. Yet this practical goal at once challenges both the history of the region and development theories and practices projected for the region by outsiders from both the West and the East. To understand the small steps, the reversals, and the real accomplishments, this study analyses SADCC – with a focus on the food and agriculture sector – in its historical and international economic-political contexts. In this way, one can begin to understand the contradictions and power struggles shaping the future of this potentially influential region.

First, SADCC simply conceptualises Southern Africa as a region and second, and more ambitiously, seeks to define and restructure that region. Most foreign scholars, newspersons, librarians, and government officials have been slow to acknowledge even the first modest proposal.[1] Scholarly analyses continue to abound on each country, e.g. Zambia or Tanzania, as if they were isolated entities and the regional context did not exist. The precarious settlement for independence in Namibia in late 1988 was heralded in both the Western and Eastern presses as an accomplishment of the Soviets, the Cubans and the Americans, not of the several African neighbours who had worked together long and hard for the sovereignty of Angola and majority rule in Namibia. Illustrative of the dominant ideology against which SADCC must work, who among the community of 'opinion leaders' acknowledges the region by the full capitalisation of 'Southern Africa'? One does not write of the 'caribbean' or of 'central America,' but in United Nations and government documents and in the Western press, the region remains 'southern Africa.' While many outsiders still look at Africa and see sub-national 'tribes,' SADCC is creating a region – not one which will replace sovereign states, but one which is altering their economic context.

Defining the region on their own terms will prove even more difficult. A leader in the formation of SADCC, Tanzania has for political and economic reasons linked up with Southern Africa, turning away from the British colonial vision of a greater East Africa. Zaire, however, has applied for membership to SADCC and been refused several times, even though historical mining ties connect Shaba province to the region. For political reasons SADCC has so far rejected this legacy; only major political changes in Zaire will change this situation. At the tenth anniversary of SADCC in 1990, Namibia joined as the tenth member; a free South Africa will be welcomed as a member, for representatives of the African National Congress (ANC) and Pan Africanist Congress (PAC) are already included in SADCC meetings and discussions.

In spite of these clear decisions and actions the United States (US) government has for ten years rejected SADCC's definition of itself. In major US government documents and in aid packages for the region, the US stubbornly continued to refer to 'southern Africa' as including Shaba province (strangely without the state of Zaire) and excluding Namibia as a future member.[2] More ominously, the US government refuses to recognize Angola and has financed the attempt to overthrow that independent government. The Soviet Union has accepted SADCC's definition of the region, but refused to attend its annual meetings for six years, arguing that they were not responsible for the problems engendered by colonialism. It remains only a hesitant participant in regional efforts.

The most ambitious and long-term goal of SADCC is to restructure the region; what exactly that means will be determined practically as the sovereign governments learn to co-operate and find new areas for co-ordination. Current SADCC programmes – illustrated in this study by the food and agriculture sector – show the strength and limitations of this goal. And powerful interests, inside and outside the region, will influence directions taken. SADCC is clear about what will not be perpetuated: subordination to South Africa, even a free South Africa, and perpetuation of the region's role in the world market as producers only of unprocessed minerals and agricultural commodities. These two concerns unite them ... and set them in opposition to dominant international economic interests.

Before analysing the current programmes and contradictions of SADCC, and the hope for the future, it is necessary to recall the colonial legacy which defines the starting point for SADCC, both in terms of regional interaction and in terms of development. The colonial background of Southern Africa restrains regional economic co-ordination and retards agricultural production and economic development.

One of the wealthiest regions in the world, Southern Africa is known for its vast mineral resources – gold, diamonds, titanium, chrome, platinum, copper. What is less realised is that commercialisation of the mines, with their ever greater demand for labour, first created a region out of the vast territory surrounded by the Indian, Southern and Atlantic Oceans. Workers came to the mines from as far away as Lake Tanganyika, over 2400 kilometres away. But the peasants did not come willingly; they preferred their small homesteads or cattle ranges. They came because they had to earn cash to pay head and hut taxes to the white colonial governments; they came because they had been pushed off their land on to sandy soil which could not sustain basic grains, only cassava. And they came because their cattle were stolen by white settlers who then congratulated themselves on the excellence of their new herds. This regionalisation, therefore, served only the white man's wealth, impoverishing the Africans.

Hostility among the European colonial powers resulted in the parcelling of the land, but the political balkanisation did not destroy the regional dominance of the mines, as all the economies (except Angola and Tanzania) were subordinated to mineral production and industrial development in South Africa (and to a lesser extent, Southern Rhodesia). However, it weakened the Africans. As each area gained political independence separately, they remained subordinate to South Africa economically.

During the independence struggle for Zimbabwe, the new states started to reformulate their region in their own way. Accepting a hundred years of political balkanisation as given, they refused to accept economic subservience to apartheid South Africa. Initially, by providing crucial diplomatic and material support, five (Angola, Mozambique, Botswana, Tanzania, Zambia) came together politically as the Frontline States to sustain the Zimbabwean nationalists in their fight for majority rule. After independent Zimbabwe joined, the Frontline States remained active in supporting SWAPO (South West Africa People's Organisation) against the South African campaign to exploit the transition to a free Namibia. As important, they formed SADCC on 1 April 1980.[3] Well aware of the political differences, the Frontline States had invited Lesotho, Swaziland and Malawi to join SADCC's efforts to build alternatives to captive economic relations with South Africa by promoting full regional co-operation. The first priority was transport and telecommunications, to rejuvenate the arteries which connect the neighbours and to avoid South African rails and ports. For the productive sectors, SADCC addressed basic needs by co-ordinating for regional food security to reduce their vulnerability to the cyclical droughts and to dependence on outside powers for subsistence. And this vulnerability is directly related to the colonial legacy of mineral production.

The first goal of colonialism was wealth – for the colonial states and for individual settlers. As individual mine claims quickly became consolidated under a few 'randlords,'[4] large capital investments were necessary to develop technology to dig even deeper; further, until the late 1960s, the price of gold was fixed. In contrast, the price of diamonds was systematically controlled by consolidating the digs and more important, by setting up a monopoly of marketing. Planned scarcity was (and is) the key to profitability of diamonds. For most of the minerals, however, profits depended on keeping costs low and the major, and sometimes only, input factor which could be kept low cost was labour. The mines remain labour intensive to this day, an anomaly in this highly technological age. Machines cannot do the job of a good 'drill boy'; they cannot trace the veins yielding ore.

White settlers complained, until well into the 20th century, about insufficient labour to make the mines – and plantations growing food to support the mining areas – profitable. The mining houses chose the form of labour with the lowest cost – migrant – but that system also has its contradictions.[5] Wages can be low because the mine owner relies on the peasant family left at home to provide for the reproduction of labour: the costs of mother/child care, of education for the children, of care for injured workers and all elders. However, a viable peasant economy offers an alternative to mine work, so peasant production had to be curbed but not actually destroyed: 'if he [the African] can work for himself to a great profit he is not likely to work for the white settler for wages.'[6]

Historical scholarship over the last two decades[7] has revealed, contrary to previous analyses of 'subsistence agriculture,' that African peasants were not only willing but skilful in taking advantage of market opportunities. Entrepreneurial and inventive, they found numerous ways to profit in the cash economy without entering European employ. As taxes were imposed by colonial governments, peasants in the proximity of the mines and cities entered the cash economy by selling produce and grain to local markets. In other areas of the region, sale of cattle was sufficient to pay taxes easily. Some, especially in the marginal areas, migrated to mines and plantations for wage labour, but in general, labour remained in critical short supply because most Africans could pay their taxes without working for white settlers. For example, in 1904, African cultivators produced over 90 percent of Southern Rhodesia's total marketed agricultural output.[8]

Brief analysis of three different areas of the region reveals the different ways by which the colonial powers reduced African agricultural production to subsistence, and to sub-subsistence, in order to obtain adequate and cheap labour for exploitation of Southern African mines. The first area is predominantly a cattle region in Pondoland in eastern South Africa; the second is Goromonzi district near Salisbury (Harare) in Southern Rhodesia (Zimbabwe); the third in Cabo Delgado, Niassa, and Zambezia provinces of northern Mozambique illustrates the use of forced production methods by the Portuguese.[9]

## Undermining African Agriculture

### Pondoland, South Africa

William Beinart has documented that the Mpondos in the Transkei region of South Africa were able to retain their economic independence from white settlers well after the 'cattle system' was promoted (about 1894; the exact date is obscure). In this 'system', 'runners' were sent out by traders to recruit mine labour from the homesteads, offering an advance of one head of cattle for the homestead for six months' labour.[10] Since this incentive was instituted soon after their herds had been reduced by rinderpest and drought, the offer was attractive.

Traders could buy cattle outside Pondoland for nine pounds sterling each, while being paid eighteen pounds sterling for the labourers' wages, making a 100 percent profit. By 1904, cattle were selling for only five pounds each, but the terms of the contract remained the same, a huge 360 percent profit.[11] If the cattle died before the mine contract expired, the worker was still required to complete his contract, as the mining company had paid all his wages to the trader. Because cattle were often imported from outside Pondoland, they were susceptible to East Coast and redwater fever, and lung sickness. Six months' work, therefore, could leave a family with 'only a hide.'

Traders then advanced more cattle to the homestead, with the result that, by 1906, advances could take four years in the mines to work off. Mpondo men would frequently defect before the contract ended; some did not even show up. As Beinart states, 'Despite pass laws, compounds and police, many Mpondo workers found it possible to desert; as their wage was at home in the shape of cattle, they had little to lose but the advance itself and a great deal to gain.' [12] The Witwatersrand Native Labour Association (WNLA) lost 6,000 pounds sterling in 1906 from such defections, not a small sum even for that conglomerate.

However, aware of their long term interests as well as their annual profit, the mine owners recognised that the cattle system was the best method for overcoming the resistance of a formerly recalcitrant rural population who would not go to the mines. Their goals coincided with the interests of elder African males because they established a pattern for junior males to migrate to the mines for work. Senior males were supportive of the system because it provided cattle to the homestead; wages could not be 'squandered,' for they were available in the form of cattle before the sons even left home. Further, receiving little or no cash, the sons would come home after their contracts finished. In addition, higher bride wealth could be demanded because cattle were more available. [13] By retaining a nucleus of a herd so necessary for cash transactions, the elders could forestall their loss of status in what was increasingly becoming a cash economy.

Mpondo women at this time were also engaged in the cash economy. They produced not only food but cash crops to supplement the minimal earnings of their men on the mines. Further, they stayed on the land because they were barred from mining compounds by owners who thereby avoided responsibility for workers' families. Because working the land was also the only way to retain access to it, women preserved the use rights of their husbands to land allocated by the clan. Maize production, mainly the responsibility of women after land was cleared, doubled in the first decade of the 20th century. [14] New crops were introduced, particularly oats for feeding to Mpondo horses. Traders, however, began to limit the value of crops, refusing to pay cash and only giving metal tokens ('good fors') to exchange for goods at their own stores at inflated prices. [15] Gradually, too, the Glen Grey Act became operative in Pondoland, bringing land increasingly under individual title so that it was no longer available for communal use. Many thus became landless, and herds and food production declined.

These adverse land ownership and trade exchange conditions enabled the state to abolish the 'cattle system' in 1908. Mpondo men now worked on the mines under the same cash contracts as others, no longer receiving advances except for their costs of transport. The rate of migration accelerated as fewer and fewer young men were able to pay taxes through the sale of cattle. Leaving wives at home to grow food for the family and some market sales, the migrants themselves earned little more than tax money. Where taxes could not be paid, cattle and/or land were seiged. When a miner was injured or became ill, he was dismissed and the family, not the mining houses, had to provide all health care and sustenance. Pondoland joined other African territories in becoming a labour reserve for the mines.

The 1913 Natives' Land Act (known to Africans as the 'law of dispossession') sealed the fate of Pondoland and all other areas of South Africa by codifying the expropriation of land. Reserving more than 90 percent of all land for white ownership and control, it prohibited even squatting or tenant farming. The President of the Chamber of Mines at the time explained the policy: 'What is wanted is ... a policy that would establish once and for all that outside special reserves, the ownership of the land must be in the hands of the white race, and that the surplus of young [African] men, instead of squatting on the land in idleness and spreading out over unlimited areas, must earn their living by working for a wage....'[16]

## Goromonzi District, Southern Rhodesia (Zimbabwe)

Elizabeth Schmidt, amongst others, has shown that near the capital of Salisbury, in Goromonzi District, Southern Rhodesia, Africans were able to resist migrant labour until the mid-1920s.[17] Rich soil and ample land enabled peasants to supply the mining communities at the beginning of the 20th century with grain and food. Women made substantial profits selling beer brewed from the maize.

In 1912, however, a series of laws began to destroy Africans' enterprise and their ability to finance taxes from the land. First, a land bank was established to attract white settlers; they were offered loans up to 2000 pounds sterling – with subsidised fertilisers, seeds, livestock, and roads for transport. In contrast, other laws alienated land from the Africans, relegating them to the worst land, often remote from transport systems and markets. At the same time, prices for maize sold by the Africans declined by 50 percent from the highs of 1903–04. By 1920 the demand for land by whites was sufficient to reduce African holdings by one million acres of the best land in all of Southern Rhodesia, and Goromonzi District was seriously affected.[18] Taxes, rents, grazing and dipping fees for cattle (against ticks and other parasites) continued to rise. The Maize Control Act of 1921 required Africans to sell to the Maize Control Board, no longer directly to the mines and cities where higher prices could be charged. The Board often delayed payment for the grain until after taxes were due, depriving peasants of cash for the payments.[19] Further, without transport, most were forced to sell to traders or middlemen at reduced prices. Finally, as in Pondoland, soon the traders refused to pay cash and only paid with tokens to exchange for goods at their stores, at inflated prices. A 1934 version of the act allocated only 20 percent of the more profitable domestic (and subsidised) market to Africans. Therefore, they were forced to sell much of their produce for the international market at lower prices.[20] Summarising these trends for all of Southern Rhodesia, Charles van Onselen concluded,

> Over a quarter century of colonial presence in central Africa, taxation, the decline of peasant markets, increases in population and restrictions on the amount of land available were all forcing a growing number of African workers into the cash markets of the regional economic system. The decline of peasant independence on the periphery of the system was making cheap labour available at a rate that undercut even *chibaro* [contract, forced labour] rates on the mines.[21]

Because Africans were turning more to the sale of cattle to obtain cash, a Cattle Levy Act of 1934 required higher dipping and other fees of Africans for their cattle; at the same time, the government subsidised the export of beef from white settler ranches. Enterprising African peasants had also increased the growing of vegetables to sell in nearby Salisbury and to white farmers who did not grow vegetables. The Native Registration Act of 1936, by attacking another means of earning cash, barred Africans from selling vegetables, chickens, eggs, and butter in European areas of the cities. Only curios and baskets could be sold there.[22]

By the 1940s – after the government took land and cattle, imposed taxes and cattle dipping fees, interdicted markets for African maize, cattle, and vegetables, restricted movement in white areas while at the same time extensively subsidising white farmers – male members of African households had to leave the land and work in the mines or on commercial farms. African women were left to provide subsistence for the children and other less productive (elderly and sick) members of the family.

With the attractive terms offered during the colonial years, enough white settlers came to Southern Rhodesia to relegate half the land to the whites. By independence in 1980, 6,000 white farmers and their families occupied half the land while 600,000 African farmers and their families were restricted to the other less fertile half.

On the African reserves (Tribal Trust Lands), average real income from farming fell by 40 percent from 1948–70, and by the late 1970s average cash household income from farming was Z$26 per year.[23] Population in the reserves exceeded the ecological carrying capacity by two and one-half times. African peasants only contributed six percent of marketed crop output, and their production was not even sufficient for subsistence: infant mortality rates and malnutrition were four times higher in the rural areas than the urban.[24] With family incomes below subsistence, the cries of malnourished babies became a national outcry for access to land and for mobilising the peasantry in the war against the illegal white regime.

As the liberation war escalated in Southern Rhodesia, the government tried to provide more health services and schools for Africans. Never was there discussion, however, of transforming the highly discriminatory system of production. At the height of the war, after 1976, conditions in rural African areas grew worse. Cattle died because the government could not maintain cattle dipping. The rural population was herded into 'protected villages' or 'keeps' to separate them from the liberation fighters, a familiar counter-revolutionary tactic. In this way, the government tried to prevent the villagers from providing food, logistical support, and hiding places for the fighters, referred to fondly by the people as the 'boys.' These 'keeps' did not succeed in their tactical goals but did increase the hardship: peasants had to walk many miles to their fields and return by dusk or be shot for breaking curfew laws.

Overpopulated areas, primitive production techniques, infertile soil, deforestation, lack of hybrid seeds for traditional crops, and no irrigation – in short the underdevelopment of African agricultural production – are directly the result of colonial exploitation for 90 years in Southern Rhodesia. This underdevelopment was in strict contrast to the white commercial farm sector which benefited for decades from the availability of fertile land stolen from the Africans, from sustained research beginning in the 1930s for hybrid crops, and from subsidised prices for crops and controlled (coerced) cheap labour. As in South Africa, this rich capitalist production in Southern Rhodesia was dependent upon the impoverishment of African land and labour. The 'backwardness' of African peasant production was fundamental to, and perpetuated by, large-scale commercial agriculture.

## Cabo Delgado, Niassa and Zambezia Provinces, Mozambique

In northern Mozambique, peasants in the nineteenth century were self-sufficient, with ample land to grow and trade crops. Because there were not enough settlers to take over land, the Portuguese resorted to forced labour (*chibalo* or *shibaru*) in 1899, which continued in various forms until 1961: 'All native inhabitants of the Portuguese overseas [provinces] are subject to the moral and legal obligations to seek to acquire through work those things which they lack to subsist and to improve their own social conditions.... if they do not comply in some way, the public authorities may force them to comply.'[25] Enforced by privileged African police (*sipais*) or hand-selected chiefs (*chefes de poste*), *chibalo* labourers were not entitled to food or lodging, often were beaten, and received little or no wages. Women were legally exempt, but often were forced to work and were sexually abused. The legal time limit of six months was frequently ignored, as the Portuguese shipped men to distant plantations for as long as two years.

Research by a collective of scholars has documented the forced cotton production initiated in 1938 to support the nascent textile industry in Portugal.[26] Peasants were required to grow a certain number of hectares of cotton in what was evaluated as a cotton growing area. One quick reaction by the peasants was to cook the seeds distributed by the Portuguese before planting them; if yields were low for three consecutive years, the area was judged not conducive to cotton growing, and they were excused from the quota. Many others fled to southern Tanzania and Southern Rhodesia as they could be committed to forced labour on Mozambican plantations for not growing cotton.

Many did grow cotton and when they took it to market, they received one-tenth of the price for the same grade as white farmers. (As late as 1957, the average yearly income earned by an entire family for cotton production was $11.)[27] Taxes increased, requiring families to grow more and more cotton for cash. Young and old, male and female worked from 5 am to 6 or 7 pm and later if there was a moon.[28] Cotton also degraded the soil as traditional crop rotation was disrupted. Records show an increase in malnutrition because peasants changed to cassava as the major food crop, mainly because it did not take much care, but it had few nutrients.

No new production techniques were introduced by the Portuguese. Increased production was achieved simply by an intensification of the exploitation of the peasantry (especially women). Food crop production stagnated and declined, along with the soil and the emaciated bodies of the peasants. Famines became frequent.

For Portuguese merchants, the system was very profitable. Cotton production increased from 338,000 kg in 1926 to 29 million kg in 1946.[29] The rate of return on investment was 400 percent, even with the Portuguese government paying only half the world price for cotton.[30]

Ultimately, however, forced cotton production did not serve the Portuguese well, for the peasants who most readily supported the liberation struggle were those under forced production. Sympathetic to the struggle, they organised with the guerrilla forces to liberate their fields from enforced cotton production; they then turned to growing food for the combatants. Their land became the sanctuaries from which the liberation war was extended, succeeding to the point where the Portuguese soldiers would fight no more and staged a coup in Lisbon in 1974.

From the above historical analyses, four additional points must be emphasised. First, colonialism intensified the exploitation of female labour in Southern Africa. As mentioned earlier, in Pondoland bride-wealth payments increased and became a commercial transaction as the elders tried to conserve control in spite of the growing cash economy. In Southern Rhodesia, women, by brewing beer which brought in cash, at first were able to help their men forestall migrating to the mines. But as the means to obtain cash deteriorated, female labour in the fields declined in status. The result was similar to Pondoland: as elders in Goromonzi District 'were not wage earners themselves, access to wealth was contingent upon their gaining control of wages earned by junior men....Thus, bridewealth deteriorated from its status as a symbol representing a bond between kin groups, to a crass commercial transaction in which women were bartered goods.' [31]

In Mozambique, the Portuguese required women as well as the men to work the cotton fields. Forced to work on plantations and in public works, women grew less food for family consumption and were less able to market goods. Removing mothers from families and reducing their ability to grow food crops destroyed the fabric of family life and reduced food consumption. Women – remaining on the tiny plots of what remained as their land in Pondoland, South Africa and in Goromonzi District, Southern Rhodesia – tried to supplement their husbands' earnings by growing maize and vegetables for the family. In all three cases, family life was disrupted to serve the colonial demand for labour.

Second, 'free market' exchange never existed in colonial Southern Africa, and each colonial regime did what it could to destroy free labour. By the 1940s, peasant agricultural production in most of Southern Africa was underdeveloped: it was no longer sufficient to sustain a family either by production for subsistence or for exchange. Most Africans were much worse off than 50 years earlier, with both wage and food production levels below family subsistence levels; malnutrition rates increased.[32] Traditional security against starvation and malnutrition – shared land, shared labour, shared harvests – was destroyed by the colonial demand for land, labour and cheap grain.

Third, although the majority of Africans suffered from this economic decline, colonialism increased social divisions among Africans. White settlers defeated armed resistance to colonial exploitation by dividing Africans. Traders who bought produce in Pondoland and paid for them with useless 'good fors' were often 'outsiders'; African tax collectors and police in Southern Rhodesia were rewarded well enough that their families did not suffer hunger; *regulos* and *sipais* in Mozambique gained economic privileges, including the ability to steal from those they were 'protecting.'[33] As will be discussed in detail for Mozambique in Chapter 2, social divisions engendered by colonialism remain important deterrents to economic transformation throughout Southern Africa.

Fourth, in addition to lowering the quality of life of the average peasant to below subsistence levels, discrimination under colonialism underdeveloped the factors of production. The crowding on African 'reserves' and the need to grow cash crops, such as cotton, year after year degraded the soil. Yields declined. Fertilisers were not available; a poor family did not have enough cattle to provide sufficient dung for use as organic fertiliser. In the effort to maintain production for subsistence consumption, peasants moved to marginal lands, even less able to sustain crops. Planting near streams became common, which increased silting of rivers and in some cases, blocked the river completely. With inadequate fuel, trees and brush were cleared resulting in a catastrophic deforestation on the 'reserves.'

Colonial governments did little or nothing to retard this ecological degradation. The independent government of Lesotho, for example, inherited a land where soil erosion had virtually destroyed the little arable land there had been. Today wood still provides a full 60 percent of the fuel in the region's rural areas.

Traditional African technology was appropriate for low density production; lands were left fallow to regain fertility; fields were rotated between crops and animals. With the crowding and demand for continuous crops, such rotation was no longer possible. Hybrids were introduced for maize, but colonial governments ignored the variety of indigenous crops that could be improved with research and testing. With the myriad of small plots, equipment was not developed to assist the farmer. The hand hoe is still the major implement in African fields as men and women spend hours bending over to cultivate and weed. Colonial control, therefore, also underdeveloped African skills and technology. Independent governments now must attend to erecting satellite disks and main frame computers at the same time as they try to develop small rototillers and tractors adaptable to the tough African soil. (Western and Eastern tractors alike are soon demolished by the laterite soil in the poorer soil regions.)

In summary, the multiple weapons used by colonial regimes in the degradation of African agricultural production are reiterated in the following general, but not all-inclusive, list:

1. Underdevelopment of agricultural production was caused by
   a) alienation of land and the subsequent over-crowding of African populations on reserves;
   b) deteriorating soil conditions because traditional crop rotation was no longer possible;
   c) forcing African producers to sell through traders, instead of selling directly to customers for higher prices;
   d) paying lower prices for food crops while raising taxes, dipping fees and rents;
   e) refusing to pay cash for crops, forcing peasants to buy agricultural inputs and basic commodities at local stores at inflated prices; the local terms of trade discriminated against African production;

f) laws which mitigated against new commercial ventures started by Africans in an attempt to find cash for taxes (e.g., Cattle Levy Act);

g) subsiding seeds, fertilisers, grain depots, irrigation and roads in white lands with few services provided for Africans; few innovative techniques were implemented on African land;

h) subsidising cattle production for white settlers;

i) arresting 'vagrants' who refused to work in the wage economy and turning them over to plantations and mines for long periods of forced labour.

2. Social differentiation increased by class and by gender. All Africans were exploited, but some much more than others. Women, as the major food producers, especially suffered, for their status declined as their work intensified.

None of the colonial powers was interested in processing local crops or minerals. Quite the reverse, they were primarily produced for the factories of Britain and Portugal. Portugal by the 1920s had actually prohibited foreign investment in cotton so it could be used exclusively in Portuguese textile mills. They were content to have the Mozambican economy used as a service economy for British interests, providing rail and port services for the rich mines of South Africa and both Southern and Northern Rhodesia (now Zimbabwe and Zambia). Such revenues provided hard currency and sustained the Portuguese state, not the Mozambican one.

Southern Rhodesia developed little small industry, choosing to export raw minerals, unprocessed tobacco leaves, coffee beans and fruits. Not until international sanctions (voluntary in 1965; mandatory but never fully enforced from 1968) began to squeeze the economy, did they develop modern engineering and steel sectors or begin to process some agricultural goods. South Africa did develop an industrial sector, but mainly for its own consumption and for some trade with the region (farm and mining equipment, small capital goods). Today all economies in the region, including South Africa, remain primary product exporters.

The colonial powers did not see it as necessary to diversify even primary commodities. Tanzania exported coffee beans, raw tea and cashews. Malawi was the source for cotton. Zambia exported only copper. Their role was to perform as pieces in the international chess board of raw material suppliers; using the wealth for local development, for diversification of production, or for creating viable economies was not on the agenda.

## South African Dominance

The colonial picture would not be complete without a brief analysis of the role of South Africa as the regional economic power. While the colonial economies were subservient to Europe, control was often exercised through South Africa. From their base in South Africa, mining houses directed operations in the region, especially in Botswana and the Southern and Northern Rhodesias. They expanded into related industries such as explosives, smelting, railroads, freight-forwarding firms and then on to insurance and banking.[34] They also ventured into wholesale and retail trade and some manufacturing.

Producing food for colonial mining enclaves and towns, plantations of tea, coffee, sugar, and fruit in Mozambique, Southern Rhodesia, Nyasaland (Malawi), and Swaziland came under British or South African corporate ownership. They also gradually developed food processing manufacturing. To support these plantations and food industries, South Africa coordinated agricultural research for the region. Although research was highly developed to meet the needs of the commercial farmers – sophisticated veterinary services, hybrids, cropping techniques, soil mapping – it was never extended beyond their farming sectors. Not until 1985 did the independent neighbours establish their own regional agricultural centre (Southern African Centre for Co-operation in Agriculture – SACCAR) separate from the dominance of South Africa. Only by 1987 did SADCC establish a regional laboratory for veterinary research to engender a common approach to diseases, eradicating their dependence on diagnoses from South Africa's Onderstepoort (near Pretoria) veterinary laboratories.

The only two countries of the region which escaped the South African web were Tanzania and Angola. Tanzania was farther afield and the British goal was to integrate it into a regional group with their ex-colonies Kenya and Uganda. Here the dominant partner was to be Kenya, with Ugandan and Tanzanian agricultural production supplying Kenya with goods for processing. The project's inherent inequity destroyed the co-operation, for neither Tanzania nor Uganda wanted to remain backwaters as raw material producers for Kenyan development.

Although few Angolans migrated to South African mines, Angolan diamonds and iron ore were mined by South African firms. Coffee plantations, however, remained under Portuguese control. Oil reserves were not discovered until late in the colonial period and were then developed by American capital.

Because the colonial links to apartheid weigh so heavily on the independent neighbours, they have documented the extent of their dependence on South Africa, discussed below by sectors. The analysis also reveals an important, but not often acknowledged, fact – a viable South African economy needs its neighbours.

## Mining

Mineral production in the region is probably the sector most penetrated by South Africa. In terms of regional economic power, South Africa's neighbours joke ironically that the Anglo-American Corporation (AAC) of South

Africa could be the next member of SADCC. The AAC-DeBeers mining consortium controls most of the region's nickel and diamond production, half of all ferro-chrome mining, and one-quarter of the copper output. In 1984 the value of mineral output owned by AAC-DeBeers was approximately 32 percent of SADCC's total mineral production.[35] South African control is exerted directly through ownership and loans, and indirectly through physical inputs (machinery and technology), foreign technicians and skilled manpower. Of the major mines, only Tanzania's diamond mine has been able to operate without expatriate personnel.[36] SADCC has criticised the foreign mining companies for their failure to train local personnel and has already opened a central isotope geochronology laboratory in Zimbabwe and a coal analysis laboratory in Malawi. In 1987 Zimbabwe ended its dependence on gold refineries in South Africa by opening its own.

SADCC mines also produce many of the strategic minerals (antimony, asbestos, cobalt, diamonds, manganese, titanium) which have been credited mainly to South Africa. With a free South Africa, it is unlikely that further development of these alternative supplies will attract immediate investment, and South African minerals and the mining houses will continue to dominate. But SADCC minerals may attract capital from non-traditional sources (e.g. Japan) who want to avoid South African monopoly prices. For example, Mozambique is developing titanium, in addition to supplies available in Malawi; Zambia and Angola have manganese not yet exploited; it is predicted that Namibia and Mozambique both have oil reserves. The only two metals for which South Africa is the world's major supplier are also available from Zimbabwe, second only to South Africa in world reserves of platinum and chromium (although Zimbabwe's deposits contain 1:1 ratio of platinum to paladium, higher than South Africa). If these supplies are to be viable, however, investments of about $1 billion for each is necessary.[37]

Local interests are beginning to look across their own borders, under SADCC auspices; the Industrial Development Corporation of Zimbabwe is considering investing in the Mozambican Pande gas fields and is a partner in Botswana soda ash production. In the near future, a growing South African economy will depend greatly on the natural gas sources in both Mozambique and Namibia and on soda ash in Botswana. It will look to the day when it can import Angolan oil (so desperately needed that it was promoted, unsuccessfully, as a South African condition for the Namibian settlement). SADCC suggests planned production for the whole region to assist rational regional exploitation of minerals, but its experience is that transnational corporations respond little to any goal but short term profit.

## Transport

In 1981, traffic through South African ports from its neighbours constituted 26 percent of overseas trade. However, South African interests also controlled freight forwarding, with centralised computers in South Africa recording the daily traffic of freight transfers within the region. Further, in some of the neighbouring countries, senior management positions are held by South Africans. A SADCC priority has been to reduce the use of South Africa's transport network, and SADCC feasibility studies have predicted that after the cessation of sabotage on the transport lines, only 20 percent of regional traffic will pass through South Africa.[38] It is for this reason that South Africa chose to bomb SADCC railways, bridges and roads. Not able to compete economically in transport, South African sabotage forced SADCC to ship 75 percent of all trade through South African ports, reduced to 62 percent by 1987. Through increased security and refurbishing under the neighbours' joint co-operation, by 1990 some two-thirds of the region's traffic was back on SADCC tracks.[39]

South African dominance in transport is neither 'natural' nor economically 'rational.' All the land-locked countries, except Lesotho and perhaps Botswana, are better served by regional ports (Swaziland by Maputo; Zimbabwe by Maputo and Beira; Malawi by Nacala and Beira; Zambia by Dar es Salaam, Benguela, and Beira; Botswana by Maputo and someday, Walvis Bay). The Beira Corridor (road, rail, pipeline) in Mozambique is now handling 18 percent of regional traffic, compared with 5 percent in 1982. The port can handle 2.5 million tonnes per year, following a 44 percent increase in traffic in 1988 and a further 16 percent increase in 1989. The plan is to rebuild the port to handle 5 million tonnes by the early 1990s.[40] From October 1986, Zambia ceased shipping copper through South African ports; Port Elizabeth had been receiving 50 percent of Zambian copper shipment, but in 1987, 80 percent was sent through Dar es Salaam, Tanzania, with the remainder through Beira. In 1990 Zambia experimented with shipping copper to Walvis Bay because Zimbabwe Railways was delaying transshipment. Botswana BCL also sent experimental shipments of copper-nickel matte northward to Beira.

A free South Africa will not be competitive in transshipment traffic, requiring the South African port cities to restructure their economies away from the transport service sector. In contrast, the neighbours will be saving precious foreign exchange by using SADCC ports and reducing transport costs of their overseas trade; Zimbabwe saves about 40 percent on tobacco shipments and 50 percent per container shipped through Beira instead of Durban.[41] Finally, with the diversity of ports available, both shortages and blockages can be avoided; planning will be possible to increase efficiency of shipments.

## Telecommunications

Perhaps the best illustration of South Africa's dominance is the fact that of 72 telecommunications links available to the nine neighbours in 1980, only 14 were direct connections from one capital city to another. In 30 cases, routing was through South Africa and 16 actually went via Europe.[42] This meant that Mozambicans could not talk with Zimbabweans without going through South Africa and could not talk with Angolans without going through Portugal. Within six years of the formation of SADCC, satellite communication facilities have made possible direct intra-SADCC telecommunications, enabling all members to bypass South African transmissions.

## Manufacturing

With the regional economy transformed to serve South African development under colonialism (and to a lesser extent Southern Rhodesia's), many SADCC members still today depend on South Africa for manufacturing of capital goods, from tractors to medical equipment to locomotives. Through the South African Customs Union, Botswana, Lesotho and Swaziland import mainly South African manufactures, but Malawi, Mozambique and Zambia are also dependent on these imports of spare parts and small capital goods. What factories do exist have often been foreign – including South African – owned. According to a UNIDO study on industrialisation, 'a major obstacle to regionally integrated industrial development is the domination of the manufacturing industry by foreign-owned enterprises, in particular large manufacturing companies and TNCs [transnational corporations].'[43]

Zimbabwe has been most successful in purchasing South African controlled companies (e.g. Astra, Chemplex and Zimphos, Delta, CAPS pharmaceutics, Wankie Colliery) and since 1980 has shifted ownership from South Africa of at least 25 percent of the total asset value of Zimbabwe's top companies. Several other companies are in the process of reducing their South African holdings. Overall, at least 30 percent of South African assets have been acquired by Zimbabwe.[44]

Mainly a primary commodity producer, South Africa does not yet have a developed capital goods sector. Because investment in manufacturing decreased, the production of capital goods fell 30 percent from 1981 to 1985.[45] Following an import substitution policy, South Africa has protected infant industries, but the manufacturing sector still expends more foreign exchange than it creates.

## Trade

South Africa has an open economy with growth depending on increased exports, for foreign trade constitutes 55 percent of its Gross Domestic Product (GDP). Not competitive in many international markets, its major market is the region, earning $2 billion per year. Estimates have also been given that regional trade provides two million jobs for South Africans.[46]

In 1987 SADCC reported that 7 percent of its exports were going to South Africa, with 30 percent of total imports originating there. However, with the exception of Swaziland's exports to South Africa and Lesotho's total trade with South Africa, the shares of all other exports to and imports from South Africa have tended to fall since 1980. Zimbabwe has shown the most dramatic results:

|  | 1980 | 1986 |
|---|---|---|
| Percentage of total exports to South Africa | 19% | 9% |
| Percentage of total imports from South Africa | 28% | 21% |

Although South Africa remains the largest supplier, Malawi cut its imports from South Africa from 37 percent in 1980 to 29 percent in 1986.[47]

South Africa had been regularly exporting grains to Mozambique, Zambia, Swaziland, Lesotho and Botswana, but in 1985 Zimbabwe exported 200,000 tonnes to South Africa. With its surplus production, Zimbabwe could be a major supplier of grain in the region. For the 1990 season, maize export earnings of South Africa was 0, while Zimbabwe had a surplus of 1.26 million tonnes and was looking for markets. As a free South Africa redistributes land and tries to resolve endemic malnutrition, it is very likely that Zimbabwe will be exporting grain to South Africa.

Intra-SADCC trade is only 4–6 percent of their total trade. However, SADCC explicitly planned that increased trade will follow co-ordinated production, so has not concentrated on trade goals. What is interesting is that over half of the trade within SADCC is manufactures, suggesting that a rudimentary regional market already exists: textiles, clothing, cement, tyres, soaps, pulp and paper, iron and steel as well as maize, sugar, meat, fish and cotton.

What will happen to trade, who dominates whom, will greatly depend on government policies. For again, South Africa's dominance is not 'natural' or even economically logical. The current government heavily subsidises its exports, especially the grains. If subsidies are reduced to spend government revenue on health care or other items, then the neighbours' goods may become more competitive. It is estimated, for example, that only 7–10 percent of Zimbabwe's imports will remain genuinely cheaper from South Africa.[48] Further, everyone involved in the changes in South Africa agrees that distribution of goods and services is key to the post-apartheid economy. In contrast to South African goods swamping the region, it may be that South Africans with more money in their pockets will become major customers for their neighbours in basic consumer items.

## Labour
With the independence of Angola and Mozambique in 1975, South Africa

started phasing out recruitment of migrant labour for the mines. In 1974 about 75 percent of the miners were from the region, which quickly dropped to 46 percent by 1976. South Africa wanted to reduce its dependence on the region and, especially, diminish the likelihood of Mozambican miners bringing in new ideas from an independent and progressive country. The drastic cut of Mozambican miners after 1975 from 115,000 to 40,000 was also an attempt by the apartheid regime to destabilise the southern Mozambique economy, for the government could not easily find them employment.

In 1987, 40 percent of the total industrial labour force in South Africa was still from the region, providing a source of foreign exchange and employment for the neighbours. Such offical figures, however, underestimate the number of workers and do not enumerate those on commercial farms. It is anticipated that a free South Africa will phase out the migrant labour conditions of segregated compounds and *de facto* job reservation for whites, but will terminate the migrants' jobs only gradually, for they provide an important source of skilled labour, not readily replaced by unemployed, but unskilled, South Africans.

Most experts expect that Lesotho will continue to provide labour, for the highly skilled Basotho are needed in the mines and the Lesotho economy is extremely dependent on their remittances. For the rest, the return of the migrants could be a gradual process, with the major disruptions to the economies already having occurred during the mid-1970s reduction. Mozambique would be most seriously affected by a return, for remittances of $50–75 million is about one-third of Mozambique's total war-ravaged external earnings; if the return is organised and gradual, however, the economy could welcome skilled workers for its own newly developed mines. In all the countries, some policy adjustments will have to be made to find employment for these urbanised and skilled workers.

## Energy

Colonial links tied Botswana, Lesotho and Swaziland into the South African electricity grid. Maputo, capital of Mozambique, its port and industrial sector, are also linked. Total import of electricity from South Africa by the nine, however, constitutes only five percent of total consumption. The only regionally integrated energy conservation project in the world, the SADCC Industrial Energy Conservation Pilot Project will initially audit about 35 factories and will prepare a five-year energy conservation plan for industry. SADCC as a group will ultimately be an energy exporter, with twice as much oil and more electricity and coal than they need for their own projected development.[49]

It is South Africa which desperately requires regional electricity, because its industrial growth needs a 100 percent increase in power supplies every eight years. To meet these needs up to the year 2020 from local resources would virtually deplete all South African non-renewable energy resources. Already the pollution from combustive power stations in the Transvaal exceeds many times the tolerated maxima in Europe and acid rain is causing damage.[50] Mozambique has provided South Africa with as much as 13 percent of its electricity, important to the industrial Transvaal.[51] However, in an example of relative power, SADCC did reject South Africa's 1989 request to import electricity from Zaire via Angola or Zambia/Zimbabwe.

## Water

In 1982 South Africa built dams in catchment areas of rivers that formed part of the water supply to Botswana's capital city, Gaborone, and a number of agricultural districts – without informing the Botswanan government. When Botswana complained, South Africa suggested it negotiate with the bantustan, Bophuthatswana,[52] which would have meant a *de facto* recognition of an illegitimate government as 'independent'.

Swaziland also competes for water with South Africa, as much of its water originates in the South African highveld to the west of Swaziland. When cyclone Domoina destroyed Swaziland's river gauging network in February 1984, SADCC created a project to reconstruct it; without a monitoring capacity, South Africa could claim prior dated use of the water and deprive Swaziland. [53] In the Swazi lowveld area, irrigated sugar and citrus fields could be expanded by at least 3000 hectares if Swaziland were able to take more water from the Usutu River. Upstream, however, South Africa has already built a dam for water as a cooling agent for Sasol 3, a thermal energy plant which reduces South African dependence on imported oil. This use of water by thermal power plants and by vast agricultural and forestry projects in South Africa has adversely affected plans for irrigation not only in Swaziland, but also Mozambique. For Mozambique, the Komati River now runs dry in low rainfall years because South Africa is taking so much of the water upstream.

Lesotho's Maluti mountains are the source of half the total flow of the Senqu-Orange River, running almost 1500 km through South Africa before emptying into the Atlantic Ocean. The Highlands Water Project will tame this 'white gold' for South Africa, and Lesotho will gain 276 MW of electricity at its completion.[54] Critics of the scheme state it transfers too much of the water to South African control and the financing will cause an onerous debt burden for Lesotho. Lesotho agrees there are risks but points out that it currently only generates about 2 MW of electricity, mostly from small diesel sets. Most of its electricity for urban use is imported from South Africa's Electrical Supply Commission (ESCOM), and rural electrification has been delayed by the shortages. The new Highlands Water Project will overcome these problems. Another example of the interlocking requirements, the Project will provide South African industry with water and will also develop Lesotho's electricity. The relationship does not provide equal benefit, but it was the best Lesotho could obtain, and it will light up the peasants' homes.

'Ironically, the survival of South Africa's industrial and agricultural heartland is in the hands of foreign states,' sounded the alarm of a South African water survey.[55] Even with the generous benefits from the Highlands Water Project, South Africa has access to sufficient water only until 2020. Engineers have proposed, therefore, 'the Zambezi connection,' building an aqueduct 1200 km from Kazungula on the Zambezi River to carry water to the industrial heartland of the Vaal triangle. Yet the countries bordering the Zambezi are Angola, Namibia, Zimbabwe, Zambia and Mozambique, not South Africa, giving these neighbours full control over whether South Africa receives one drop. SADCC is currently implementing a Regional Legislation for Management of the Zambezi (ZACPRO2) and an Integrated Water Management Plan for the Zambezi Basin (ZACPRO5) to decide their own priorities for sharing water.

One reason for South African extreme dependence on its neighbours for water is that the apartheid government has been providing it cheaply to the farmers. Irrigation consumes 70 percent and the water has been sold to farmers at 10 percent of real cost. The inability to import as much oil as they needed because of sanctions also increased demand for hydroelectric power and for the thermal energy plants. Economic growth will require even greater amounts, and in this vital sector, it is South Africa which is vulnerable.

## Conclusion

For most of this century South Africa has had the capital, information, technical control, transport links, and ownership patterns to maintain its hegemony of the region. That domination did not result from open competition within a free market; military force had established it while economic power and coercion sustained it. The liberation of Angola and Mozambique in 1975 and Zimbabwe in 1980 produced a situation where Pretoria chose to use greater force to keep the region in line. South Africa's response to the formation of SADCC in 1980 was to call up its military option and to launch its programme of aggressive destabilisation. The long succession of acts of economic blackmail and sabotage, of assassinations, bombing raids, covert military operations and the sponsorship of surrogate armies have been well documented and will not be repeated here. Table 1.1 summarises the range and extent of this openly interventionist attack on the governments and people of the region.

The response of Western governments to South Africa's destabilisation ranged from toleration to outright support by the Reagan and Thatcher

Table 1.1: *South African Sanctions Against its Neighbours, 1981–1987*

| | Angola | Botswana | Lesotho | Malawi | Mozambique | Swaziland | Tanzania | Zambia | Zimbabwe |
|---|---|---|---|---|---|---|---|---|---|
| Sponsorship of insurgents | X | | | | X | | | X | X |
| Government intervention (e.g., assasination, coup attempts) | | | X | X | X | | | X | X |
| Military raids | X | X | X | | X | X | X | X | X |
| Embargo on rail traffic | | X | X | X | X | X | | X | X |
| Delay of border traffic | | X | X | | | | | X | X |
| Removal of technical personnel | | | X | | X | X | | | X |
| Threat/removal of investment, finances | | X | X | | X | X | | | X |
| Delay of trade payments/transactions | | X | X | X | | X | | X | X |
| Currency smuggling | | | | | X | | | X | X |
| Threat/return of migrant labour | | X | X | X | X | X | | X | X |
| Petrol/diesel sabotage/blockage | | X | X | X | X | X | | X | X |
| Unilateral diversion of rivers | | X | X | | X | X | | | X |

N.B.   Neither Angola's nor Tanzania's economy is linked to South Africa; therefore, the apartheid regime has less economic leverage against them, although its war against Angola exacts a very high economic price.

*Source:* Tabulated from multiple sources. Refer to works on destabilization in the bibliography. This chart understates the extent of South African sanctions against its neighbours, for many covert threats and actions have not been registered.

administrations. A particular convergence of US and South African ideological goals and strategies for the shaping of the region emerged. With the Reagan administration simultaneously destabilising its Central American 'backyard', the decade of the 1980s saw a very special relationship develop between Washington and Pretoria, which will be examined in the next chapter.

# Notes

1   One illustrative example suffices: even after 11 years of existence, not one American library systematically collects SADCC documents, not the Library of Congress, not even one of the libraries at the prestigious African Studies Centers at ten American universities. More internationally, only the World Bank has established a SADCC desk (1988); other international agencies do not, such as the International Monetary Fund, which demands major national economic restructuring without acknowledging the regional economic impact of the national changes. Analyses of such problems are the core of this study.

2   United States Department of State. 'An Initiative for Economic Progress in Southern Africa,' January 29, 1987.

3   Carol B. Thompson. *Challenge to Imperialism: The Frontline States in the Liberation of Zimbabwe.* Harare: Zimbabwe Publishing House, 1985 and Boulder: Westview Press, 1986.

4   Geoffrey Wheatcroft. *The Randlords.* New York: Atheneum, 1986; Charles van Onselen. *Chibaro: African Mine Labour in Southern Rhodesia, 1900-1933.* London: Pluto Press, 1976.

5   Two other contradictions of semi-proletarian labour are daily absenteeism, as workers try to avoid work or are ill from the adverse conditions, and the fact that use of impermanent labour is possible only at a lower level of productive skill; manufacturing requires a disciplined and permanent labour force. For an excellent analysis of the contradictions in the system of semi-proletarian labour, see Issa G. Shivji, *Law, State and the Working Class in Tanzania.* London: James Currey and Dar es Salaam: Tanzania Publishing House, 1986, chapter 1.

6   Notes of interviews with Lord Selborne, Salisbury, October 12, 1906, quoted in Ian Phimister, 'Commodity Relations and Class Formation in the Zimbabwean Countryside, 1891-1920,' *The Journal of Peasant Studies* 13:4 (July 1986): 242.

7   Giovanni Arrighi. 'Labour Supplies in Historical Perspective: A Study of the Proletarianization of the African Peasantry in Rhodesia,' *The Journal of Development Studies* 6:3 (April 1970): 197-234. Colin Bundy. *The Rise and Fall of the South African Peasantry.* Berkeley: University of California Press, 1979. Mohamed Lamine Gakou. *The Crisis in African Agriculture.* London: ZED Books, 1987. Eduardo Mondlane. *The Struggle for Mozambique.* London: ZED Press, reprinted 1983 (originally 1969). Colin Murray. *Families Divided: The Impact of Migrant Labour in Lesotho.* New York: Cambridge University Press, 1981. Michael Painter. 'The Value of Peasant

Labour Power in a Prolonged Transition to Capitalism,' *The Journal of Peasant Studies* 13:4 (July 1986): 221-39. Robin Palmer. *Land and Racial Discrimination in Rhodesia.* London: Heinemann, 1977. Robin Palmer and Neil Parsons. *The Roots of Rural Poverty in Central and Southern Africa.* London: Heinemann, 1977. Ian Phimister. 'Peasant Production and Under-development in Southern Rhodesia, 1890-1914, with particular reference to Victoria District.' *African Affairs* 73:291 (April 1974): 217-228.

8    Ian Phimister, 1986, *op. cit.*, p. 244.

9    William Beinart. *The Political Economy of Pondoland 1860–1930.* Cambridge: Cambridge University Press, 1982. Elizabeth Schmidt. 'Ideology, Economics, and the Role of Shona Women in Southern Rhodesia, 1850-1939.' Ph.D. dissertation, University of Wisconsin, 1987. Allen Isaacman, Michael Stephen, Yussuf Adam, Maria Joao Homen, Eugenio Macamo and Augustinho Pililao. 'Cotton is the Mother of Poverty – Peasant Resistance to Forced Cotton Production in Mozambique, 1938-1961,' *International Journal of African Historical Studies* 13:4 (1980):581-615. Allen and Barbara Isaacman. *Mozambique: From Colonialism to Revolution* (Harare: Zimbabwe Publishing House, 1985). Allen Isaacman. 'Chiefs, Rural Differentiation and Peasant Protest: The Mozambican Forced Cotton Regime 1938-1961,' *African Economic History* 14 (l985): 15-56. Allen Isaacman. 'Forced Cotton Production in Mozambique,' lecture at University of Zimbabwe, Department of History, June 20, 1986.

For recent documentation which present similar analyses for Malawi, Swaziland, Tanzania and Zambia, see Thandika Mkandawire and Naceur Bourenane, eds. *The State and Agriculture in Africa.* Dakar: Codesria, 1987. I.K.S. Musoke. 'Capitalist Penetration and the Underdevelopment of African Peasant Agriculture: Swaziland, Southern Rhodesia, Nyasaland,' in African Centre for Applied Research and Training in Social Development (ACARTSOD). *Understanding Africa's Food Problems: Social Policy Perspectives.* London: Hans Zell, 1990, pp. 22-60.

10    Beinart, *op. cit.*, p. 58.

11    *Ibid.*

12    *Ibid.*, p. 60.

13    *Ibid.*, p. 69.

14    *Ibid.*, p. 50.

15    *Ibid.*, p. 52.

16    Ernest Harsch. *Apartheid's Great Land Theft: The Struggle for the Right to Farm in South Africa.* New York: Pathfinder Press, 1986, p. 11.

17    Schmidt, *op. cit.*

18    *Ibid.*, p. 178-9.

19    *Ibid.*, p. 186.

20    *Ibid.*, pp. 186-9, 234.

21    Charles van Onselen, *op. cit.*, p. 117.

22    Schmidt, *op. cit.,* pp. 189-90.

23    Whitsun Foundation, 'A Strategy for Rural Development and Data Bank No. 2: The Peasant Sector,' Harare, 1978. Roger Riddell, *The Land Problem in Rhodesia: Alternatives for the Future.* Harare: Mambo, 1978.

24    Food and Agriculture Organization, 'Policy Options Paper for Agrarian Reform in Zimbabwe,' 1985, pp. 18-20.

25    Isaacman and Isaacman, *op. cit.*, p. 34.

26  Isaacman, *et al., op. cit.*, 1980. Isaacman, *op. cit.* Isaacman, *op cit.* seminar, 1986.
27  Isaacman and Isaacman, *op. cit.*, p. 46.
28  Isaacman, 1986, *op. cit.*
29  Isaacman and Isaacman, *op. cit.*, p. 45.
30  Isaacman, 1986, *op. cit.*
31  Schmidt, *op. cit.*, p. 204.
32  Even mountainous Lesotho used to be a granary, exporting 150,000 bags of maize in 1908 but importing 320,000 bags 60 years later. Colin Murray, *op. cit.*, p. 18. Swaziland was a self-supporting nation until the cattle epidemics of the 1890s and the appropriation of two-thirds of the land for white settlers by the British in the 1907 Partition Proclamation. The country then became a chronic importer of grain, which continues to today. Alan R. Booth. *Swaziland: Tradition and Change in A Southern African Kingdom.* Boulder: Westview, 1983, p. 23.
33  Today in South Africa the white regime is still trying to forestall majority rule with the same old tactic: appointing and assisting ethnic leaders so they serve the white master not their African constituents.
34  Duncan Clarke. *Foreign Companies and International Investment in Zimbabwe.* London: Catholic Institute for International Relations, March 1980. Duncan Clarke. 'Economic Linkages in Southern Africa,' Geneva, April 1982.
35  W. Sweta *et al.* 'The Minerals Sector of the States of SADCC: Possibilities for a Regional Minerals Policy,' Lusaka: SADCC Mining Sector Coordination Unit, 1988, p. 2.
36  SADCC, Gaborone: SADCC, September 1985, pp. 99-101.
37  Paul Jourdan, 'US Mineral Dependence on South Africa: Exploding the Myths,' Institute of Mining Research, University of Zimbabwe, August 1988, pp. 11-13.
38  SADCC, (1985), *op. cit.*, pp. 63-64, 126.
39  *Financial Gazette* (Harare), July 3, 1987. Colleen Lowe Morna, 'What Lies Ahead Now for the SADCC Countries?' *African Business* (February 1990): 16.
40  *Financial Gazette* (Harare), July 7, 1987; *Tanzania Daily News*, April 18, 1988. *BCG (Beira Corridor Group) Bulletin* (Harare), no. 16 (March 1990): 8.

| BEIRA *(port tonnes)* | 1986 | 1987 | 1988 | 1989 |
|---|---|---|---|---|
| Total Trade (excluding petrol) | 164.5 | 941.4 | 1176.3 | 1293.0 |

41  Beira Corridor Group *Bulletin*, no. 19 (August 1990), p. 7.
42  *Ibid.*, p. 65.
43  UNIDO, 'Industrial Cooperation through the Southern African Development Coordination Conference (SADCC),' 1985, p. 90. For a case study of how domination by TNCs has limited regional development of the tractor sector, see Tom Ostergaard, *SADCC beyond Transportation: The Challenge of Industrial Cooperation*, Uppsala: Scandinavian Institute of African Studies, 1989.
44  Roger C. Riddell, 'Zimbabwe in the Frontline,' paper presented to conference, Sanctions against South Africa: What Works? What Doesn't? Howard University, October 30-31, 1987, p. 9.
45  Tom Ostergaard, 'Industrial Development in Southern Africa and the Role of SADCC,' Working Paper 89.4, Centre for Development Research

(Copenhagen), November 1989, pp. 31-2.

46  Simba Makoni, press conference, August 15, 1985 and interview, *Financial Gazette*, March 6, 1987.

47  SADCC (1985), *op. cit.*, pp. 39, 42. Economist Intelligence Unit, country reports of all the SADCC members for 1989-90.

48  Joseph Hanlon. *SADCC in the 1990s*. EIU Special Report no. 1158 (September 1989): 32.

49  SADCC (1985), *op. cit.*, pp. 49, 55. *SADCC Energy*. 3:21 (1990): 13-14.

50  *BCG Bulletin*, no. 12 (May 1989): 7.

51  After 1981, South Africa chose to instruct the Mozambique National Resistance (MNR) to attack the electricity pylons from the Cahora Bassa dam in northern Mozambique, apparently in an effort to disguise their support of the MNR. As South Africa began to need the electricity more in early 1988, they initiated talks with the Mozambican government about the rebuilding of the pylons and their protection by South African troops. Unless relations change drastically, such an arrangement would mean that South Africa would be financing troops to protect the pylons, while financing other troops to burn villages and kill peasants within a few kilometers of the pylons. For discussion of MNR, see Chapter 2.

52  Olusegun Obasanjo, 'Southern Africa: the Security of the Front-Line States,' Report of a Special Mission, Commonwealth Secretariat, June 1988, p. 12.

53  SADCC, *Food, Agriculture and Natural Resources*, sector report for annual meeting, Gaborone, Botswana, February 5-6, 1987, p. 68.

54  'Commercial Energy without Dependence?' *SADCC Energy* 5:13 (1987): 27.

55  'Water. A Survey.' Supplement to *Financial Mail*, 1 March 1985, p. 5.

# 2.

# Fire Force:
# Invasion and Destabilisation

The degree of congruence in the goals and tactics of South Africa and the United States in the first decade of SADCC (1980s) was remarkable. The Total Strategy of South Africa (1977) and the Reagan Doctrine (1981) echoed similar themes: perpetuation of regional dominance and control through the 'roll-back of communism.' The policies were not always consistently followed, and certainly some in each government opposed them, but the themes remained predominant for the decade. Most similar in regard to South Africa's destabilisation of Mozambique and the United States' efforts to destabilise Nicaragua,[1] the policies were not just comparable for each in its own region; the US abetted South Africa in its attempt to overthrow the Angola government, and South Africa assisted the US in Central America. Policies were not fully congruent and the differences will be discussed, but the commanding interests in each created a special relationship during this decade.

The essential first condition for success of the policies was for each to maintain ideological hegemony; thus, both governments cast events in terms of a 'communist onslaught' and used such propaganda labels as 'terrorist' to stigmatise the perceived enemy. Second, they shared military goals to reverse the gains made by revolutionary forces in each region. The Reagan administration worked overtly and covertly to overthrow the Sandinistas in Nicaragua; both governments worked to overthrow the Angolan government. After the Nkomati Accord of 1984, the US government officially supported the Mozambican government over the South African-backed Mozambique National Resistance (MNR); however, evidence has emerged to show that private US foundations, the same 'off-the-shelf' financing as in the Iran–contra scandal, took on some of the expense of the MNR. Third, the partnership was not simply the coincidence of tactics and goals; the two provided mutual assistance to reassert their dominance. Finally, these strategies and tactics led to the privatisation of foreign policy in both countries, albeit in very different ways. Each of these points will be discussed.

The first formal articulation of South African policy was a 1977 *Defence White Paper* outlining what came to be known as the 'Total

Strategy.' The paper argued that a 'total onslaught' threatened the apartheid government. Calling on the full resources of the state to effect internal reforms and restructure external relations within the region, this strategy planned to end internal revolt as well as the pariah status of the South African government. The central policy for overcoming this pariah status was to reorganise the region under the 'Constellation of Southern African States' (CONSAS). In this proposal, South Africa would provide loans and development projects, increase trade and investment, and promote technical training for the 'independent' bantustans, along with the neighbouring African states – all to make South Africa the brightest star in the constellation. As stated earlier, the independence of Zimbabwe under the leadership of Robert Mugabe and the formation of SADCC effectively thwarted any hopes for CONSAS.

CONSAS, however, was only one component of the regional policy. More limited objectives demanded the neighbours accept the following conditions:

1) refrain from supporting the ANC and SWAPO and further, act as policing agents for Pretoria against South African refugees in their countries;
2) refuse even normal diplomatic relations with 'Soviet bloc powers';
3) 'maintain and indeed strengthen' existing economic ties in the region;
4) oppose calls for mandatory sanctions against South Africa and shield South Africa from sanctions;
5) moderate anti-South African rhetoric.[2]

The SADCC nine as a group not only defeated CONSAS, but frustrated all five goals. The whole purpose of SADCC is to overturn the economic status quo in the region (#3), and the members regularly included SWAPO, ANC, and PAC as observers in their meetings (#1). SADCC has continually condemned apartheid (#5) and called for comprehensive sanctions, with even Malawi and Swaziland concurring (#4). Although the USSR has only recently given due regard to SADCC, the German Democratic Republic provided development funds, and members like Zimbabwe and Lesotho (before the 1986 coup) increased their exchanges with the USSR (#2).

Coming to power in 1981, the Reagan administration refined and vigorously promoted two consistent themes in US policy toward Southern Africa: anti-communism and counter-revolution. There was little new in these themes: interpreting events in the region from the perspective of superpower rivalry, US governments, under both Republicans and Democrats, have looked at the region and seen only Moscow. Arms sales and trade continued with Southern Rhodesia despite international sanctions, not only because the exchange was profitable, but because the liberation groups were too 'communist.' Angola was 'lost' to the Soviets, even though the trade and investment pattern remained overwhelmingly with the West. The US Congress asked the CIA to investigate the communist influence inside the ANC (and the CIA reported it was minimal, if at all).

The second theme of counter-revolution was consistent with a long-held aim of the US government to manage national liberation struggles. From the Congo to Namibia, the US has tried to control – sometimes quite directly – those taking power in the new governments. Britain, the US and South Africa supported Bishop Abel Muzorewa for the leadership of independent Zimbabwe; they legitimised his bid for the office and came close to recognising his internal settlement under Ian Smith in 1979. In the elections of 1980, they provided him with campaign materials and funds.[3] In the transition to elections in Namibia in 1989, Herman Cohen, the US Assistant Secretary of State for Africa in the new Bush Administration, referred to the United Nations (UN) Special Representative for Namibia as 'our agent.' When questioned in the congressional hearings what he meant, Cohen claimed that the US paid the UN bills so the US controlled what the UN did in Namibia.[4] Pursued so consistently, this policy offers an insight into the US attitude to change in South Africa: the US seeks to manage the transition to majority rule.

## Ideological Offensive

The ideological mission of the US and South Africa in Southern Africa has been to depict the Pretoria regime as the 'stabiliser' and its neighbours as the 'destabilising' force. Systematic denigration of the MPLA (Popular Movement for the Liberation of Angola), for example, tries to convince Americans and South Africans that it is the 'enemy,' and tagging a government 'communist' goes a long way to achieving that goal.[5] The first dimension of the offensive, therefore, is literally a war of words. Because of the presence of Cuban troops, both South Africa and the US governments labelled Angola a Soviet enclave. Responding to this relatively successful campaign, prominent black leaders in the US (such as Charles Evers, Dick Gregory, and Maurice Dawkins) have spoken in support of Jonas Savimbi's 'anti-communist' war.

For Nicaragua, President Reagan escalated the word game by attempting to attach a second label to the Sandinistas: 'terrorist'. In July 1983 they were 'counterfeit revolutionaries;' by mid-1984 Nicaragua was a 'communist totalitarian state' conducting a 'reign of terror.'[6] For Mozambique the propaganda accusations were equally serious. After bombing a jam factory and a child-care centre outside Maputo, South Africa insisted that an ANC base had been eliminated. When it attacked ANC offices in Maputo, South Africa announced it had destroyed a military base.

The propaganda campaigns in the 1980s reached new levels of international co-ordination and of sophistication. Right-wing groups organised to 'roll-back communism' have existed since the 1950s, but they gained importance in the 1980s as right-wing 'think tanks' to provide analysis directly to the government. The Council for Inter-American Studies (CIS) wrote the Santa Fe Report which was the blueprint for Reagan's Central American policy in his first term (1981–84); four CIS members joined the administration to carry out the plan.[7] In 1985 the International Freedom Foundation (IFF) was established with offices in Washington, Johannesburg and London. They published an anti-sanctions monograph, 'Understanding Sanctions,' held hearings on alleged repression of children by the ANC (in response to US Congressional hearings on South African detention of children) and published tracts on the same subject, one of which called the head of the anti-apartheid TransAfrica organisation a 'spokesman for Soviet and Cuban supported terrorist groups.' The *International Freedom Review* Advisory Board has included members of Congress, Philip M. Crane and Robert Dornan as well as Senator Jesse Helms.[8]

Tactics of other right-wing organisations are even more comprehensive. Such groups as Reverend Moon's Unification Church, the World Anti-Communist League (WACL), and Citizens for America provide everything from media campaigns and conferences to material aid and contacts with corporate executives for counter-revolutionaries. For example, the WACL, led by retired Major General John K. Singlaub (a major figure in the Iran–contra affair),[9] held a conference in San Diego, California, in September 1984 where the MNR arrived with a shopping list: 500 surface-to-air missiles, small arms for 15,000 troops, AK-47 ammunition, bazookas, and demolition equipment (as well as 'access to the media and important legislators').[10] In late 1988, Singlaub toured inside Mozambique with the MNR, referring to them as the 'good guys.'[11] And the ties are interlocking, for the IFF attends the conferences of the WACL and of Moon's front groups. Documentation on Reverend Moon's organisations is extensive, because they have been fully involved in destabilisation in Central America, providing free trips and money for anti-government Nicaraguans such as Steadman Fagoth and Edgar Chamorro. Moon's *Insight* magazine advertised South African tours, one of which included a stop in London to meet with the former Commander of NATO, General Walter Walker.[12]

Another set of organisations is more specialised, acting only as a cash conduit to the counter-revolutionaries from corporations and foundations. The list for Central America is long, including groups that claim only 'humanitarian' aid: Friends of the Americas, Human Development Fund, Americares, Knights of Malta, Refugee Relief International, and World Medical Relief (which has worked closely with the CIA for many years, supplying Hmong mercenaries in Laos and other anti-communist forces).[13] Evangelical churches, in pursuit of anti-communist Christianity, also operate relief networks which gather intelligence. Paralife Ministries in El Salvador co-ordinates with the government; Shekinah Ministries in Mozambique work closely with the MNR.[14] As a 1987 US Senate Committee report stated:

> The provision of humanitarian aid and civic assistance activities to the civilian populace of developing foreign countries potentially confronted with low intensity conflict should be explicitly recognised as a valid military mission.[15]

One group, Food for Africa, did receive permission from the Mozambican government to distribute food, even though it is South Africa-based; when asked about allegations of its supporting the MNR, the director replied that they were simply feeding hungry people. Back in the US, Food for Africa was raising money from other evangelical groups which openly supported the MNR, received assistance from a lawyer who also raised funds for the contras against Nicaragua, and hired the same publicity firm, Lichtenstein and Co., which provided publicity for fund-raising for the contras.[16]

The organisations, which assist counter-revolutionaries by lobbying parliamentarians, media campaigns and with analysis from think tanks, provide an international network which gives the 'freedom fighters' a legitimacy far beyond their own capabilities. The *Internationale de la Résistance*, for example, paid for an advertisement in *Le Monde* on 12 March 1985[17] calling for the US Congress to finance the contras against Nicaragua; it was signed by several prominent politicians, including Malcolm Frazer of Australia, who became co-chair of the Commonwealth Eminent Persons Group of Southern Africa. The United States Global Strategy Council has former ambassador to the UN Jean Kirkpatrick, Henry Luce III, and Donald Rumsfeld on the board; the council offers favorable analyses of the MNR and distributes interviews of MNR leaders.[18] The few listed here provide only a glimpse into the extent and diversity of private support for the counter-revolutions.[19] By attending international conferences, speaking to government officials, appearing on television, the counter-revolutionaries gain credibility; in fact, with little legitimacy at home, international 'respectability' is crucial to their success.

The reasons for the proliferation of these organisations go beyond legal lobbying or international networking. With funds for counter-revolutionaries threatened in elected parliaments, these organisations represent the 'privatisation of roll-back.' The congressional cutting-off of funds to the contras was not much of a problem for their continuing operations because private donors were willing conduits. Similarly, the South African government can argue that funding for the MNR continues by way of private Portuguese interests not under South African control. Likewise the US government can officially support Mozambique, while its top leaders privately raise funds for the MNR.

A second important raison d'être for the organisations is that, as 'private' entities, they are not subject to as much public scrutiny as government administrations. In the US, private organisations are used explicitly to circumvent the Freedom of Information Act, for they can avoid disclosing documents or keeping records and can hold closed meetings. Further, they are exempt from the restriction prohibiting involvement in the internal affairs of other countries.

Third-party funding from other governments also sustained the networks. The 'problem' as defined in a 1985 memo from General John Singlaub to National Security Council staff member Oliver North and CIA Director William Casey was the following: 'With each passing year, Congress has become increasingly unpredictable and uncooperative regarding the President's desire to support the cause of the Freedom Fighters despite Soviet oppression.' The solution was 'to create a conduit for maintaining a continuous flow of Soviet weapons and technology, to be used by the United States in support of Freedom Fighters in Nicaragua, Angola, Cambodia, Ethiopia, etc.' The memo proposed a three-way trade in which the US would provide high technology equipment to another country, that country would deliver from its stockpiles military equipment of equal value to a third country, and the third country would export Soviet-compatible arms to a trading company at the direction of the US.[20]

As early as 1982, CIA Director William Casey had already flown to Pretoria apparently to arrange for Saudi Arabia to assist in the funding of UNITA. Saudi officials were described as willing to take on the 'burden of support for Savimbi.'[21] The Saudi arms dealer, Adnan M. Khashoggi, who purchased arms for Oliver North to supply the contras against Nicaragua, reportedly also arranged a $200 million loan to Zaire guaranteed by King Fahd. The US delivered some of the arms via the Boma and Matadi ports of Zaire.[22] Others went by air on St. Lucia Airlines via Cape Verde for refuelling to a southern airstrip in Zaire.[23] All of these possible transactions occurred while the Clark Amendment, prohibiting US government covert funds to UNITA, was US law. John Stockwell, former CIA Task Force leader in Angola during 1975–6, states that it is likely UNITA has received hundreds of millions of dollars from Saudi Arabia, Brunei, and Morocco.[24] In similar third-party operations, Mozambique has traced assistance for the MNR directly to Portugal, Oman and the Comoros.

Israel was key to the whole Iran–contra affair, particularly in regard to the transfer of arms. In the 1987 Congressional hearings exposing the deals but deferring to sensitive relations with allies, Israel was not mentioned by name but merited the designation 'country #1' (Saudi Arabia was #2, South Africa #6 and Portugal #15). The Israeli–South African connection has been well-documented,[25] as the Israelis regularly trade arms with South Africa, providing not only their own manufactures but also captured PLO weapons for UNITA and the MNR in order to conceal their source. Given the close ties of Israel to the US and to South Africa, this 'third-party' option was probably used frequently.

However, the Israeli connection goes far beyond financing by a third party in that they also have helped train South Africans in counter-insurgency against internal insurrection in South Africa; SHABAK, the Israeli security police, has a permanent mission in South Africa. Further, Israelis have also died and been captured while fighting against the governments inside Angola and Mozambique.[26] Israelis were reported training MNR troops in Malawi, only one of four African countries that maintained relations with Israel after the Organisation of African Unity 1973 diplomatic boycott. After re-establishing relations with Zaire in 1982, Israel began training both Zairian forces in Shaba province and UNITA forces in Namibia: 'Israeli Defence Minister Ariel Sharon was personally involved in the organisation, training and equipping of "commando" units of the army of Zaire, especially organised for missions along the borders of the RPA [People's Republic of Angola].'[27] From 1975, Israelis were permanently stationed in Namibia and participated in various invasions of Angola.[28]

## Shared Goals and Tactics

The goals of South Africa and the US were identical in their desire to establish non-communist, or even non-socialist, governments, friendly to Western interests. But the shared tactics for how to pursue this objective varied from country to country. In Angola, this goal was translated into a sustained attempt by both governments to overthrow the MPLA government. From the independence struggle (1961–75) against Portuguese colonialism when the two supported Portugal, including direct invasions of independent Angola by South Africa (begun in August 1974 just before independence), to the defeat of South African forces at Cuito Cuanavale in 1988, they have collaborated to defeat the MPLA. From 1975–85, the Clark amendment was in effect, prohibiting US government covert operations but, as discussed above, the amendment was probably circumvented (just as the Boland amendment stopping government funds for the Nicaraguan contras was abrogated by the White House). The US repeatedly vetoed UN Security Council resolutions condemning South African invasions, often trying to blame Angola for them. And the US devised the policy of 'linkage' – the independence of Namibia required prior removal of Cuban troops from Angola. After the military defeat of South Africa in the summer of 1988, compromise was reached on Namibia. A Mozambican minister commented on the dramatic victories by the MPLA: 'Cuito Cuanavale was the most important setback for the South Africans;' they used to brag about their military superiority by claiming 'they could have breakfast in Johannesburg, lunch in Nairobi and dinner in Cairo. But they never even reached Cuito Cuanavale.'[29] As a direct result of the defeat, the time table was set for transition to Namibian independence, with Cuban troops being gradually withdrawn over three years.

However, the settlement did not change US policy toward Angola, for the first foreign policy act of the new Bush Administration in 1989 was to assure Jonas Savimbi of continuing US support to overthrow the Angolan government. By 1988 UNITA was mainly supplied from six air bases in Zaire and operated more from northern Angola; the US had taken over the financing and supply of UNITA from beleaguered South Africa.

The goal of South Africa and the US for the region was translated in a second way into the destabilisation of Mozambique; in contrast to Angola, the two partners were not necessarily interested in the direct overthrow of Frelimo, but openly discussed wanting to 'change behaviour.' Deon Geldenhuys, a prominent South African academic analyst, wrote:

> As the regional leviathan, South Africa is of course placed to exert economic and military pressure against relatively weak and vulnerable black states....*The object of destabilisation is then to promote (or force) profound political changes in the target state.* These may or may not involve structural change – in effect toppling the regime in power and seeing it replaced by a 'moderate' one – *but would certainly involve a major change in the target state's behaviour.*[30]
> [emphasis mine]

South Africa's repeated invasions of Angola and its war in Namibia made the cost of another invasion of Mozambique prohibitive and impractical; putting an army on two extreme borders was risky (and by 1985 the army was also needed in the townships). Destabilisation is a tactic, therefore, when the dominant country judges it cannot invade another, but it also cannot coexist. It seeks to destroy the government from within, to render the country ungovernable. It is implosion. To appear legitimate, sabotage is done by nationals of the target country or from neighbouring countries, not by the army of the destabiliser.

One reason why the Frelimo government has been regarded as 'unacceptable' and the two have wished to change its behaviour is the view that it is 'exporting revolution.' Before the Nkomati Accord in 1984 Mozambique did allow ANC guerrillas to traverse Mozambican territory on the way to South Africa, but they never allowed the ANC in-country bases. After the Accord, ANC activities were strictly curtailed, but South African destabilisation continued. It became clear the support of the ANC was only an initial reason for the policy; the real target was the Mozambican government, its own experiments in social transformation. Schools and health centres were targeted, in order to prevent the Mozambican government from serving the people: from 1983–89 the MNR destroyed over 3000 primary schools or 52 percent of the total; over 900 health clinics were razed.[31] The main goal of destabilisation was to destroy any attempts to take control of the domestic economy. To maintain the market and production relations under old patterns of dominance, the regional power has to show the nationals that the new system cannot work. Social and economic transformations are threatening examples to the status quo.[32] Apartheid South Africa in the 1980s was threatened by the example of Mozambique, not by any armed insurgents. As President Samora Machel so graphically stated,

> A few days ago the South African regime alleged that Mozambique is threatening it by concentrating sophisticated weapons on its border. What are those sophisticated weapons that the regime is referring to? The sophisticated weapon is making the home the centre of fulfilment....The sophisticated weapon is having children as the only privileged sector of our society....The sophisticated weapon is the people's right to create their own history by directing their own destiny, by exercising their sovereign power....the sophisticated weapon that really threatens apartheid is the alternative of civilisation that our society now represents.[33]

The US never officially recognised the MNR, but it also has never condemned South African support and financing of the MNR. For two years, 1978–9, US aid was withheld because of alleged violations of human rights in Mozambique. During one of the most severe droughts in Southern African history (1982–84), the US provided food aid but cut off development aid to Mozambique – until the government signed the Nkomati Accord. In 1984 over 100,000 Mozambicans starved to death because government efforts to send food supplies were sabotaged by the MNR who blew up trucks and burned warehouses. South Africa never honoured the Nkomati Accord, and captured documents reveal that it supplied the MNR just before the Accord was signed and continued to do so in the months thereafter. South African military commanders and the Deputy Minister for Foreign Affairs flew to bases inside Mozambique to direct and assist the MNR.[34]

The US is not on record condemning South Africa's duplicity in signing the accord and continuing the aggression. In fact, US policy toward Mozambique has been complicated and has often appeared contradictory.

By 1986 the US had become the largest food donor to Mozambique, certainly a triumph of Frelimo diplomacy in that the Reagan Administration did not agree with the Congressional right-wing to add the MNR to the list of 'freedom fighters.' In June 1987 Republican presidential candidate Robert Dole and Senator Jesse Helms held up the appointment of Melissa Wells as ambassador to Mozambique, insisting that the State Department talk with the MNR. Tolerated by the US government, a MNR public relations office in Washington, DC, promoted 'multi-national' representation in a multiparty system in Mozambique. However, then Assistant Secretary of State for Africa, Chester Crocker, countered, 'The MNR has no policy but to overthrow the Frelimo government....'

Although not formally recognising the MNR, other US tactics were less supportive of the Mozambican government. The American aid agency, CARE, took over air delivery of food and supplies, trying to run the whole operation in Tete province. The Mozambican government had to remind CARE that Tete was part of its sovereign jurisdiction, not an autonomous unit under CARE. By 1988, Mozambique was asking for development, not just food, aid; when the US did donate a small amount of development aid, it was only to the private sector, a message to the Mozambicans against any state intervention in production or marketing. The US refused security aid for the projects, although other Western nations included the cost of security for development projects to respond to the obvious: new pumps or roads are not much use if they are blown up the day after they are built. Yet the 1988 State Department Gersony report described in detail the atrocities of the MNR, concluding it recruited mainly by terrorist threats to civilians.[35]

These apparently conflicting policies of the US government appear less contradictory if the primary goal is to change the behaviour of the Mozambican government. Putting no pressure on South Africa about its support for the MNR allows the surrogate to continue its atrocities which target trained workers, demobilise the rural population, and virtually halt production – crippling the government so it cannot serve the people. Villagers turn away from organising, for the leaders are the first ones killed or maimed (ears and breasts cut off) by the MNR; they logically turn against a government which cannot provide basic protection or food after the fields have been burned. The US can then move in with donor food, with efficient deliveries, and with equipment for water supplies in resettlement areas; the development aid rewards private farmers, not the cooperatives. The US message is clear: the socialist experiment in Mozambique failed to provide the most fundamental needs, and private enterprise and expertise can 'remedy' the problems.

In the face of this onslaught Mozambique has changed its behaviour. The economy is now open to foreign investment, with few restrictions. The Fifth Party Congress (July 1989) affirmed its belief in socialism but reduced references to workers' and peasants' control. The new constitution (30 November 1990) explicitly embraces a market economy, but strong dissent throughout the country against an unbridled market nuanced the constitutional language by prioritising the value of labour and legitimising state intervention in the economy. The people also rejected the privatisation of land, and the state will remain the sole owner, providing titles for the use of land. What new economic relations will flourish depend on the response of workers and peasants not only to private initiative but also to the greater economic inequities. With the state dependent on Western funds for its own survival, new relations have begun to form a pattern: fields can be replanted and wounds healed, but the social organisation promoted by Frelimo has been the real target of military and economic destabilisation. In the remote areas, its destruction has been pervasive, if not complete. Aid projects are now administered in an hierarchical, command manner – not in the Frelimo style of community participation and organising. Plans and supplies are provided from outside, not as a result of 'the people organised' (*o povo organisado*).

In a third and different way, the goal of the US and South Africa for the region was translated by South Africa into commando raids and economic de-linking from the neighbouring countries. They were accused of harbouring 'terrorists' and frequent commando raids have bombed civilian residences, which are then labelled terrorist bases. As stated earlier, the goal was to convince the outside world that the independent governments in the region were the source of destabilisation, not apartheid. When the US bombed civilian homes in Libya in April 1986 and declared the target a 'terrorist base,' Southern Africans discussed in the media how South Africa would copy that tactic and attack them. Within six weeks (25 May 1986), South African commando raids into Botswana, Zambia and Zimbabwe bombed civilian houses and offices, all of which were proclaimed to be 'terrorist bases.' The US has protested such raids (which also were regularly staged against all the neighbours except Malawi). However, in a major 1987 policy statement, 'An Initiative for Economic Progress in Southern Africa,' the devastation by South Africa against its neighbours was reduced to a brief reference to the 'spill-over effects of internal political conflict in South Africa.'[36]

Although its use of surrogate forces has been mainly in Angola and Mozambique, the Pretoria government has also supported surrogates in Lesotho, Zambia and Zimbabwe. From 1981 until late 1988, despite the failure of the 'Constellation of States' and with growing evidence that the internal bantustans were bankrupt economically and politically,[37] South Africa offered no compromise for its policy of forced dominance and control in the region.

Complementing acts of military sabotage, South Africa also attacked economic targets. In Angola and Mozambique, the surrogate forces targeted health workers, teachers, agricultural extension workers, and skilled craftsmen in an effort to disrupt production; they burned crops and workshops in rural areas and factories in industrial sites. Referring to similar tactics by the contras in Nicaragua, Duane Clarridge, chief of covert operations for the CIA's Latin American division, admitted the contras were routinely murdering 'civilians ... in the provinces, as well as heads of cooperatives, nurses, doctors and judges.' Revealing the attitude of the US government, he said 'there were no rules, no restrictions and no restraints at all on what the contras did in Nicaragua....After all this is war....'[38]

Hitting SADCC directly, South African commandos blew up rail lines and roads, to keep the landlocked states of the region dependent upon South African routes. Sophisticated commando groups operating in Mozambique also blew up oil storage tanks in the port of Beira and electricity pylons from the Cahora Bassa dam; in Angola they tried unsuccessfully to attack the Cabinda oil enclave.

Economic de-linking, purposefully disrupting long-term relations to hurt the weaker partner, paralleled the economic sabotage. This approach ranged from threats which were not carried out, to disruption of 100-year old economic links, to a total embargo. The threats have been manifold, the first was against Zimbabwe in 1981 to abrogate a preferential trade agreement. Botswana complained that railway cars were being held too long inside South Africa; the apartheid regime told Botswana to appeal to the neighbouring Bophuthatswana authorities, which would have been a *de facto* recognition of the bantustan. Lesotho experienced several slow-downs at its border posts, disrupting supplies, then limited border closures, and finally a full embargo in January 1986 which toppled the government.

Mozambique, however, was hardest hit by economic de-linking. As early as 1976, the South Africans responded with severe economic retaliation as Mozambique enforced sanctions against Southern Rhodesia. By 1979, shipments through Maputo port had been cut to 61 percent of immediate pre-independence (1975) levels. By 1980 the number of Mozambican workers in South African mines was 40 percent of the 1975 level. On 10 April 1978, the South African government unilaterally ceased the sale of gold to Mozambique at the fixed price of 29.75 rand per ounce, a practice which had allowed the Portuguese colonial government to sell it at a much higher rate on the world market to finance its balance of payments deficits.[39] In short, the South African government began imposing sanctions against Mozambique in 1976, exacting a high price for its support of majority rule in the region.

The Reagan administration used exactly the same tactics in its region against the Sandinista government. The US suspended all loans to Nicaragua, complaining that its payments were in arrears (although the government and banks seemed to have supplied Anastacio Somoza with all he needed). When Nicaragua approached the Inter-American Development Bank for $60 million, Secretary of State Schultz threatened no new financing for the bank if the directors granted the loan; they bowed to the US. In October 1982 Standard Fruit, the only banana export company in Nicaragua, terminated a five-year contract it had signed only a year before. Exxon refused to transport Mexican oil to Nicaragua. By April 1985 President Reagan issued an executive order to impose a trade embargo, unilaterally breaking three treaties with Nicaragua (General Agreement on Trade and Tariffs, Organisation of American States, Treaty of Friendship).

Reagan administration embargoes have not only been used in neighbouring regions, however; the US also abetted South Africa by sanctioning its neighbours. For example, in 1986 the US cut all aid to Zimbabwe, the economic power in the region doing the most to help the Mozambican government withstand South African-inspired aggression. First to open an embassy at the independence of Zimbabwe (1980), the US provided a major foreign aid package to the new government, to assist in its goals of both primary education and primary health care for all. By 1985, however, relations had deteriorated. After the drought was over and Zimbabwe had a bumper harvest, the government pledged more support to Mozambique and increased the number of its forces in joint manoeuvres. The government became increasingly critical of the US' 'constructive engagement' policy toward South Africa, arguing that it only encouraged the apartheid regime in state terrorism against its own people and its neighbours. From the beginning of 1986, the US government responded by threatening to cut off aid to Zimbabwe. On 4 July 1986, it obtained the pretext: at American independence celebrations hosted by the US Embassy, the Zimbabwe government official invited to speak criticised constructive engagement, citing how conditions inside South Africa and aggression by South Africa had become worse, not better. Ex-President Jimmy Carter, a guest at the reception, walked out. In August the US informed Zimbabwe that all aid would be cut, and it was not restored for a full three years, during which time apartheid aggression in the region increased. In October 1986, President Reagan vetoed a sanctions bill against South Africa, choosing to sanction Zimbabwe, not the apartheid government.

In contrast, the US Congress, responding to increased pressure from their constituents to act against apartheid, passed the 1986 sanctions bill over the President's veto. The mild sanctions became US law, with many loopholes allowing the executive branch to avoid full enforcement. Continuing to resist any sanctions efforts, however, the Reagan administration vetoed a 1987 UN Security Council resolution which was worded exactly like the US sanctions law, creating the anomaly of a government vetoing an international resolution identical to one of its own statues. During the same period, the US also abstained when the UN General Assembly called for special economic assistance to the Frontline States, arguing cynically 'that no realistic amount of aid would be sufficient to insulate the front-line [sic] States from the adverse effects of economic measures taken by or against South Africa.'[40]

Although the US Congress did pass the sanctions bill, a year earlier it had also renewed overt aid to Jonas Savimbi, a decision perceived by the Southern African states as an act of hostility. In mid-1987, the US Congress reduced a proposed aid package to SADCC from $140 million per year for five years to only $37.5 million for one year. (For comparison, US economic aid to El Salvador for fiscal 1987 was $417 million, not counting supplemental funds nor military assistance.) In addition, the Congress passed an amendment requiring that the SADCC nations condemn 'necklacing' in South Africa. No government had ever expressed support for 'necklacing', and the ANC condemned it. However, the Congress depicted the SADCC members as supporting this vigilante act – when, in fact, they never had – serving the purpose of deflecting attention from South African brutality. The response from Southern Africa was vehement; President Mugabe of Zimbabwe expressed the anger felt by SADCC: 'Your 30 million...pieces of silver for the enslavement of our fellow blacks in South Africa, please keep to yourself. Our humanity and personality come first.'[41]

The direct and indirect costs of military and economic sabotage to the nine members of SADCC through 1988 was estimated at $60 billion in 1988 prices, equalling the total production of the region for four years. It was $800 for every man, woman and child in the region; in comparison, the average annual income in Mozambique is less than $200.[42]

The military costs to Zimbabwe and Tanzania for supporting Mozambique are prohibitive. Estimates for Zimbabwe's military range from $3–6 million per week. For a country committed to development, per capita growth has been less than half what it would have been in peace.[43] A Commonwealth report on destabilisation estimated the bill for Zimbabwe at about $7 billion, about the same amount as its total debt in 1990 ($7.2 billion), showing the government would have had a balanced budget but for apartheid aggression. Tanzanians have supported Frelimo since its inception in 1962, stating they themselves cannot be free or develop their economy until Mozambique is free from South African dominance. Over 6000 Tanzanian soldiers operated as far south as the Zambezi River, beyond the Swahili-speaking provinces of northern Mozambique. There are no public estimates of the Tanzanian costs, but they involve expenditures which could have been put to better use in agriculture or industry. In 1988, they withdrew the troops, a decision quite related to demands by the IMF for the government to cut costs. (This financial destabilisation will be analysed in Chapter 5.)

Angola has estimated the cost of destruction from 15 years of war at $20 billion, excluding the cost of defence which consumes about 40 percent of the annual government budget. Consequently, Angola's debt, only $300 million in 1977, soared to $6 billion by 1990,[44] and this oil-rich country joined the ranks of the many trying to borrow from the IMF. Mozambique estimates a cost of $15 billion or ten times its GDP.

More important, these financial costs do not measure the human suffering. UNICEF reported in early 1987 that Angola and Mozambique had the highest mortality rate of children under five in the world...more than Iran, Iraq, or Afghanistan. In the 1989 update, a child was dying every 3.5 minutes, a higher rate than 1987. Since 1980, 1.5 million Southern Africans have been killed, more than the total number of soldiers lost by the US in all its wars since 1776.[45] The reports document the cause of this suffering as South African aggression, not the neglect of governments, not corruption, not even drought.

## Mutual Assistance

The US and South Africa directly assisted each other in their shared goal of anti-communism and desire to manage national liberation efforts. Until the sanctions bill, the Reagan administration increased the sale of 'para-military' equipment and sophisticated computers to South Africa; increased the exchange of military personnel and nuclear scientists; and increased loans from the IMF and banks. Licences for sale of aircraft components and unfinished assemblies of computers and communication equipment almost doubled in Reagan's first term (1981–84).[46] The 1986 sanctions bill did curtail overt expressions of some of these activities.

Information, however, has begun to emerge which would help to explain the perpetuation of a policy which did not have the support of either the American people or the US Congress. It seems that South African adventures not only paralleled the American destabilisation policy, but directly assisted the Reagan administration in Central America. In a 'vest pocket' operation run outside normal channels, a South African cargo corporation, SAFAIR, provided planes to Southern Air Transport which regularly flew weapons to the contras. Lieutenant-Colonel North met Southern Air Transport pilots and said that 'third country' [South Africa] pilots would fly weapons into Nicaragua from El Salvador.[47] This South African assistance to the Reagan Central American policy helped buy tolerance and patience from the US administration for apartheid's slow reforms and continued aggression in the region.

According to an intelligence report dated February 1985, the CIA learned that contra leader Eden Pastora, operating from Costa Rica, had received 200,000 tons of weapons from South Africa. However, the CIA said it had no role in the shipment. In testimony to congressional committees on 4 August 1987, CIA Latin American division chief Duane Clarridge denied that any transactions resulted from official trips to South Africa. However, he did testify that an April 1984 trip related to the 'Nicaraguan Project;' the rest of his testimony giving more detail was censored from the public transcript. Reporters, however, attributed the official talks to complicated negotiations by which the CIA was sharing intelligence with South Africa to be passed on to UNITA in Angola,[48] at the time when US law barred the administration from directly assisting UNITA.

Eden Pastora testified that a CIA Costa Rican operative, Daniel Pacheco, arranged a meeting for him with South African security forces in San José in late 1984; he also stated that he received no assistance from the South Africans.[49] Mario Ferro, editor of the Mozambican *Noticias*, however, found in his investigations that Pastora had been in Portugal several times and met with the MNR to 'discuss the formation of a broad front to seek support from international organisations.'[50]

As the use of land mines by UNITA forces increased, it was reported that 60 UNITA men had been trained in explosives by US experts along with Nicaraguan contras in Central America. One of the weapons both were trained to use was the Claymore antipersonnel fragmentation mine, made in Louisiana and developed to maim its victims by exploding 700 steel projectiles when detonated. UNITA's use of these mines on footpaths to fields of the peasants has given Angola the highest amputee rate in the world.[51]

Finally, in 1985, South Africa began to emulate one of the more odious Central American practices; death squad assassinations escalated against anti-apartheid activists inside South Africa; less cumbersome administratively than detentions, the method has been used against both black and white leaders in South Africa and Namibia.

## Privatisation of Foreign Policy

Destabilisation of a neighbouring country has been part of the increasing militarisation of both the US and South African foreign policy. Negotiations, diplomacy – which mean compromise – played a lesser role until the very end of the 1980s. Choosing the military option, however, has not simply been seen as the most effective means for attaining stated policy objectives; it has also served the domestic goal of strengthening the executive in both countries. Secret military operations cannot be scrutinised fully by the legislature, which has the purpose of debating policy openly. Instead, executive control and secret operations extend reliance on individuals and networks who share ideological goals; other parties and branches of government cannot be trusted – an attitude which leads to the privatisation of foreign policy.

After the exposés of the Gulf of Tonkin incident (1964) and of the bombing of Cambodia (1969) without congressional consent, the US Congress tried to reassert its role in foreign policy. The War Powers Act (1973) allows the President to introduce armed forces overseas only when US forces are under attack, and then only for 60 days unless Congress declares war. In 1974 the Congress also limited cash sales of arms overseas, and from 1975 it required the CIA to report covert operations to the Senate and House Intelligence Committees. Finally, Congress passed the Freedom of Information Act requiring the US government to release files of citizens who had been under surveillance.

Many viewed these laws as a return to the balance and separation of powers between the executive and legislative branches. However, the conservatives saw them as an attack on the ability of the US government to act expeditiously against its enemies, citing the 'loss' of Vietnam, Cambodia, Iran, Nicaragua and Angola from the American sphere of influence. The Reagan administration had as its major goal the restoration of presidential authority in order to reassert American interests; Congress, with all its committees and factions, was a hindrance to incisive assertion of power. The American President must 'stand tall,' not only over the rest of the world, but over the law-makers.

Reagan was successful with this agenda throughout both terms of office. The general climate of anti-communism, promoted through the various foundations discussed above, set the theme for the President. With his personal popularity, he was able to act unilaterally and deflect polite Congressional questions. After Nicaragua twice took the US government to the World Court, over the mining of the harbour and over the embargo, President Reagan removed the US, which had been a founding member, from the court. When questioned about the constitutionality of such a unilateral executive action, he claimed that the constitution required US Senate approval for international treaties, but it said nothing about Senate consent to abrogate them.

Resurgence of the CIA was signalled when President Reagan appointed William Casey, one of its founders, as director in 1981. From 1973–81, when the CIA came under closer congressional scrutiny, the central intelligence analysis (information-gathering) wing gained prominence over the covert operations wing, but Casey moved immediately to restore the latter to its previous prominence. He won new restrictions on the Freedom of Information disclosures relating to the CIA, as well as harsh legal reprisals for anyone disclosing CIA activities.

As is now well documented, the expanded role of the CIA was not sufficient for some in the executive branch. More than one national security advisor ran extensive covert operations, referred to in the May–August 1987 congressional hearings as the 'secret government within our government' (Senator Daniel Inouye), for many foreign policy decisions were made in this way, from financing and supplying 'freedom fighters' to trading arms for hostages in the Middle East.

Because the secret operations were mainly for military goals, several military officers were key to the policy (Colonel MacFarland, Admiral Poindexter, Lieutenant-Colonel North, Major-Generals Secord and Singlaub, Colonel Richard Dutton, Lieutenant-Colonels Richard Gadd and Robert Earl). They also boasted of their 'can-do' skills, the ability to execute plans expeditiously. Through their military connections, against explicit congressional laws, they acquired ships, weapons, missiles and requisitioned military flights for the covert operations.

One feature of the privatisation of foreign policy is that CIA and National Security Advisor operations were closely intertwined with private firms. Yet there are strict restrictions on activities of non-profit organisations which must remain 'educational' and refrain from supporting a particular political line; many of the right-wing groups claim this non-profit (tax-exempt) status. Since 1794 (when French agents were seeking private US support in the expanding European war), it has been against the US Neutrality Act for any private citizen to support or participate in military action against any country at peace with the US. In working closely with several private groups, the executive branch ignored these laws. As important for current conflicts, even if the operations out of the National Security Advisor's office have since been curtailed, little has yet been done to delimit the private business operations in funding 'freedom fighters' (e.g. UNITA or MNR).

President Reagan denied he knew private profits from arms sales to Iran were used to fund the contras. As the congressional hearings proceeded, however, he admitted knowing about extensive extra-legal operations, not under the scrutiny of his own National Security Council or the Congress. Secret operations greatly strengthen the hand of the executive against the Congress and the American public, who are kept misinformed about activities and relationships. The arms deals are not secret to the adversary (Iran), for they are involved. The wars are not secret to the people bombed. It is the American public and many of their elected representatives who become redundant in the privatisation of foreign policy.

Also a move to strengthen the executive and remove policy decisions from legislative debate, President Reagan issued approximately 300 National Security Decision Directives (NSDD). Unlike executive orders which are listed in the Federal Register or presidential findings which are sent to the House and Senate Intelligence Committees, NSDDs do not have to be revealed to any other branch of government. Unless cancelled or modified, they continue in force into the next administration. A NSDD initiated the funding of the contras as well as the invasion of Grenada. Ostensibly, NSDDs are merely internal memorandums from the President to his bureaucracy, but some have ordered actions contrary to the government's stated policy and infringed on basic civil liberties. Analysts say that President Reagan's proclivity to use them was 'apparently because it [the Reagan White House] didn't have to make them public.'[52] More than 200 Reagan NSDDs remain classified. After failing to receive a list of NSDDs dating from 1981, House Speaker Jim Wright stated, 'Congress cannot react responsibly to new dictates for national policy set in operation by the executive branch behind closed doors.'[53]

The extent of increased executive power was demonstrated in a startling transfer of constitutional powers by a Florida federal judge in a ruling on July 13, 1989. Judge Norman Roettger dismissed indictments against six contra supporters for violations of the Neutrality Act, ruling that the US was not 'at peace' with Nicaragua because the executive branch pursued hostilities, despite a congressional ban on assistance to the contras. The Reagan administration's defiance of Congress meant that private citizens were allowed to join the executive branch in warfare against Nicaragua. The judge wrote that 'declarations of war between nations are passé....'[54] The Supreme Court had ruled that congressional passage of appropriation bills authorising military actions, even without formal declarations of war, legalised a war, but the six contra supporters were indicted with violating the Neutrality Act when Congress had *explicitly prohibited* military assistance to the contras. The Roettger ruling virtually takes all war-making powers away from Congress. Unlikely to be appealed by the Bush administration's Justice Department, the ruling will have to be taken up by the Congress in order for it to retain its own constitutional powers.

The South African government is very different from the US, but there are three important similarities: 1) the executive has been strengthened relative to the legislature; 2) the role of covert actions and of the military in policy formulations has increased; 3) the liaison of private business and organisations with the executive facilitates avoidance of public debate about foreign policy.

The 1984 constitutional change was widely publicised because it established three racial houses of parliament: white, 'coloured,' Asian. An element of the new constitution which did not receive much press attention was the increased powers of the executive. If one or more houses rejects a bill from committee, it is referred to the President's Council for arbitration. Dominated by whites, Council decisions cannot be vetoed by parliament. The President's Council can, therefore, impose its will even though its majority party (white) has a minority of total MPs in parliament. With parliament reduced to a debating society, real power has shifted to the executive branch, to the Presidency and the myriad of institutions which are a part of it. Such a concentration of power reached its apogee under President P.W. Botha with the real focus of power being the State Security Council (SSC), a committee of the cabinet. Under Botha it advised on the formulations and implementation 'of national policy and strategy in relation to the security of the Republic,'[55]an assignment broad enough to cover almost any policy. In contrast to other cabinet committees, decisions did not have to be circulated as appendices to cabinet minutes and meetings were not open to cabinet ministers not formally appointed to the SSC. The President took the chair, with the Ministers of Defence, Foreign Affairs, Justice and Police as well as the head of the National Intelligence Service, the police and the defence forces as members. The increased role of the SSC in foreign policy downgraded the Ministry of Foreign Affairs and considerably increased the role of the military. Philip H. Frankel of the University of Witwatersrand noted:

> Military men are in general placed at strategic points to influence virtually every aspect of public policy. This influence has progressively increased since 1980 as Botha and his military allies have moved to an ever more embracing conception of 'national security' which penetrates into virtually every aspect of political, economic and cultural life and as the powers of the legislature have been eroded to the advantage of the office of prime minister [now president] and the state security network.[56]

It was this unique and powerful body which caused analysts to refer to the shift in the balance of power within the government as a 'creeping coup d'état.' For example, the SSC was solely responsible for the Directorate of Military Intelligence (DMI) which handled almost all intelligence work, including commanding the MNR in Mozambique. The ex-head of DMI, Lt. General P.W. van der Westhuizen, served as a secretary to the SSC. Heading a staff of 87 to serve the SSC, his role was not too different from that of the US National Security Advisor to the US National Security Council.

In contrast to the US, however, under the SSC the penetration of the South African military into all levels of administration was very systematic. Twelve Joint Military Commands (JMCs) operated at the level of the old provincial councils; these were subdivided into 60 sub-JMCs at the level of metropolitan regions. Mini-JMCs (448 of them) worked with local authorities or town councils. The purpose of this network was to contain political resistance, co-ordinate a broad 'hearts and minds' strategy by improving conditions in black areas and act as an early warning system to the SSC for potential problems.[57]

It is this national security management system (NSMS) which both militarised foreign policy and strengthened the executive:

> The structures of the NSMS, and particularly the SSC, have been the vehicles through which the military have come to exercise a preponderant role in foreign and particularly regional, policy making. At the same time, it must be stressed that the NSMS has also brought about a centralisation and 'rationalisation' of decision-making within the executive.[58]

The most important link between business and the military has been Armscor (Armaments Corporation of South Africa), which is the sole procurement agent of arms for the defence forces. Except for a few wholly-owned subsidiaries, Armscor relies on close co-operation with private corporations for research, development and the manufacturing of armaments. Its ten-member board is appointed by the President and is responsible to the Minister of Defence, yet it has only two government representatives on it. The chair and most directors are from the private sector, but their names are not revealed for fear of jeopardising their foreign business interests. In fact, most of what Armscor does is highly secret, for it is against the law to disclose 'any information in relation to the acquisition, supply, marketing, importation, export, development, manufacture, maintenance or repair of, or research in connection with armaments, by, for, on behalf of, or for the benefit of the Armaments Corporation or a subsidiary company.'[59] Armscor, therefore, is a state corporation run almost exclusively by private enterprise, sub-contracting thousands of contracts to large and small private corporations.

The South African government has institutionalised the executive-military dominance over parliament, a major structural difference from the separation of powers between the US Congress and the executive. The Congress could reassert its control of the purse over foreign policy and its oversight of covert operations. The use of private business and foundations to promote covert operations is not new in US history, but Congress could once again tighten those controls; most of the laws needed are already on the books. The South African parliament, in contrast, has been reduced to an impotent rubber-stamp of the executive will.

In the last decade, many in Southern Africa have died as a direct result of the congruence of US and South African policy. The pervasiveness of the destruction makes any attempt to analyse SADCC's efforts to develop almost arrogant. What is more remarkable than US–South African collaboration, therefore, is the ability of the members to co-ordinate for development while resisting aggression.

One other component – in addition to the colonial legacy and continuing South African aggression – must be analysed as part of the context for regional co-ordination, namely, the degree of diversity which characterises the SADCC member states and which places a limit on both their development potential and the degree of SADCC co-operation.

# NOTES

1 Some parts of this chapter have been elaborated in Carol B. Thompson, 'War by Another Name: Destabilization in Nicaragua and Mozambique.' *Race and Class* 29:4 (1988): 21-44. For a discussion of Total Strategy as one version of 'low-intensity conflict,' a term coined by the Reagan administration, see Steven Metz, 'Pretoria's "Total Strategy" and Low-Intensity Warfare in Southern Africa.' *Comparative Strategy* 6:4 (1987): 437-69. 'Low-intensity conflict' is a concept consciously avoided in the analysis in this chapter, for it is never 'low-intensity' to those being assaulted; the word is simply a euphemism to describe an unproclaimed war which does not necessarily include a full-scale invasion. The concept 'destabilisation' is analysed here to explain that type of war.

2 Department of Defence, *White Paper on Defence,* Cape Town, 1977. Deon Geldenhuys, 'Some Strategic Implications of Regional Economic Relationships for the Republic of South Africa,' *ISSUP Strategic Review* (January 1981): 17-24.

3 Carol B. Thompson. *Challenge to Imperialism: The Frontline States in the Liberation of Zimbabwe.* Harare: Zimbabwe Publishing House, 1985 and Boulder: Westview Press, 1986.

4 National Public Radio, 11 August 1989.

5 For a thorough history of the US governments' misrepresentation of the MPLA, see Gerald J. Bender. 'Washington's Quest for Enemies in Angola,' *Regional Conflict and U.S. Policy: Angola and Mozambique.* Richard J. Bloomfield (ed.) Michigan: Reference Publications, Inc., 1988, pp. 186-206.

6 Roy Gutman. 'Nicaragua: America's Diplomatic Charade,' *Foreign Policy,* no. 56 (1984): 16.

7 Jerry Sanders. 'Terminators,' *Mother Jones* (August-September 1983): pp. 36-41. Although this analysis focuses on the US, such private think-tank activities were also carried out in other Western countries. The Hans Siedel Foundation of the conservative CSU in Bavaria held strategy sessions on Southern Africa, attended by South African Foreign Minister Pik Botha and UNITA leaders. The Konrad Adenauer Foundation of the CDU party in the Federal Republic of Germany helped formulate the constitution for the Multi-Party Conference, the South African-controlled government in Namibia. *Africa Confidential* (28 November 1984). Sam Nujoma, 'Conspiracy between FRG and Racist South Africa,' press statement, Luanda, 23 May 1985.

8 David Ivon. 'Touting for South Africa: International Freedom Foundation,' *CovertAction,* no. 31 (Winter 1989): 62-4.

9 Retired Army Major General Singlaub was fired from his job as head of the US forces in South Korea after he publicly challenged then President Carter's proposal to withdraw troops from that country. With Oliver North's knowledge, Singlaub became one of the major conduits of arms to the contras, while a congressional ban on such aid was in effect. He was chosen to be the 'lightning rod,' to deflect attention from higher officials who were also involved in the secret illegal deals.

10 Jerry Sanders, *op. cit.,* p. 40.

11 Speech, Benefit for the Conservative Caucus Foundation, 1 April 1989, Ramada Renaissance Hotel, Herndon, Virginia.

12 *Manchester Guardian Weekly* (24 February and 3 March 1985), both p. 13.

Fred Clarkson. 'Privatizing the War,' *CovertAction*, no. 22 (1984): pp. 31-3. David Ivon. *op. cit.*, p. 63.

13   *Guardian* (New York), March 12, 1989, p. 3.

14   Prexy Nesbitt. 'Terminators, Crusaders and Gladiators: Western (private and public) Support for Renamo and Unita,' *Review of African Political Economy*, no. 43 (1988): 118, 120.

15   *Ibid.*, p. 118.

16   'Ex-HUD aide solicited for charity allegedly linked to African rebels,' *San Jose Mercury*, 27 August 1989. The Mozambique government is now investigating Food for Africa. Food for Africa is possibly linked to the Housing and Urban Development scandal in the US government; Housing Commissioner (1986-88) Thomas Demery raised over $290,000 from housing contractors and developers for Food for Africa. An investigative report on conflict of interest was not prosecuted by the Justice Department, and Demery denied any wrong-doing.

17   Advertisement in *Le Monde*, 21 March 1985, p. 6. Internationale de la Résistance, Declaration of Principles and List of Support Committee Members, mimeo, 4 May 1983. *Afrique-Asie*, 14 January 1986.

18   Sibyl Cline. 'The Fight Goes On: RENAMO – Anti-Communist Insurgents in Mozambique,' United States Global Strategy Council, 30 June 1989.

19   For a list of those who supported UNITA and the MNR, see Prexy Nesbitt, *op. cit.*, pp. 122-24.

20   *Report of the Congressional Committees Investigating the Iran-Contra Affair*, abridged edition, New York: Times Books, 1988, pp. 233-4. For a discussion of the philosophy behind the use of private donors and third-country funders, see Thomas Shackley. *The Third Option: An American View of Counterinsurgency Operations*. New York: Readers Digest Press, 1981.

21   Robert Knight. 'Iran Arms Profits,' *Guardian*, 31 December 1987; *Guardian*, 28 July 1987. On 1 July 1987 at the House Foreign Affairs Subcommittee hearings, Sam Joseph Bamieh, a Republican businessman from California and a friend of King Fahd, testified that Saudi officials agreed to finance UNITA (and other 'anti-Communist' movements) in 1981 in exchange for the Reagan administration's support for the Saudi purchase of the AWACs. *New York Times*, 2 July 1987. At the same hearings, he also testified that Saudi officials asked him in February 1984 to help start an offshore company that would buy oil from the Saudis and then resell it to South Africa, making 75 cents to one dollar profit on each barrel to provide funds for 'freedom fighters.' He was to work with Richard Secord and Albert Hakim. This deal has not been confirmed, but its idea is the same model as the arms and drug sales for the contras. Saudi Arabia received American AWAC planes, but South Africa? Representative Edward Boland, inquiring about Clarridge's mission to South Africa, noted that Pretoria would support the contras 'in exchange for...'– the rest of the sentence was deleted in the public record of the hearings. 'South Africa Link,' *The Nation*, 12 September 1987, pp. 221-2.

22   *Africa Confidential*, 7 January and 13 May 1987; *Africa Report*, May-June 1983.

23   'Tiny St. Lucia Airline used in Iran Missions,' *Washington Post*, 24 February 1987.

24   Prexy Nesbitt, *op. cit.*, p. 113 and personal conversations with John

Stockwell. David Ottaway. 'Savimbi Warns Oil Firms in Angola,' *Washington Post*, 4 February 1986.

25    James Adams. *The Unnatural Alliance: Israel and South Africa*. London: Quartet Books, 1984. Benjamin Beit-Hallahmi. *The Israeli Connection— Who Israel Arms and Why*. New York: Pantheon, 1987. Jane Hunter. *Israeli Foreign Policy: South Africa and Central America*. Boston: South End Press, 1987. Richard P. Stevens and Abdelwahab M. Elmessiri. *Israel and South Africa: The Progression of a Relationship*. New Brunswick, NJ: North American, Inc., 1976.

26    Benjamin Ben Beit-Hallahmi. *ibid.*, chapter five and Jane Hunter, *ibid.*

27    Jane Hunter, *ibid.*, p.59.

28    Benjamin Beit-Hallahmi, *op. cit.*, p. 121.

29    Sergio Vieira, quoted in Ecumenical Documentation and Information Centre for Eastern and Southern Africa (EDICESA) 2/2 (February-March 1989): 12.

30    Deon Geldenhuys, 'South Africa's Regional Policy,' paper presented at the Golden Jubilee Conference of the South African Institute of International Affairs, Cape Town, 6-7 March 1984, p. 28.

31    Mozambique Information Agency Bulletin, 16 December 1989 and 6 July 1990.

32    This same policy and tactic were used by the Reagan Administration against Nicaragua. See Carol B. Thompson, 1988, *op.cit.*

33    'Hell-Bent on Destabilisation,' *Social Change and Development* (Zimbabwe), no. 7 (1984): 17.

34    'Documentos da Gorongosa (extractos),' 1984, captured and released by the Mozambican government after the fall of the MNR camp in Gorongosa, August 1986.

35    Robert Gersony. 'Summary of Mozambican Refugee Accounts of Principally Conflict-Related Experience in Mozambique: Report submitted to Ambassador Jonathan Moore and Dr. Chester A. Crocker.' Washington: Department of State Bureau for Refugee Programs, April 1988.

36    United States Department of State, 'An Initiative for Economic Progress in Southern Africa,' 29 January 1987, p. 3. This paper was presented to Congress by the President as a 'comprehensive multi-year program designed to promote economic reform and development in the black-ruled states of southern Africa.' p. 1.

37    In early 1988, there were two coups in the so-called 'independent' bantustans or homelands, the Transkei and Bophuthatswana. In Bophuthatswana, the South African military restored the old order within minutes of taking action. For discussion of South Africa's regional policy, see Centro de Estudos Africanos, Universidade Eduardo Mondlane, 'Re-Structuring the Southern African Region: Research Support for the SADCC Strategy,' a paper presented at conference on Priorities in Southern Africa, Roma, Lesotho, 23-27 November 1981. Deon Geldenhuys, 1984, *op. cit.* Dan O'Meara, 'Pretoria's Strategy in South and Southern Africa,' paper presented at conference on Peace and Security in Southern Africa, Mohonk Mountain House, New York, 7-9 December 1984.

38    Johnathan Marshall, Peter Dale Scott and Jane Hunter. *The Iran Contra Connection—Secret Teams and Covert Operations in the Reagan Era*. Boston: South End Press, 1987, p. 131.

39 People's Republic of Mozambique, Economic Report, Maputo, January 1984, pp. 30-1.
40 United Nations General Assembly, Report of the Secretary-General, 'Special Assistance to front-line States and bordering States,' Addendum, A/42/422/add.1, 17 September 1987, p. 4.
41 *Herald* (Harare), 26 May 1987.
42 Reginold Herbold Green *et al. Children on the Front Line.* New York: UNICEF, 1989, p. 23.
43 *Ibid.*, pp. 20 and 22.
44 Southern African Research and Documentation Centre, 'Destabilisation Update,' Harare, 15 December 1990.
45 *Ibid.*, p. 11.
46 *Washington Post,* 24 February 1985.
47 Transcript, ABC World News Tonight, 25 February 1987. Safair did acknowledge leasing aircraft to Southern Air Transport. Baltimore *Sun,* 27 February 1987. See also The National Security Archive, *The Chronology- The Documented Day-by-Day Account of the Secret Military Assistance to Iran and the Contras.* New York: Warner Books, 1987, pp. 31, 35. Johnathan Marshall *et al., op. cit.*, p. 237.
48 *New York Times,* 20 August 1987.
49 *The Nation,* 12 September 1987, *op. cit.* 'Inside the Shadow Government,' Declaration of Plaintiffs' Counsel, filed by the Christic Institute, US District Court, Miami, 31 March 1988, p. 111.
50 Radio Mozambique, 11 GMT, 31 December 1984.
51 Renee Simar, 'Land Mines in Angola,' mimeo, 28 September 1988; 'Exploding Mines: US Claymore Mines in Central America,' mimeo, 10 July 1988. 'Angola: UNITA at the Crossroads,' *Africa Confidential* 29:16 (12 August 1988): 5.
52 Eve Pell, 'The Backbone of Hidden Government,' *The Nation* (19 June 1989): 853.
53 *Ibid.*, p. 852
54 Christic Institute, 'A Dramatic Transfer of Constitutional Power,' memo-randum, 19 July 1989.
55 Deon Geldenhuys. *The Diplomacy of Isolation: South African Foreign Policy Making.* Johannesburg: Macmillan South Africa, 1984, p. 92.
56 Philip H. Frankel. *Pretoria's Praetorians.* Cambridge: Cambridge University Press, 1984, p. 106.
57 *The Cape Times,* 9 July 1987; *Guardian,* 3 October 1986.
58 Mac Maharaj. 'Internal Determinants of Pretoria's Present Foreign Policy,' paper given at seminar in memory of Aquino de Bragança and Ruth First, Universidade Eduardo Mondlane, Maputo, 21-22 January 1988, p. 14.
59 Armaments Development and Production Act, 1980 Amendment, cited in South African Institute of Race Relations, *Survey 1980.* Johannesburg: Institute of Race Relations, 1981, p. 213.

# 3.

# A Region
# Defined by Diversity

Dominance of mining in the region set a pattern: white settlers in larger numbers than elsewhere on the continent, vast wealth potential and migrant labour production. Such a regional overview, however, should not obscure the vast diversity – both economic and political. Again, colonialism directs the course, modified only slightly in the periods since independence.

Although SADCC members derive over 60 percent of their foreign exchange from mineral exports, mineral dependence ranges from 0 percent in Malawi to 96 percent of exports for Angola.[1] In fact, only four of the members provide almost all (97 percent) of the region's mineral output.[2] And three of the four remain vulnerable as mono-mineral exporters, with one mineral accounting for over 60 percent of all exports (Angola–oil, Botswana–diamonds, Zambia–copper). In contrast, Zimbabwe has a more diversified mineral sector; gold is the second export after tobacco; chrome, asbestos, coal all contribute to industry and exports.

Despite these valuable resources, not all the mineral wealthy members have prospered from its exploitation; for example, Angolan mineral wealth has financed only war. Diamonds were discovered in Angola in 1912, but oil became important to the Portuguese economy only after Gulf Oil began its operations in the late 1960s. Oil helped finance the Portuguese war effort against the liberation armies in its three African colonies. Unfortunately, over 20 years later, oil is still financing war in Angola; the fact is that independent Angola could not have resisted multiple South African invasions or UNITA destabilisation without the oil revenue, reaching almost $2.1 billion in 1987 (after a serious decline in 1986 to $1.1 billion because of price declines). The proportion of government revenue financed by oil varied between 40–60 percent in the late 1980s because of oil price fluctuations. War has adversely affected production from the rich diamond mines, ample iron ore reserves, magnite, copper, phosphate, gypsum, uranium and gold deposits.[3]

Mozambique appears to have much mineral potential, but almost all is undeveloped (less than two-thirds is sufficiently mapped for geological baselines). The vast Moatize coal fields were closed by MNR sabotage of the coal rail line. Mozambique's mineral resources – oil, tantalum, titanium, iron ore, nepheline syenite (for aluminum), tin, bauxite – offer a wealthy potential to this poor country,[4] but war has deterred exploration and mining.

In contrast, Botswana, an arid cattle country, has been able to use much of its wealth in agricultural support and social service programmes. In aggregate figures, Botswana is the wealthiest of the SADCC states with reserves equivalent ($2.9 billion) to 30 months' imports by the end of 1989, one of the highest rates in the world. Trying to use the wealth to develop the economy, government leaders have been acutely aware of the short life of mineral bonanzas, as prices can fluctuate wildly and mineral veins diminish. Underlying the need for diversification is the fact that in recent years, Botswana has produced only 5 percent of its grain consumption, and agriculture represents only 3 percent of GDP (1989). The regional example of the problems of mono-exports is not far away; since the disastrous fall in the price of copper in the mid-1970s, followed by fluctuating prices, Zambia's economy has experienced multiple crises as the government tries to diversify production.

In spite of the historical importance of minerals in defining the region, agriculture is the priority production sector for all of SADCC because family incomes are based on it. In four member states over 80 percent of the population is dependent on agriculture for their livelihood (Malawi, Mozambique, Swaziland, Tanzania) but even in mineral-rich Angola and Zimbabwe the number is still over 70 percent. Zambian dependence is more than 50 percent. While Botswanan families have had to rely on food aid for several years because of drought, almost 80 percent derive their livelihood from cattle raising. In contrast, household incomes in Lesotho come mainly from wages of migrant labour to South Africa. Overall, agriculture contributes to 24 percent of regional GNP and 26 percent of total regional export earnings.

Table 3.1 illustrates the diversity of the SADCC economies, with Angola, Botswana, Zambia, and to a lesser extent Zimbabwe, relying on their mineral resources as the primary contributor to their Gross National Products (GNP). Malawi and Mozambique reflect the lowest GNP/capita in the world, with Tanzania not far behind. The table also reveals the crisis in Southern African agriculture in that per capita production has not been sustained from the 1979–81 index, for 1984–86 was a period of drought. However, the decline in per capita production continued to 1989 for most members, with Zimbabwe and Tanzania the notable exceptions (and Zambia and Malawi in occasional years). In 1989, for the first time, regional agricultural production surpassed the population growth rate, yet many members remained chronic food importers. These aggregate figures, therefore, only reveal the effects of the diversity. The patterns of land tenure and distribution begin to explain the variance and reveal the contradictions for SADCC in pursuing its agricultural priorities.

*Table 3.1: SADCC Basic Data (with South Africa for comparison)*

| Country | Population (millions) Mid-1988 | Area (1000s) of sq kms | GNP/capita (US Dollars) 1988 | Life Expectancy 1988 | Food prod. per capita (1979–81=100) 1986–88 |
|---|---|---|---|---|---|
| Angola | 9.4 | 1,247 | 470* | 45 | 87 |
| Botswana | 1.2 | 582 | 1,010 | 67 | 69 |
| Lesotho | 1.7 | 30 | 420 | 56 | 80 |
| Malawi | 8.0 | 118 | 170 | 47 | 85 |
| Mozambique | 14.9 | 802 | 100 | 48 | 83 |
| Namibia* | 1.5 | 823 | 1,290 | 49 | n.a. |
| Swaziland* | 0.7 | 17 | 936 | 55 | n.a. |
| Tanzania | 24.7 | 945 | 160 | 53 | 89 |
| Zambia | 7.6 | 753 | 290 | 53 | 96 |
| Zimbabwe | 9.3 | 391 | 650 | 63 | 81 |
| South Africa | 34.0 | 1,221 | 2,290 | 61 | 84 |

* World Bank figures quoted in International Coalition for Development Action (ICDA), SADCC-NGO Newsletter, October 1990, p. 1.
n.a. not available.
*Source:* World Bank, *World Development Report 1990,* New York: Oxford University Press, 1990, pp. 178-9, 184-5.

## Ideological-Political Differences

### Land Tenure and Distribution

With a majority of the people living in rural areas, agriculture is a strategic sector in Southern Africa. To the people, land is the key resource in Southern Africa, for access to land determines the patterns of distribution – for income, employment, and food. As the Food and Agriculture Organisation (FAO) bluntly stated, 'Land is the major input of production; when it is inadequate, or its tenure uncertain, the outcome is usually poverty levels of income.'[5] Although the general pattern is that of the small peasant producer on communally owned land, actual distribution and tenure of land vary greatly. And the divergences delimit SADCC policy.

Clarification of terminology is important, for 'small peasant' does not mean the same as 'small farmer.' In Western terms, small farmer implies private ownership of land, animals, tools. Small farmers do exist in Southern Africa, especially in Zambia, Zimbabwe and Malawi. 'Small peasant', however, most often implies small-scale production on communally held land. The land is not owned by the family or individual, but they have a right to use it, given traditionally by the chief or council of elders, most often today by the state. In Zambia, Zimbabwe, and Botswana where the relations of production are capitalist, over 50 percent of the land in each is still not privatised, but held in trust by the state for the people. In Mozambique, Tanzania, Angola all land is nationally 'owned.' In short, state control of land does not differentiate 'capitalist' versus 'socialist' in Southern Africa.

For most Africans, privatisation of land is an alien concept, for land is accepted as a public good. All the SADCC countries do, however, permit large- and small-scale private production. In Tanzania, Mozambique, and Angola private production is on leased land or in partnership with the state. Responding to considerable donor pressure to encourage private initiative, the proposed Mozambican constitution allowed for privatisation of land. During the long debates, people flatly rejected this land alienation, affirming the tradition that land is a collective resource. Frelimo had to back down and the 1990 constitution preserves state ownership in the name of the people, only to be leased to private interests. In Botswana, 100-year leases are now available, along with communal production. For the others – Zambia, Zimbabwe, Malawi, Lesotho and Swaziland – about 50 percent of the land is under private legal claim and control, another colonial legacy.

Zimbabwe and Malawi have been the two food surplus countries of the ten. Except in years of very bad drought (1981–83 and 1986–87 for Malawi), they have annually produced surplus maize, sorghum, millet and other crops for export. Both, however, have a serious land distribution problem which may retard future production increases.

The Zimbabwe land distribution problem was outlined in Chapter 1. There the settler regime systematically deprived Africans of land, access to markets, seeds and fertilisers. The 1981 economic policy statement of the independent government started with a clear recognition of the need to redress the gross inequities of the inherited land distribution and to reverse the neglect of African agriculture in order to effect the following policy goals:

• acceptable and fair distribution of land ownership and use;
• rapid reduction in the levels of absolute poverty;
• a system of land tenure where no one has absolute ownership and its use is entrusted to the people;
• food self-sufficiency and regional food security.

The 1982/85 Transitional Development Plan proposed to resettle 165,000 families. By 1986 only 40,000 families had been resettled on 2 million hectares of purchased land.[6] With the 1985 land bill the government gained all the legal tools necessary to define 'under-utilised' land, decide on a price to be offered to the commercial farmer, allow an appeal process if there is dispute, and redistribute the land to the landless peasant. Very little land has been redistributed in this way, although much land is under-utilised. For example, in fertile Mashonaland, more than three million hectares of Zimbabwe's best highveld is not being used, even allowing for grazing and fallow lands.[7] By the end of 1990, only 52,000 families had been resettled on 3.3 million hectares. Under the 1990 National Land Policy, the government proposed that 5 of 11 million hectares of commercial farm land be purchased to resettle 110,000 families. The government announced it will control land prices fixed by natural region and value of permanent improvements. Further, foreigners cannot own land and the time of 'telephone farmers' is over, with only a few absentee landowners to be tolerated.[8]

The major constraint has been political, with the government unwilling to alienate economically powerful whites, many of whom have strong links with South Africa. Most important, the government did not want to antagonise them in such a way that would reduce production. President Samora Machel is said to have advised Prime Minister Mugabe to sustain the large-scale commercial farming sector in order to avoid national food deficits which would make the new economy even more vulnerable. For these reasons, the white commercial farmers appear to be more politically powerful than the peasants who sustained the guerrilla war on the promise of more land. Many wealthier peasants are organised and receive credit, agricultural inputs, and agricultural extension services from the government; poor peasants, who can afford few of the inputs and receive no credit, are not well organised. A few, however, joined together as squatters to take over under-utilised land, while the government looked the other way. In areas suitable for cattle, some peasants still pay 'grazing rents' to ranchers; others herd cattle on unused land, and some cut fences to 'trespass.' As elsewhere in SADCC, land is a volatile political issue in Zimbabwe.

In contrast to the colonial legacy Zimbabwe still confronts, Malawi's land distribution problems result directly from the post-independence government's policy. Although some settlers established large plantations under colonialism, recent policies have made access to land even more inequitable. Rewarding 'master farmers' with more inputs and price incentives, land has been consolidated away from the poorer farmers, leaving 55 percent with less than one hectare.[9] The World Bank claimed success of a land reform project in Lilongwe, arguing that privatisation gave farmers greater security, but then contradicted that by asserting that a market in land would ensure that land reached its commercial potential and could then be sold.[10]

Large commercial farms, run by agribusiness firms, have also increased in size. Expansion of large estate acreage is recent – from 2 percent of cultivable land in 1970 to 15 percent in 1981.[11] Malawi, therefore, has had surplus grain production along with impoverishment of the peasants and increased unemployment. According to a SADCC document, the constraint on food crop production is the limited amounts of land available to the small producer.[12] In the late 1980s, an influx of nearly one million Mozambican refugees, some of whom were allocated small plots, constricted land availability even more. Many who cannot afford to buy the food and do not have plots large enough to sustain a family have migrated to Zimbabwe and Zambia.

Land distribution in Swaziland is also inequitable, resulting in large part from the tripartite land tenure system imposed in 1907 by the British colonial administration. It divided land into a) an individual freehold sector into which settlers were encouraged, indeed, induced, to move; b) crown land, that is, land held by the colonial authority for its disposal; and c) a communal sector for exclusive occupation by the Swazi people. This sector amounted to a mere 33 percent of the total land area which, in turn, was sub-divided into 34 so-called reserves. Under the control of the traditional Swazi authorities, plots were allocated by the chiefs on a leasehold basis.[13]

After World War II, foreign capital began to flow into Swaziland developing vast timber, sugar and citrus estates. Much of this development occurred in the freehold sector which became dominated by corporate South African and British agricultural interests; only about one-third of this sector is now owned by individual title deed farmers, an increasing number of whom are, however, Swazis – mostly members of the royal family or individuals with strong royalist connections. The freehold sector has a virtual monopoly of commercial production and the communal sector produces to all intents and purposes only for consumption. The sugar industry is the single largest user of land and consumes the most water,[14] indicators of a monoculture. At the same time, maize production, the national staple, has declined because of insufficient land for the small family plots. With a rapidly growing population, land in the communal sector is under pressure and the average size of a plot has in recent years been shrinking. Overgrazing has also contributed to its declining productivity. In the early 1980s, the FAO warned that 'the continued pre-emption of the best agricultural land by a few large estates relegates most farmers to small-holdings on poor land, with little hope of adequate returns for their labour.'[15]

Botswana has been unable to produce much more than five percent of its grain production for several seasons due to the five-year long (1982–87) drought which ravaged the country. Too arid to become self-sufficient in grain, the government has attempted to increase production by encouraging massive irrigation schemes for 'whomever will develop it,' whether it be agribusiness or individual farmers (in areas such as Tuli, Chobe, Maun Ngamiland).[16] Rural wealth is measured by the number of head of cattle, not land, and concentration of wealth has occurred, especially with the decimation of up to one-half of the national herd during the drought (official statistics not available). With its mineral wealth, the government has been able to provide food staples to the rural poor and supplemental feeding to school children. Only this massive and efficient relief effort, paid for largely by diamond exports, has kept Botswana off the list of countries with starving populations.

Mountainous Lesotho is even less fertile than Botswana. Soil erosion and degradation are at crisis levels. Landlessness is the highest in tropical Africa – about 20 percent – and growing.[17] Not able to eke out a living on the mountainous terrain, 45 percent of the labour force work in South African mines. The women stay at home, struggling to produce a few bushels of grain and tending goats and small animals. South Africa is Lesotho's major food supplier.

Tanzania, Mozambique and Angola have the most fertile land, with more than adequate land available for all; in Tanzania, for example, the policy is that every household is entitled to at least five hectares for cultivation. All three shared the experience of colonial plantation production, but alongside of viable African peasant production.

In Tanzania white settlers never came in large numbers, but did set up some plantations in the central region for sisal. In the north there were settler tea plantations, but coffee production was never taken away from African peasants, and coffee producers remain a relatively wealthy and politically influential group in Tanzania. In the southern coastal regions, peasants tended the cashew trees and marketed the nuts. Subsistence production in the central region was adequate, but attempts to increase production in cotton, maize and tobacco have been unsuccessful, with inadequate rain often the killing factor. Schemes for irrigation have not been developed because of a lack of finance.

The southern area, also rich in arable land, has not been developed. Seasonal flooding still cuts the region off from the rest of the country for almost half of every year. Until the end of the 1970s, the government did not try to develop dams, roads and bridges, but the area became the training ground and sanctuary for Mozambican and Zimbabwean nationalists fighting for independence; this delayed development is just one of the prices Tanzanians have paid to support their neighbours. Further compounding the area's burden has been the influx of an estimated 100,000 Mozambicans, refugees from MNR atrocities. In addition, members of the ANC's military army (*Umkhonto we Sizwe*) were transferred to southern Tanzania when asked to leave Angola as part of the 1988 Namibian peace settlement.

Tanzania, therefore, has more than adequate land and no land tenure problems. Its potential is not reached because of chronic problems with agricultural inputs and an export dependence on a few crops (coffee, tea, cashews) whose world market prices vary considerably and are not often high. Peasant production expansion depends on a more reliable water supply, more inputs and better crop collection facilities.

Mozambique also had a combination of plantations and individual peasant plots under colonialism. As discussed earlier, peasant production was permitted in the north, if they grew cotton and collected cashews. If not, both men and women were conscripted to work on the plantations. In central Mozambique the plantations dominated, with forced labour producing sugar, sisal and copra. In the south individual family production suffered from male migration to the mines of South Africa and Southern Rhodesia. The more viable peasant sector in the north was important to Frelimo, for there peasants quickly became independent of the Portuguese economy, and reverted to food production. It was they who sustained the Frelimo guerrillas.

At independence, the government chose to spend most of its agricultural budget to establish state farms on abandoned plantations (e.g., the Boror company loaded their entire 1975 copra crop on four ships and sailed away[18]). The Portuguese not only fled but destroyed tractors and dumped trucks in rivers. Large production schemes in fertile valleys seemed an easy answer to feeding the small urban population and producing for export. However, the schemes were too large and too highly technical for the skill level of the workers. Production levels were abysmal and the policy was criticised from 1979; change was only made in 1983 when large tracts were sub-divided into more manageable units of 1000 to 1500 hectares, such as the Limpopo Agro-Industrial Complex (CAIL) which was broken up into ten units. On these state farms, workers remain in control of production, organising themselves for various tasks. However, other tracts have been converted into joint ventures of the state with private transnational corporations, such as Lonrho, to develop areas the state can no longer finance.

Individual family production was discouraged as co-operatives were given priority. But input for that sector was also inadequate and the co-ops were not successful. Neglect of the family sector is now seen as one reason why some Mozambicans joined the MNR; peasants could not obtain inputs (seed, fertiliser) which were first distributed to state farms and co-operatives. What they did produce could not buy essentials. Major rural trading centres were reduced to selling tea and sisal rope from otherwise barren shelves; kerosene, cloth, matches and pots were unavailable, let alone bicycles or radios.

Under colonialism, rural traders were a regular reminder to peasants of their exploitation, because consumer prices were high relative to payments for crops. At independence, in an effort to destroy colonial exploitation, the Mozambican government nationalised both retail and wholesale trade, causing the traders to flee the country. It soon became clear that the centralised state could not manage retail sales, and goods did not arrive. The retail stores were privatised in 1979, but by that time, the rural trading network had been seriously disrupted. State policy, with its emphasis on state farming and its control of retail sales, systematically decimated the family peasant sector.

Angolan coffee was produced mainly on plantations in the east owned by Portuguese. Other plantations in the central highlands produced cotton, rice and fruits. With ample arable land, however, peasant production continued, constrained in the same way but to a lesser extent than Mozambique, by the colonial state's demand for labour on plantations and in the mines. *De facto* forced labour existed until about 1961 which meant that many families did not have the labour to produce much beyond subsistence. As in Mozambique, plantations were nationalised in Angola because their Portuguese owners fled. By providing wages and some worker control, coffee production reached pre-independence levels after four years, but then the war with South Africa led to neglect of the trees. The breadbasket of the central plateau has been hampered in production because of land mines planted on paths to the fields, burning of crops, and disruption of transport to markets. In 1984, rich and arable Angola became a food importer.

Zambia also has adequate fertile land for its small eight million population, with only 16 percent of the arable land presently cultivated.[19] White settlers took the best land along the rail line and some still produce there today. Under colonialism peasant production was discouraged by the same tactics, described in Chapter 1, of price discrimination against their crops, inadequate transport, and virtually no inputs provided by the colonial government. Taxes also forced men to work in the copper mines.

The independent government of Zambia did little to cultivate the underdeveloped peasant sector; some roads were built but prices for producers were kept low to keep consumer prices low, for Zambia is 40 percent urban, the highest in the region. When drought caused shortfalls in production, the government imported maize from South Africa, paid for by copper exports. This pattern changed in 1974 when Zambia closed the border to the south as a sanction against the illegal white regime in Southern Rhodesia. However, the government did not really overcome its neglect of agriculture until well into the 1980s when little financing from copper was available to buy food during the devastating drought which hit the region. Now Zambia is producing surplus maize, with almost self-sufficient amounts in rice. The majority of the farms are small peasant plots, with the commercial farmers still producing most of the grain.

Ideological labels do not work in Southern Africa; they confound more than inform. Appearances are also not to be trusted. Large waving fields of grain can be indicative of large commercial farms or co-operatives or state farms with labour relations ranging from capitalist to socialist (how much or whether workers are in control). Neither the West nor the East nor South Africa seems to understand this complexity. In the 1980s, Mozambique and Angola were repeatedly denied US aid because they are too 'Marxist-Leninist,' while the USSR excluded them from the East European common market (Council for Mutual Economic Assistance – CMEA or COMECON) because they were 'not truly Marxist-Leninist.'

Large waving fields of grain in Zimbabwe are no longer unique to commercial farmers. Some abandoned land has been given to collective co-operatives of ex-combatants who plant large tracts of maize and wheat. Other fields of grain in Zimbabwe are run as commercial farms, with wage labour, by the state. In Mozambique the large fields are state farms or joint ventures with foreign capital. In Swaziland, such fields could be owned by members of the royal family, underwritten by South African or British capital.

Zimbabwe is capitalist but not exactly in the Western mould. What does 'mixed economy' imply for Angola and Mozambique or a free South Africa? Does monarchy mean monopoly in Swaziland? Land tenure and distribution discussed above reveal the complexities. Malawi, Swaziland and Lesotho are increasing the privatisation of land. Large estates are growing in Malawi and Swaziland, at the expense of the communal peasant. In Lesotho individual peasants are obtaining title to land, which will marginalise others. Botswana is also increasing privatisation, with the constraint of a lease not outright ownership. Zambia has not changed its tenure laws, but its policies are assisting the large farmer more than the small peasant, with the poorest possibly losing out to the more 'efficient.' Zimbabwe has the most inequitable land distribution in the region (except for South Africa), and land distribution and tenure persist as controversial political issues. Tanzania, Mozambique and Angola have no land distribution or tenure problems. The states own all the land but encourage private production. State farms have been most favoured, but other sectors are now receiving attention. Similar to Zambia, the poor may lose because of lack of inputs (to be discussed later) but not because of land distribution.

## Marketing

Ideological differences are also apparent in other agricultural policies, such as marketing. The Zambian state has become the buyer only of last resort, allowing the co-operatives to handle the marketing. The National Agricultural Marketing Board (NAMBOARD) was dissolved in July 1989 and its functions taken over by the Cooperative Federation and Nitrogen Chemicals (distribution of inputs). Because the Swazi Milling Company in Swaziland will pick up and market no less than 30 bags of 70 kg each, it is not of much assistance to the small producer. In Tanzania, the marketing boards are limited to acting as auction or marketing agents for the co-operatives as well as providing quality control and information.all three, the private traders are expected to move grain and supplies. In contrast, in Botswana, Lesotho, Zimbabwe, Angola and Mozambique, state corporations or parastatals still play a major role in marketing grain. In Malawi, ADMARC (Agricultural Development and Marketing Corporation) no longer has a monopoly, as commercial and small-scale producers can sell directly to the private sector. Private trading is not prohibited but the state sets prices and still moves much of the grain.

This increasing congruence in marketing policy toward a greater role for private traders obscures some important differences. In Zimbabwe, three farmers' unions (large-scale, small-scale and communal) meet with the government to determine prices; the cabinet officially sets the final prices. In no other country do the farmers participate even to that extent. The Botswana Agricultural Marketing Board sets higher prices for remote areas to encourage sales, but many small-scale producers sell among themselves. Co-op Lesotho, set up in 1980, buys all agricultural goods, but transport costs are high and communication irregular to remote areas. The National Milling Corporation of Tanzania has come under repeated attacks for inefficiency and corruption; the state has often set prices so low that the parallel market flourishes. Such problems are being addressed but not yet eradicated.[20]

For Angola and Mozambique, it is difficult to assess their present marketing operations because of the wars. At times, food must be air transported in both countries. Private traders cannot operate any more effectively than the state in the war-torn areas. Both countries have successful 'green zones' around the cities which have kept the urban populations alive. Women have organised themselves in efficient cooperatives to grow and market the food; the state only stepped in to help with marketing after the women had proven their success.

The differences in regard to these few agricultural policies show the impossibility of labelling the Southern African economies. Land ownership patterns vary greatly; most have fundamental state intervention in agricultural production and marketing. Tanzania, Zimbabwe and Zambia all have capitalist labour relations co-existing with collective production. Mozambique and Angola, which have proclaimed a commitment to socialism, still rely on individual peasant production to feed their people.

## The Zimbabwe 'Success' Story
Zimbabwe is singled out in the region and by international prizes (Child Survival Award of the US National Council for International Health and the Leadership Award for the Sustainable End of Hunger) as exemplary

in transforming agricultural production. In many respects, it is emerging as a model for agricultural reform, yet its lessons in food production and distribution also offer caveats to its diverse neighbours.

Zimbabwe has accepted the 'agrarian reform' approach promoted by the World Conference on Agrarian Reform and Rural Development, organised by the FAO in Rome in 1979. More broad than simply 'land reform' or 'food security,' the term implies structural transformation of the agrarian system. Two objectives are primary: greater equality in access to land and in income, with special attention to the needs of the poorest, and the removal of structural constraints that inhibit the continued expansion of agricultural production. Zimbabwe's success relates mostly to the second.

In comparison with the six percent of marketed output produced by peasants before independence, the peasant sector by 1989 accounted for nearly 70 percent of national production of maize or about 55 percent of marketed maize. In addition, the large-scale commercial sector has increased its output by 300 percent. The phenomenal rise in peasant marketing results from a comprehensive approach by the government. First, seed or production packets were distributed in the communal lands, providing peasants with appropriate hybrid maize seeds, sufficient fertilisers and pesticides, ready for use. Agricultural extension workers were trained in large numbers and sent to the communal lands; over 25 percent of these were women in order to guarantee that female producers would also learn the new techniques. Equally important, but not often mentioned in the context of agricultural policies, health clinics were built in the rural areas, making primary health care accessible to hundreds of thousands for the first time. Not only are mothers more healthy for work in the fields, but they now spend less time taking the children to the nearby health clinics.

In some areas, farmers' clubs and co-operatives were formed to share oxen or the occasional tractor for ploughing. Many of the clubs were related to savings clubs which initiated small funds for local credit. Through the Agricultural Finance Corporation (AFC), credit to the communal lands increased by 350 percent from 1980–85 (but still reaching only eight percent of all communal households and only 10 percent by 1988[21]). Because the AFC set up offices in the rural areas, credit was cleared and funds allocated in time for the necessary purchases.

The Grain Marketing Board (GMB) also set up many collection points to reduce the transport distances to the market for the small peasants; the goal is to have a depot within 15 km of every farmer. Real prices for maize were maintained in order to encourage marketing. The peasants' own union joined the Commercial Farmers Union in discussing prices for the next season with the government before they were set.

The Batsiranai District Council 'Radical Land Reform Programme' in

Mwenezi is one of a number of experiments in Zimbabwe that illustrates the comprehensive approach to agrarian reform. Located in the worst land area (natural region V), it is very dry and suffered almost a total absence of crops and a serious loss of cattle in the 1982–84 drought. The plan formulated by the councillors attempted to reorganise land in the following ways:

1) re-establish demarcated grazing areas that had been encroached upon during the war, including the removal of houses and introduce village management of grazing;
2) consolidate arable holdings into blocks to reduce a need for draught power;
3) cater for the need of the stockless by giving them rights in the grazing areas, encouraging the spread of traditional custom of lending out cattle for use of those herding;
4) planting nut and fruit trees as additional income-generating activities;
5) building a series of medium- and small-size dams and other water installations for cattle and domestic needs, and potentially for irrigation.[22]

Most of the different elements have been implemented in some of the wards, though the rate of implementation naturally varies; still, the experiment is instructive in many ways. Commitment developed from grass roots discussions and processes which sustained interest. The priority given to cattle, not crops, makes it relevant to the driest areas in the region. The interests of the stockless are not ignored; rather, cooperative efforts assist in providing them access to livestock, and to low-cost draught power.

Many other cases (e.g., Gutu, Wedza, Vukuzenzele) reveal local initiatives which mobilised to take quick advantage of the new services provided by the government. And some are initiatives taken in spite of the government; for example, the savings clubs and credit schemes are local (and precarious) attempts to address the lack of credit to the poorest of the poor from both government and the banks.

Zimbabwe's success extends to peasants, but several studies reveal its limited impact. Those communal lands in the better natural regions (I–III) are disproportionately contributing to the increased production; the three Mashonaland provinces contributed a full 96 percent of the maize deliveries to the GMB in 1983–4 (a drought year). In more ordinary times, one-third of all national maize deliveries were from only six communal lands, and regularly, over 40 percent of peasants market no grain.[23] In short, the national statistic of impressive peasant deliveries masks considerable regional disparities.

Further evidence of the continuing desperate conditions of many Zimbabweans are to be found in surveys which reveal that 20 percent of children under five are malnourished. These children are found not only in the poorer farming regions but are also among workers on prosperous commercial farms and among female-headed households in all areas. Class differences in Zimbabwe seem to be based – not simply on numbers of cattle, nor on the amount of land, nor even access to water – but on remittances from the urban areas. The ability to accumulate, and for many to simply survive, depends on remittances from wage-earning relatives. For some it provides as much as 73 percent of household income.[24] Classes cut across the usual urban–rural divide or so-called 'dualism.' Very related to the colonial legacy of migrant labour, the ability to prosper in Zimbabwe depends on both rural production and urban wages. Wages can purchase seed and fertiliser after depletion of resources by drought, and rural land and production is a hedge against inflation in consumer prices and unemployment. Again, the poorest of the poor are most often rural female single heads of households – until and unless the children can become wage earners.

The experience of Zimbabwe demonstrates that attention to one factor will not improve agricultural performance. Multiple inputs increase peasant production – availability of seed, fertiliser, pesticides, water, draught power, grain depots, roads, transport, and government guaranteed crop prices which are not neutralised by inflated prices for inputs or consumer goods. The lesson contradicts dominant development theories of the World Bank or Western aid agencies, for the Zimbabwean state is very much involved in the above tasks, considered too daunting and too important to be left simply to profit margins of private corporations. Yet it also shows that an impressive mobilisation of state planning and resources is inadequate without land distribution. Insufficient lands force young people to urban areas; if wage employment is also inadequate, food is not put on the tables. The few prosper as aggregate figures impress the world. Growth with equity remains a goal.

## Ideological-Political Congruence

### Sovereignty

What the members have in common is more important than their differences. In fact, theories of regional co-ordination suggest that political congruence is key to the success of regional programmes.[25] What most binds the SADCC states together is the desire for a greater degree of sovereignty, particularly vis-a-vis South Africa. Because the colonial legacy left them vulnerable to outside forces, they agree that their independence so far has been superficial; their people are not yet in control of the wealth of their lands.

Botswana, Lesotho and Swaziland (BLS) will aim to rewrite the terms of the Southern African Customs Union after South Africa gains majority rule. At present they are less 'sovereign' in their exports and imports than say, the state of Tennessee. The relationship of South Africa to the BLS is as if Alabama told land-locked Tennessee the prices it will enjoy for its imports and exports. Further, Alabama alone would decide who gets what share of any tariffs (set by Alabama) on goods coming in the area. Finally, Alabama requires that Tennessee only use Alabamian roads and rails to send its goods to the sea for shipment overseas, even though a shorter and less expensive route might be through North Carolina. Such a relationship is not one between equal sovereigns. That it endures decades after 'independence' of the BLS states explains their commitment to SADCC's regional coordination efforts.

The seemingly contradictory model SADCC has chosen – to maintain sovereignty while cooperating – will be discussed in detail in the next chapter. Even the brief historical overview, given above, of false integration under the dominance of South Africa reveals why the neighbours desire to preserve national authority. SADCC is highly decentralised, to allow each member to participate, while respecting fully each other's problems and concerns. In the first years of SADCC, this model has maximised SADCC's activities, and gained it plaudits from outsiders in regard to the effective implementation of its projects.

## Reduced Dependence on South Africa

As long ago as 1929, Southern Rhodesia's Legislative Assembly was told that South African policy is 'inimical to the interests of the people of this Colony, whether they were producers, consumers, or the Treasury itself.'[26] In 1980, when Southern Rhodesia became Zimbabwe, the neighbours in the region pledged to reduce their dependence on apartheid South Africa. Even the more conservative of them saw the advantage of having alternative economic relations for trade and transport. South Africa of course still dominates the region but important steps have been taken along the road to collective self-reliance, as discussed sector by sector in the previous chapter.

## State Intervention in the Economy

The ten disagree about the role of private national businesses, but they do agree on one basic: reserving the right of the state to intervene in the economy and to take control of production. That process will be played out differently in the ten, but all find foreign control and foreign intervention to dictate economic terms of trade or investment intolerable. All reserve the right to set national economic plans, not to allow them to be written by South Africa or foreign interests.

As will be discussed in Chapter 4, included in these plans are their choices for the extent of state intervention in marketing or in production. Further, each will choose different combinations of private ownership, joint ventures or state ownership. The mix of 'private' versus 'public' varies, but none will erase 'public' from the control of production.

## Non-Alignment

President Robert Mugabe of Zimbabwe, as the leader of the Non-Aligned Movement (NAM) from 1986–89, was more than a symbol to the region; such leadership was a powerful diplomatic tool. The members view non-alignment as a process, not a status. Because of the colonial legacies, they cannot simply declare themselves 'non-aligned,' knowing their economic linkages reveal otherwise. What they mean by non-alignment is that, as they transform their economies, they will establish and maintain open relations with both the East and West. They invite both the East and the West to participate in their development plans and to trade.

Such a position is usually only considered radical if the professed non-aligned state is in the 'backyard' of a major power. Nicaragua and Afghanistan both know the limitations which stem from their proximity to the powerful. Southern Africa is geographically remote from the major powers but what turns that advantage around is its mineral wealth. Interests in the West still act as if the minerals are their private reserves; indeed, minerals form the economic base not only for several Western corporations but for development of Western technology because titanium, vanadium, platinum and several others are essential for production of jet engines and rockets.

So far the West has not been willing simply to trade the minerals for a fair price. When a government declared itself open equally to relationships with the East, there was more than a nervous twitch in the board rooms and cabinet offices of the West. The Reagan Administration in particular was quick to punish those who tried to appear neutral. Indeed, if Mugabe's leadership of NAM symbolised SADCC's commitment to non-alignment, an American-built and run airstrip in the remote areas of southern Zaire continues to symbolise Western rejection of non-alignment. Upgrading the Kamina air base, the US in early 1987 sent two battalions of American troops for exercises there. On March 6, 1987, US Chargé d'Affaires in Zimbabwe, Edward Fugit, said, the base 'would possibly be for our use if needed....we are looking at the region as a superpower needing various options...[and] planning for contingencies and the possibility to have the means in the future.'[27] With such proprietorial attitudes, non-alignment becomes a threat.

# Notes

1   W. Sweta *et al.*, 'The Minerals Sector of the States of SADCC: Possibilities for a Regional Minerals Policy,' mimeo, Lusaka: SADCC Mining Sector Coordination Unit, 1988, p. 1

2   This analysis of SADCC in the 1980s does not take into account the considerable mineral sector in Namibia which joined SADCC in April 1990. Uranium, diamonds and base metals (primarily copper, lead, tin, zinc) account for one-third to one-half of Namibia's GDP. Two transnational corporations (Rio Tinto Zinc and Anglo-American Corporation, including DeBeers) control most of the production.

3   Paul Jourdan. 'The Effects of South African Destabilisation on Mining in the States of SADCC.' *Raw Materials Report* 5:1 (1987): 42-53. Economist Intelligence Unit. *Angola,* Country Profile, 1988-89, p. 23.

4   Paul Jourdan. 'The Minerals Industry of Mozambique,' Raw Materials Report, University of Zimbabwe, 1986, pp. 18, 22-26.

5   Food and Agricultural Organization, United Nations. *SADCC Agriculture Toward 2000.* Rome: FAO, 1984, p. 6.3.

6   Lionel Cliffe. 'Zimbabwe's Agricultural "Success" and Food Security in Southern Africa.' *Review of African Political Economy.* no. 43 (1988): 16.

7   *Africa South* (May–June 1990): 15-16.

8   Text of speech by Minister of Lands, Agriculture and Rural Resettlement, Witness Mangwende, on the National Land Policy. *Financial Gazette* (Harare), 3 August 1990. Commerical farmers' reply, 'CFU sees Red over the New Land Policy' is in the same issue.

9   Guy C.Z. Mhone. 'Agriculture and Food Policy in Malawi: A Review,' *The State and Agriculture in Africa.* Thandika Mkandawire and Naceur Bourenane (eds.) Dakar: Codesria, 1987, pp. 63–4. *Africa Economic Digest,* (27 August 1990): 5. See also A.K. Mwakasungula. *The Rural Economy of Malawi: A Critical Analysis.* Bergen: The Chr. Michelsen Institute, 1984.

10  Edward Mason and Robert E.Asher. *The World Bank Since Bretton Woods.* Washington, D.C.: The Brookings Institution, 1973, pp. 713-14.

11  Ian Livingstone. 'Agricultural Development Strategy and Agricultural Pricing Policy in Malawi.' *Marketing Boards in Tropical Africa.* Kwame Arhin *et al*, eds. London: KPI, 1985, p. 176.

12  D.R.B. Manda, Benjamin H. Dzowela *et al.* 'Malawi,' *Agricultural Research Resource Assessment in the SADCC Countries,* Gaborone: Consultative Technical Committee for Agricultural Research, SADCC, 1985, p. 106.

13  Robert Davies, Dan O'Meara, and Sipho Dlamini. *The Kingdom of Swaziland.* London: Zed Press, 1985, p. 26.

14  *Ibid.* British capital dominates the sugar and citrus production, which is marketed through South African marketing boards. Patricia McFadden. 'The State and Agri-business in Swazi Economy,' *The State and Agriculture in Africa, op. cit.*, pp. 100-10.

15  FAO, *op. cit.*, p. 6.3.

16  Interviews of officials in the Ministry of Agriculture, Republic of Botswana, July 1985.

17  FAO, *op. cit.*, p. 6.1.

18  Joseph Hanlon, *Mozambique: The Revolution Under Fire.* London: Zed Books Ltd, 1984, p. 48.

19  Robina K. Chungu and Livingston Singogo. 'Zambia,' *Agricultural Research Resource Assessment in the SADCC Countries,* Gaborone: Consultative Technical Committee for Agricultural Research, SADCC, 1985, p. 19.
20  L.A. Msambichaka. 'State Policies and Food Production in Tanzania,' *The State and Agriculture in Africa, op. cit.,* pp. 117–143. Ernest Harsch. 'Tanzania: Difficult Road to Recovery,' *Africa Recovery* (July–September 1990): 10–15.
21  AFC also loaned large scale farmers $136,000 per farm compared to $680 per peasant farm. *Herald* (Harare) 12 July 1988.
22  FAO, 1985, *op. cit.,* pp. 61–2.
23  FAO, 1985, *op. cit.,* pp. 29–30. J.C. Jackson, P. Collier and A. Conti. 'Rural Development Policies and Food Security in Zimbabwe, Part II,' Geneva, Employment and Development Department, International Labour Office, 1987, p. 82. See also Jayne L. Stanning. 'Contribution of Smallholder Agriculture to Marketed Output in Zimbabwe 1970-85; Recent Experience and Some Future Research,' Working Paper 5, Department of Land Management, University of Zimbabwe, 1985. Daniel Weiner. 'Land and Agricultural Development.' *Zimbabwe's Prospects: Issues of Race, Class, State and Capital in Southern Africa.* London: Macmillan, 1988. Lionel Cliffe, *op. cit.*
24  J.C. Jackson, *et. al., op. cit.,* p. 65.
25  W. Andrew Axline. 'Underdevelopment, Dependence and Integration: the Politics of Regionalism in the Third World,' *International Organization* 31:1 (Winter 1977): 83-105. Germanico Salgado Penaherrera. 'Viable Integration and the Economic Co-operation Problems of the Developing World,' *Journal of Common Market Studies* 19:1 (September 1980): 65-76.
26  Ian Phimister. 'Industrialisation and Sub-Imperialism: Southern Rhodesia and South African Trade Relations between the Wars,' paper presented at conference on Alternative Development Strategies in Africa, Oxford, September 1987, p. 6.
27  *International Newsbriefing on Namibia,* no. 46 (April 1987): 1.

# 4.

# The Regional Response to Food Insecurity

Southern Africa is a focal point of conflict. It is not the quest for liberation but the entrenched racism, exploitation and oppression (by South Africa) which is the cause of conflict....The power behind this is in large measure economic. *Economic liberation is, therefore, as vital as political liberation.*
SADCC, Lusaka Declaration, 1980

Too diverse economically and politically to expect any one state to accept a loss of sovereignty to a supra-national entity, the SADCC members chose a decentralised consensus model for co-operation, one which would not threaten the political status quo of any state. Nor would it dictate national decisions. Thus, when Zimbabwe pursued its own Hwange coal power station and Kariba South Extension hydro-electric scheme instead of buying excess Zambian power, SADCC could only complain. When Zambia negotiated construction of a steel industry with the USSR, SADCC could only remind the government of plans for one integrated steel industry in Zimbabwe.

SADCC also is not a ' mode of production' or ' transition to socialism' scheme: no discussions address workers' control of production, and modest indeed are proposals to adjust wage differentials across borders within a sector (e.g., railway workers on regional lines). Yet the decentralised consensus model provides co-ordinated action that already has proven more effective than disparate national efforts. From the call for reduced dependence on South Africa to the co-ordinated sale of beef to the EEC by Botswana and Zimbabwe, the region is promoting shared interests. Further, its choice of co-ordinating production before trade is an effort to reduce historic inequities and wasteful competition while expanding economic mutuality. Given the decades of a hostile international economic environment with declining commodity prices and insignificant investment from outside the region, it is not, for example, in the interest of Zimbabwe for its neighbours to remain economic backwaters; efficient Zimbabwean growth very much depends on healthy neighbouring economies that can do their share in research, training, production and trade for regional development.

Contrary to most other regional economic organisations, the

decentralised conference demands no subscription fees or sweeping protocols. Instead, the organisation assigns each member with responsibilities for a particular sector. After making decisions by consensus, execution of projects is co-ordinated by one state. Zimbabwe, economically the strongest member, has not been assessed a large subscription fee to maintain a central administration, as Nigeria in the case of the Economic Community for West African States (ECOWAS). Instead, Zimbabwe agreed to co-ordinate the food security sector, meeting the requisite salaries and other costs. Scarce foreign exchange is not expended on some high-rise glass and steel headquarters sponsoring grandiose projects. The commitment is low-key and daily with Zimbabwean officials seconded to the food-security office located in the Ministry of Agriculture; they administer concrete programs, not general protocols.

*Table 4.1: Sectoral Responsibilities*

| | |
|---|---|
| Angola | Energy Conservation and Development |
| Botswana | Agricultural Research and Animal Disease Control |
| Lesotho | Soil and Water Conservation and Land Utilization; Tourism |
| Malawi | Fisheries, Wildlife and Forestry |
| Mozambique | Transport and Communications, Culture and Information |
| Namibia | Not yet assigned |
| Swaziland | Manpower Development |
| Tanzania | Industry and Trade |
| Zambia | Southern Africa Development Fund and Mining |
| Zimbabwe | Agriculture |

Zimbabwe was chosen as overall co-ordinator for all agricultural sectors because of its strong agricultural potential. Botswana co-ordinates the more specific sectors of agricultural research and animal disease control; Lesotho, soil and water conservation; Malawi, fisheries and wildlife. In certain cases, a state which was weak in an area was given co-ordination responsibilities so as to stimulate its own national sector (industry for Tanzania, soil conservation for Lesotho, manpower training for Swaziland). If the strongest economy had been chosen in each area, Zimbabwe would have several key sectors. Instead, SADCC' s chosen structure reflects a concern for equity in decision-making and administration.

Such an arrangement also stimulates greater accountability, for if Zimbabwe, for example, slacks off or makes mistakes, criticism by other members is concrete and specific: why does the food-marketing project not discuss advantages of state facilities? Why was a consultant paid before fulfilling the terms of reference? These questions and their required responses evoke more direct accountability than yet another plea from a distant bureaucrat about paying a subscription. Further, complaints can be addressed at several levels from the teams for different projects to the agricultural ministers and eventually up to the heads of state.

This model lets nationalism prevail; some would say too much so. For example, in designating priority food industry projects of supposed benefit to the whole region, Tanzania submitted proposals for its beer and wine production – not exactly food priorities and with little regional impact. Lesotho submitted a proposal for the processing of asparagus and artichokes, not a regional food priority but an export overseas cash crop.[1]Reflecting the reality of the regional political economy, the model acknowledges that co-operation would be seriously limited without consensus. The hope is that, as co-operation develops, the area of mutual interests expands, and tolerance of differences increase. Enthusiasm for ' our way' is kept in check as the debates continue at various levels.

Real economic contradictions will not of course disappear by way of protracted discussion but the approach of SADCC is that, given the colonial legacy, there exists a large area of shared interests to pursue. This approach is obvious in infrastructure: connecting electricity grids and operating cost-efficient railroads help capitalist and socialist economies alike.

SADCC has proceeded further than that, however. Members rejected from the outset the notion that co-operation would simply result in a co-ordination of marketing. From experience in the Central African Federation, the East African Community and the Southern African Customs Union,[2] member states learned that lower tariffs and open markets mostly boost the economies of the stronger members and foreign capital. Zimbabwe would be able to take advantage of the enlarged market, much more than Lesotho or Mozambique. The President of Botswana explained:

> Intra-regional trade can increase without the creation of a free trade area or a common market. Each of our states in SADCC has experience with those models of trade creation. The Federation of Rhodesia and Nyasaland [Central African Federation], the Portuguese colonial 'economic union,' the East African Common Market, the Southern African Customs Union – all were, or are, free trade areas or common markets. *All have served to limit our development, to enrich externally based firms and interests and to hamper national planning.*[3] [emphasis added]

SADCC chose to co-ordinate production first. Market forces (often dominated by transnational corporations) will not dictate production priorities, size or location; rather, planned production will.

Three different levels of planned and co-ordinated production exist.

First, planning designates that no co-ordination is necessary in some industrial fields: for example, any and all states can pursue textile and hand-tool production for national consumption; consumer demand is sufficient and technology adequate enough for each to benefit from production in these sectors. The second is the reverse case with SADCC specifying that only Zimbabwe should develop a full steel industry and only Angola a petrochemical industry. The first chemical pulp and paper mill is in Mgololo, Iringa in Tanzania; the first aluminum smelter will be in Mozambique taking advantage of its bauxite and hydroelectric power, and the first inorganic chemical industry in Botswana will be based on its soda ash deposits.[4]

Where planning is especially important and difficult is at the third level of co-ordination: production complementarity. First, industrial priority sectors are selected: fertilisers, agricultural equipment, transport equipment, pharmaceuticals, and telecommunications equipment. Second, in industrial areas where competition among members could be detrimental to all, SADCC tries to decide by consensus which member will produce what type of product. For example, it has been agreed that Zimbabwe will at present produce all the phosphate fertiliser for regional use and for export (used for maize, beans, wheat and cotton), with later additional plants in Zambia or Botswana. Several natural gas fields in the region could supply ammonia plants, but it has been agreed that the Tanzanian Kilamco plant will begin to meet the current shortfall in regional ammonia supplies; new production in Inhambane, Mozambique will take care of medium-term deficits. From the ammonia, nitrogenous fertilisers will be formulated in Tanzania, Mozambique, Angola, Malawi, Zambia and Zimbabwe. (Much more in demand, nitrogenous fertilisers are used for maize, rice, vegetables, sugar, coffee, tea, cotton and tobacco.)[5] Such planning includes not only cost-benefit decisions, but also equity considerations. It makes sense to establish a fertiliser plant where raw materials are available, but planning tries to recommend which member will pursue development of the resources first.

Completed regional studies propose investment for increased productive capacity to satisfy existing regional demand in pesticides, textile chemicals, salt and tractors. To produce pesticides, copper oxychloride plants are in Zambia and Zimbabwe, but another is planned for Tanzania. Formulation plants already operate in Zambia, Zimbabwe, Tanzania, Mozambique and Angola, with new ones planned for Malawi and Swaziland. A good example of complementarity is the production of tractors, for Swaziland already produces low-cost tractors and Tanzania will assemble conventional tractors to service the whole region. Each will thus increase national production, employment and capital – fulfilling regional needs, while avoiding potentially ruinous competition.

# Agriculture: A Priority Sector

Right at the outset in 1980, SADCC chose food security as a priority second only to co-ordination of transport and communication, the infra-structural base for any production efforts. The choice was easy to make, for African agriculture was in an abysmal state after decades of under-development. Production of grains repeatedly fell short of domestic needs, with any adverse weather conditions bringing not just hardship but starvation. At the end of the 1970s, President Nyerere of Tanzania, attending a conference in Rome, was angry he had to learn from the FAO (which monitors crops via satellite) – not from his own agricultural minister – that Tanzania's next harvest would produce a serious shortfall; the word was too late to find alternatives to purchasing grain on the international market where prices had risen because of world demand.

Problems and mistakes in agriculture by the independent governments of Southern Africa fall into three interrelated areas: technology, finance, and distribution. Technological problems involve insufficient innovation and inadequate implementation of the available technology. On a continent that has contributed significant plant genetic material to the world, distorted development priorities allocated only two percent of government agricultural budgets to research. Few new strains were developed, and imported ones were not conducive to harsh African climates. In some areas, the failure was not for lack of trying: research over 40 years from 1931–75 in West Africa failed to achieve any improve-ment in yields of sorghum or millet. Only in 1984, after 12 years of research of 5000 varieties in the Sudan, could researchers release one new strain.[6] Southern Africa did develop hybrid maize and wheat in the 1930s, but nothing comparable was accomplished in the first decades of independence. Successful development of new strains takes financing, training of scientists, transfer of plant material and continuity of investigation, none of which was sufficiently promoted in Southern Africa.

When innovative ideas were available, they were often not im-plemented. Racism in Southern Rhodesia certainly contributed to the disparity between small-scale African farmers who produced one ton of maize per hectare and white commercial farmers who produced on average four tons, often on similar soils. The African farmer not only was crowded into the reserves, but rarely received information from extension workers about innovative techniques, seeds, or the use of organic fertilisers. The minority government did not even provide small-scale irrigation for the semi-arid reserves. After independence in many of the countries, class was no doubt a factor in producing a government bias towards the large and so-called modern sector. In Swaziland, Malawi, Zambia and Zimbabwe, large-scale farmers use the latest methods, right in the same neighbourhood where small peasants continue to rely on a hoe. And gender discrimination affects almost all the countries. Innovative techniques were shared in Tanzania, for example, but for the cash crops grown and controlled by men. Following the bias of state policy, often encouraged by international agencies, Tanzanian male extension workers ignored female producers whose responsibility was food crops, rather than priority cash crops.

Southern African governments are now most self-critical about their financial mistakes. Low prices to agricultural producers, to keep food costs low for urban consumers, discouraged marketing and even production. Farmers in Africa in general receive a share of the final value of a food grain product that is almost half that received by their Asian counterparts.[7] Offering the same price throughout the country, irrespective of soil conditions or transport costs, distorted production and acted as a disincentive. Policies existed so that maize was grown where conditions were more conducive to sorghum (Botswana, Tanzania, Zambia, Zimbabwe); when drought hit marginal lands, the losses were multiplied, for sorghum can survive with less water than maize. The lack of official prices or marketing channels discouraged increased production of some crops, such as legumes and groundnuts.

Peasants respond rationally to low prices by smuggling food crops to cross-border markets with higher prices, a response endemic in Angola, Tanzania, Zambia, Mozambique, and Malawi. Estimates for Zambia suggest that peasants have smuggled 30,000–60,000 metric tons of maize a year into Zaire, costing the government $3 million. The profit margin in smuggling maize from Ndola to Lubumbashi has been put as high as 481 percent.[8] Smuggling also drastically alters production figures; for example, much of the 'surplus' Malawian maize in the early 1980s was actually Mozambican in origin.

Inadequate credit, either from government or commercial banks, also deters production. The policy prevails that peasants must have substantial collateral in order to borrow; programmes of credit for marginal farmers, who need it the most, are non-existent or minimal. In Zimbabwe, for example, only about 10 percent of the peasants receive loans compared to 95 percent of the large-scale commercial farmers. In some of the least endowed communal lands, the percentage of peasants receiving loans is as low as 2 or 3 percent. This is consistent with the policy of the Agricultural Finance Corporation (AFC) to avoid loans to 'high risk' producers; yet it defeats the 'growth with equity' goal of the government, producing the same discrepancies in incomes as in production.

Zimbabweans have organised themselves to try to overcome this bias, one notable example being the Dondolo-Mudonzwo ('Walking stick') national co-operative of women. If small peasants are discriminated against in credit allocations, female producers are virtually ignored.

Dondolo-Mudonzwo was organised to provide loans as little as Z$50 (US$35) to women organised in co-operatives which accepted ultimate responsibility for paying back the loan; policy stated that no other co-operative in the province would receive a loan if any one member of a co-operative in that province defaulted. The provincial representatives of the co-operatives participated, therefore, in deciding who would receive loans and assisted with the management of the finances. Savings clubs in villages and credit schemes among co-operatives have also been instituted, some of them quite successfully.[9] But the amount of money mobilised by grass roots efforts is minuscule compared to what is available from the AFC. Most credit schemes in Zimbabwe will continue to support the 'master farmers,' rather than assist the marginal farmers over the threshold to lucrative production.

Credit for peasant production has the same negative bias in virtually all the SADCC countries, and solutions are not easy to find. Not exactly an example to emulate, this contradiction between bankers and farmers has been resolved in most Western countries by driving out the small farmers and consolidating land under the ownership of large agribusiness. In Zimbabwe a possible solution might be to encourage a high repayment rate which would then release more funds, and the AFC has tried to obtain repayment by way of the peasants' sales to the Grain Marketing Board (GMB). Payment for the delivered grain is first credited for repayment of a loan, but too often, there is absolutely nothing left after deductions; the peasant's harvest provided no cash, only debt relief. In such a circumstance, a peasant farmer will naturally look to alternatives, such as intermediary traders who pay cash, but often cheat by under-grading the grain and underweighing the bags.

Finally, the financial capacity of the government to purchase and store grain is sometimes subverted by other spending priorities, outside interference, or corruption. In Swaziland in 1985 and 1986, maize production outstripped the capacity of the National Maize Corporation (NMC) to purchase and store it. Small Swazi farmers were left with no sales outlets for surplus harvests, although the country continued to import maize (mainly from South Africa) of 40,000 tons a year (to April 1986).[10] In Tanzania in 1986–87, the World Bank recommended higher producer prices for maize and cotton resulting in a bumper crop, but then IMF conditionality left the crop purchasing authorities (National Milling Corporation and the co-operatives) with insufficient funds to purchase the harvests. They rotted at the depots.

Such distribution problems invariably involve transport obstacles – delayed delivery of seed, fertiliser or pesticide inputs preventing timely sowing; inadequate collection of harvests, allowing grain to rot; insufficient delivery of consumer goods to rural shops. Part of the problem is the poor state of the transportation infrastructure with roads and railways in disrepair. After two decades, potholes large enough to deter four-wheel drive vehicles still plague the gathering of Tanzanian harvests. Mozambique still does not have a north–south all-weather road running the length of the country, and feeder roads to highways quickly diminish to trails. Rural transport costs per ton mile in Africa are twice those in Asia.[11]

However, much of the problem also stems from government inefficiency and/or overt corruption. Depots for collecting grain are widely scattered and often too far from small peasant plots. Collection vehicles often do not arrive in time so that grain rots. In Zimbabwe the problem is often a shortage of bags for the grain; with no bags available, even the most industrious would probably revert to subsistence production or sell in the parallel markets. If the peasant has managed to overcome all of the above and has cash to spend, rural shops are often empty or poorly stocked – again often a delivery problem. Seed is not delivered on time for planting; new tools or clothing or cooking oil are not available to buy. And these conditions prevail in areas in which there is state control in marketing, as well as where private traders are dominant. Private traders have demonstrated over the years that they will not market in remote areas where the profit margins are low because of the high cost of transport and low volume.

Consistent with its highly decentralised model, SADCC leaves national planning for agricultural production to each government. However, it does raise important issues and implement programmes to reduce obstacles to production and to put food on all the tables. The most crucial issue for SADCC – indeed all over the world – is who can best feed everyone.

## Production by Whom?

A distinctive feature of SADCC's agricultural policy is their attention to the 'small producer.' Concerned primarily to increase grain production, it chose to pursue research and genetic development of grains grown by peasants, such as sorghum and millets, legumes, and cow peas. Only recently has wheat, grown on large and irrigated commercial farms, become part of the agenda.

SADCC has not specifically defined 'small producer,' but some of the SADCC documents indicate the meaning, as summarised in Table 4.2. Average holdings per family in communal areas in Malawi is 1.7 hectares, but 55 percent of the peasant farmers have less than 1 hectare and only 5 percent are over 3 hectares. For Lesotho, with the most severe land shortage, the average per family is 1.4 hectares. Each Tanzanian family is allocated 5 hectares, and up to 10 hectares in more arid areas, by the government. Botswana changed eligibility for assistance through the Arable Land Development Programme (ALDEP) to those with up to 10 hectares because of the long drought. Angola, Mozambique and Zimbabwe have not given figures, although discussions elicit estimates of 2–3 hectares for average size of peasant holdings.

Table 4.2: 'Small-Scale' Producers – SADCC
(Comparison of average size of plot to qualify as 'small peasant')

| | |
|---|---|
| Angola | 2–3.0* hectares |
| Botswana | 10.0 (increased to 10 because of years of drought) |
| Lesotho | 1.4 |
| Malawi | 1.7 |
| Mozambique | 1–3.0* |
| Swaziland | 2.75 |
| Tanzania | 5.0 (10. 0 hectares for arid areas) |
| Zambia | 3.0 (2 hectares considered subsistence) |
| Zimbabwe | 1–3.0* |

* estimates
Sources: *Agricultural Research Resource Assessment in the SADCC Countries*, I and II. Gaborone: Consultative Technical Committee for Agricultural Research, SADCC, 1985. Vakakis and Assocs. 'Overview of Food Reserve and Food Aid Policies in SADCC Member States,' consultant interim report, Regional Food Reserve/Food Aid to SADCC Food Security Administrative Unit, June 1986.

With wide variability in soil conditions and availability of water, no one figure or average adequately describes the conditions. A family with two hectares could, for example, be better off than one with ten. In general, however, 'small' means only 'adequate'. Even with the best of conditions – weather, soil, labour availability, inputs – a family averaging 6–7 members with 2–3 hectares would not become wealthy; most often they would be living on the margin, especially during adverse market or weather conditions.

SADCC chooses, therefore, not to follow simplistic cost-benefit requirements for increasing production. It does not allocate subsidies and inputs to those able to increase production most quickly and efficiently, i.e., the commercial farms. Instead, its programmes address the vast majority of the population on small plots of land. It attempts to generate surplus small-scale production to keep families 'employed' and to create a potential for rural industries based on agricultural goods. By encouraging growth in this sector, SADCC hopes to make migration to the cities less attractive.

Another important reason for SADCC paying attention to the small producer is the question of equity. Most policy makers reject a policy of growth without equity considerations: 'trickle down' in poor societies means those at the bottom can starve, not just suffer. For some leaders, the decision is one of political expediency to reduce possibilities of political instability; for many in SADCC, however, it derives from a logical economic analysis that growth can only be sustained if the majority benefits. SADCC, however, avoids dictating the specifics of such a policy; therefore, actual implementation within the individual economies varies widely. The 'small producer' is the target of the regional projects, but a wide variety of producers and social conditions fall into that category. An extension worker trained by SADCC may be sent to wealthy peasants in Malawi, but assigned to the poorest of the poor in Mozambique. Such decisions are national policy.

A plant breeder in Botswana, explaining their policy,[12] says they are happy to let SADCC work with hybrid sorghum and millet, but quickly point out that most Botswanan peasants will not be able to use them. Variability in water availability is too high to sustain a hybrid, which needs the exact amount of inputs (water, fertiliser and pesticides) at the correct time or it yields less than indigenous strains. The smaller peasant often has insufficient cash or credit to assure purchases at exactly the time required. Committed to assisting this sector, Botswanan research is, therefore, focusing on 'stable producers,' indigenous strains which will not yield as much as hybrids, but will not fail as miserably as the hybrids under less propitious conditions.

In contrast, Malawi's use of SADCC projects seems to be for the larger peasant producers, not those with 1–2 hectares. A coffee project submitted for SADCC funding was written for 'small' producers who have 8–9 hectares of coffee. Under 10 hectares is not large-scale production, but neither is it marginal. Zimbabwe also seems to be helping those peasants with more land and who are relatively better off. Increased marketed grain production from the communal lands is coming from less than 20 percent of the peasantry who live within the most favourable agro-ecological regions (about 30,000 households).[13] A few producers have increased production remarkably; others still suffer malnutrition.

Irrigation is another example of how the debate over target producers continues. SADCC is discussing projects for large-scale irrigation because of the high variability of rain throughout the region. Botswana, for example, has decided that large projects are needed in order to even begin the goal of increased production in grain; therefore, government subsidised irrigation projects are mainly for large farms. Estimates for Zimbabwe indicate that irrigation (with some tsetse fly eradication) of 300,000 hectares in the Zambezi and Save valleys could almost double the total area which was under irrigation in 1985. In tandem with these large-scale national plans, SADCC will develop small-scale irrigation in the region, training technicians in the building of small dams which will benefit the smallest farmer.

Most SADCC members are not simply adopting the 'easy answers' to increased agricultural production, such as an open invitation to large agribusinesses to farm their land. Lonrho is farming in Mozambique, and South African firms are rehabilitating citrus estates near Chimoio; Lonrho is also back producing tea in Tanzania after being expelled in the late 1970s for economic and political reasons. Botswana is encouraging corporate investment in newly irrigated areas. However, in all, the state will regulate the terms and be a partner. The governments have learned from their colonial heritages that agribusiness is often not efficient and, certainly, uses more foreign exchange and less labour – the former a scarce commodity and the latter an abundant commodity – than small-scale production. Further, the firms grow what brings the best profit, not necessarily basic food crops; Lonrho was told by Mozambique, therefore, that it could farm in the rich soil of Manica and Sofala provinces only if it grew a quota of maize. As fundamental, during nation-wide discussions on the new constitution, the peasants spoke out vehemently against the privatisation of land, fearing its alienation to large capital interests; land remains in the public domain. Botswana also restricts most of the large-scale irrigated production to grains.

Zimbabwe has long established agribusiness, especially in sugar and citrus production. The firms received special subsidies from the colonial government. For example, Huletts (Anglo-American Corporation) successfully lobbied in the late 1950s for the Southern Rhodesian government to build the Kyle dam for the cane, contributing only $600,000 of the $4 million cost for the project; with the additional water, 25,000 hectares were added to private cane production. The firms grew sugar and citrus for export, while paying workers less than subsistence wages. Zimbabwe knows well, therefore, how exotic crops are grown for the few while the many are malnourished. Consequently, at independence the government established state farms under the Agriculture and Rural Development Authority (ARDA) to manage large estates. When some foreign corporations pulled out of tea production at independence, the state took over and several are now part of ARDA's 18 farming estates growing not only tea, but also wheat, cotton, soya, beans, and some vegetables. Because dairy farming had been the exclusive preserve of large commercial farmers, ARDA began a project resettling small-holder dairy producers on four hectares of land.

Although the above policies are mixed, holding only some constraints on agribusiness, the regulations are much greater than in Swaziland and Malawi where local ruling classes have linked up with foreign agricultural interests to expand corporate holdings, in particular sugar in Swaziland and tobacco in Malawi. With solid bases in agribusiness, the Tibiyo Fund in Swaziland (an investment company controlled by the royal family and immune from any form of public scrutiny) has expanded to acquire shareholdings in local banking, manufacturing and trading operations.[14] These policies have reduced food production to such an extent that most maize consumed in Swaziland must now be imported from South Africa.

In Malawi large-scale producers are increasing their control over land, producing 90 percent of total exports. Press Holdings (run on behalf of President Banda until the World Bank protested) is the largest estate holder in the country, growing 40 percent of tobacco produced on estates. It is a conglomerate with controlling interest in two national banks and ownership of retail stores, industrial and commercial concerns. Because land is so scarce for the small peasants, according to SADCC, 'political pressures are being exerted to degazette or excise some of the land in watersheds for agricultural production and resettlement' (with potential disastrous effects on the ecology).

As a regional organisation, SADCC focuses on the 'small producer,' which generally means those with 2–5 hectares. However, the pattern of holdings in SADCC is complicated, and one must analyse the class interests supporting each state to understand the various interpretations of 'small' for national production. SADCC does not dictate policies, but by promoting regional efforts to assist the smaller producer, it may be possible to begin modifying the context for national class interests.

## Reducing Obstacles to Development

In agriculture, SADCC's first goal is increased production of food grains. Because of the diversity of agricultural conditions within the region, projects emphasise reducing obstacles to production, rather than promoting the complementarity of production as in the case of industry. Food grains are considered too strategic an item for any member to forego the target of self-sufficiency; even arid Botswana is trying to grow more maize in order to reduce its dependence on outside sources, be it apartheid South Africa or Zimbabwe. In other agricultural sectors, such as fruits and flowers, SADCC is just beginning to discuss co-ordinated production.

For funding, SADCC favours agricultural projects designed to reduce constraints on production. In a world of computer data bases, it is astonishing that the Southern Africa region had no regional co-ordination of weather information, no regional maps of soil, few satellite pictures of terrain, and vastly different data collection techniques. Little comparable data exists. This deficiency reflects once again the region's colonial legacy. Many of the weather reports still come from stations in South Africa. Agricultural research for the whole region was directed and dominated by the South Africa-based SARCUSS (Southern Africa Regional Commission for the Conservation of Soil) until the independence of Angola and Mozambique in 1975. It was not until after the Zimbabwean liberation war that an alternative could be established.

Only in 1986 was phase one of the Food and Agriculture Organisation's (FAO) early warning system in each country completed; members now have a better chance to detect yields below expectations while crops are still in the fields. A Regional Resources Information System and a Regional Inventory of Agriculture Resources Base have begun the arduous task of the standardisation and collection of data. Since 1986, project teams have been collecting data in each country, but historical records of weather patterns, of crop yields and of disease had been tabulated in diverse ways, hindering analysis.

Supervision of agricultural project proposals was first performed by three consultative technical committees (CTCs) working with the food security sector, co-ordinated by Zimbabwe: economics and marketing, agricultural extension and training, and agricultural research. Experts from each member country attended meetings to offer technical advice on proposed projects, select consultants and review projects. They organised workshops on difficult issues such as pricing, credit and land tenure, crop yield forecasts, land use planning, irrigation and extension services.

As part of their review brief, the CTCs have occasionally rejected completed feasibility studies. One study on agricultural marketing done by a private Canadian firm, showing little knowledge or sensitivity to Southern African views, referred to the war in Mozambique as 'internal strife.' Insensitive to the colonial legacy of the region, the firm also assumed that agribusiness would be most effective in marketing goods in Southern Africa. Finally, the firm failed to consult with Mozambique, responsible for transport within SADCC, in regards to the transportation aspects of regional marketing. After rejecting this study, members of the CTC assigned the task of drafting a marketing co-ordination proposal to a team of SADCC nationals.

Even in technical details, therefore, SADCC operates by consensus with all members participating. They do not view technology as 'neutral' politically or ideologically. As the marketing proposal illustrates, even transporting goods from one point to another has political overtones: by small-scale carriers, transnational corporate carriers, or the state? how does pricing affect marketing? how is regional marketing possible in the midst of war? how can trucks be co-ordinated with trains (which are state owned)?

In 1987 the Food Security Technical and Administrative Unit (FSTAU) replaced the CTCs with a board of agricultural economists from each member state. Called 'national sector contact persons', they co-ordinate the implementation of projects in their own countries, as well as bring proposals to FSTAU for new projects.[15] Projects provisionally accepted by FSTAU are referred to a standing committee of officials which examines feasibility and technical questions; thereafter they proceed to ministers of agriculture of each state for approval. Finally, they require adoption by the SADCC Council of Ministers. Decisions at all these stages are by consensus. This long process provides each member many opportunities to critique, revise and reject a project; it is also a process which can augment compromise and agreement.[16]

FSTAU also establishes and directs technical teams needed for project implementation. Just one example reveals the many ways in which SADCC works to reduce obstacles to agricultural production. The team for the Regional Inventory of Agriculture Resources Base, composed of a Tanzanian soil scientist, a Malawian land use planner, an Irish agriculturalist and a cartographer first investigated the problem of the comparability of data that is available from only four members: Malawi, Tanzania, Zambia, Zimbabwe. Then they organised collections of new data through national agricultural reserve inventories. A major goal is to determine the impact of inputs on the population-supporting capacity of the land, information necessary for land use planning to designate areas useful for food production. Raising questions of appropriate technology, they investigate the impact of various amounts of fertilisers and degree of mechanisation on the land. The Tanzanian soil scientist on the team cited the type of problems SADCC land use planning will try to overcome: 'Man is land use; he usually degrades it....Tanzania cannot pay back World Bank loans taken out to increase tobacco production because fertilisers are no longer producing good tobacco yields after only 2–3 years....Irrigation depends on the saline, alkaline nature of the soils. In the lower Moshi and Same areas of Tanzania, the soil was depleted after only 3 years of irrigation.'[17]

The most important institutional development in the agricultural sector has been the establishment of SACCAR (Southern African Centre for Co-operation in Agricultural Research). Based in Botswana and directed by a Tanzanian, the Centre co-ordinates and offers grants for research and holds training workshops to strengthen national agricultural research. Technical Advisory Panels provide policy guidance and monitoring. Commodity specific steering committees, such as for sorghum and millet, co-ordinate the research. A 1988 review praised the implementation of co-ordinated research and training projects, but criticised the lack of formal agreements between SACCAR and the executing agencies.[18] Because several, such as ICRISAT (International Centre for Research on Agriculture in Semi-Arid Tropics) and IITA (International Institute for Tropical Agriculture), are from outside the region, this shortcoming could encourage foreign interference and control.

SACCAR is the depository for research results in sorghum, millet, cow peas, beans, and groundnuts conducted in the other member states. Not only developing new seeds, a key aim of the sorghum/millet project has been the discovery of alternative uses of the grain in animal feeds, blended flours for biscuits, cakes and buns, and the brewing of beer. Zimbabwe now produces bread in rural areas using 20 percent sorghum flour, reducing the need to import wheat. Breads of various kinds can be made from sorghum flour, mixed with wheat and maize flour. Research on sorghum and millet has revealed their suitability for the making of pasta, breakfast cereal, porridge (for weaning also), salty snacks and for paper cardboard and chipboard. Boiled white sorghum is like rice and many dishes based on rice can be successfully prepared substituting sorghum.[19] The invention of a better sorghum dehuller in Botswana, manufactured for the regional market in Tanzania, supported this development of new foods; because removing the hard outer shell is so labour intensive, this task had deterred broadening the use of sorghum.

An urgent and controversial project in agricultural research has been the establishment of a SADCC gene bank. Development of hybrids have diminished the number of genetic pools around the world, and SADCC does not want to lose its original genetic stock to hybrids or to transnational corporate control. The Chalimbana Research Station in Zambia has ideal humidity and temperature for the gene bank, and has been made responsible for the collection, characterisation and storage of germplasm. Duplicate seeds will be kept in the Nordic gene bank and with the FAO network. As Angola, Lesotho, Namibia, and Swaziland have no seed conservation facilities, National Plant Genetic Resources Committees will be set up in all ten states to direct the national selection of genetic material, of storage sites and of trainees for instruction in preservation of seed.

Although only 30–40 percent of the SADCC area under basic cereal crops is planted with improved seeds, Zimbabwe, Tanzania and Zambia all produce quality seed. Zimbabwe has, in fact, been elected to the executive of the germination committee of the International Seed Testing Association. The committee arbitrates disputes over quality of seed traded among its 110 members.[20]

Cross-breeding of hybrids can take hundreds of crosses over several years. Genetic engineering – splicing and restructuring genes – revolutionises the painstaking process with scientists able to insert a wider variety of beneficial genes into plants in a matter of days. New varieties of disease-free plants can be developed for many crops, reducing the need for foreign exchange to buy pesticides and decreasing the use of chemicals in the fields. Tanzania has already bred a coffee strain resistant to coffee berry disease and a sugar cane resistant to fungus and white scales, saving the cost of expensive fungicides.[21] Zimbabwe spends almost $20 million per year on pesticides and still loses $6 million of the maize crop to the stem-borer, so the potential for savings are great. Biotechnologists at the University of Zimbabwe have developed a virus-free cassava clone which produces 50 tonnes of cassava per hectare, compared to the regional average of 2–8 tonnes.[22]

In January 1989 SADCC held its first conference on biotechnology. Numerous indigenous strains of maize, sorghums, millet, beans and medicinal plants have not been collected, and SADCC would like to involve the small peasants in gathering them. But the whole question of the ownership and outside use of the genetic material has not been resolved. Experience from other developing areas, such as Latin America, is not encouraging. The highlands of the Andes constitute one of the richest pools of plant resources in the world, but 'their wealth [of genetic material] leads to their impoverishment,'[23] for foreigners control the resource. The US state of Colorado produces more quinua (cereal with high protein content) than both its native Peru and Bolivia combined. Foreign interests take the original genetic material and create new strains, which are then patented and treated like highly-guarded commercial secrets, as is the technology used to derive it. SADCC material is supposed to be duplicated in 'designated crop-specific gene banks in the IBPGR (International Board for Plant Genetic Resources) network,' which is anywhere from Fort Collins, Colorado to Tsukuba.[24] These freely-donated genetic resources could become patented plant varieties from which corporations would collect royalties. SADCC would have to buy back the improved seed.

In 1984 at a FAO meeting a resolution was adopted that germ plasm, including patented seed, should be a common heritage and freely available to all; the US was alone in opposing the resolution. The FAO, however, is trying to establish an international network of base collections in which existing gene banks, including private ones, are brought together under FAO's auspices, to guarantee safe storage and free access of stored germ plasm. Given the above problems, regional co-ordination of collection and development of germ plasm is probably the only way to try to protect this non-replaceable heritage of Southern Africa.

## Distribution – Food on all the Tables

Another crucial area of concern to SADCC is the distribution of production. Drought from 1982–84, continuing into 1987 in Botswana as well as parts of Zimbabwe and Mozambique, underlined the importance of storage and distribution. The Post Production Food Industry Advisory Unit (PFIAU) has been studying traditional as well as modern techniques of storage, looking at the question of transport depots in rural areas, and at agro-processing in the rural areas so that grain does not have to travel far from the villages.[25]

By 1986 Zimbabwe and Malawi had become surplus producers of grain; Zimbabwe had approximately two million metric tons surplus (three years' normal domestic sales) which was stored in large silos and in bags piled high in pyramids near the silos. Four years' supply of sorghum was also in storage. Plans for regional storage under SADCC control have been delayed by donor interference in regional agricultural policy and pricing (see Chapter 5). However, national committees of the PFIAU in Angola, Botswana, Lesotho, Malawi, Tanzania, Zambia and Zimbabwe are also looking at small, local storage schemes. A traditional method successfully used among Nguni peoples was to store grain under the cattle byre. A hole was dug and lined with a mixture of soil, dung and water to protect the grain from insects and rodents. A slab was put over the small hole at the top and covered with the same mixture. Placing the cattle kraal over it would maintain the dung-soil mixture over the hole. This storage was particularly effective against moisture and insect deterioration in certain soil types. This and other appropriate technology methods for the village have been under study. SADCC is therefore not relying only on large silos for its needs, but trying to develop different methods for different areas.

Repeated marketing proposals call for attention to rural depots to collect grain. Poorer farmers cannot take grain long distances to the market and, with inadequate storage, it rots on the farm. As discussed in Chapter 1, under colonialism in Southern Rhodesia, the white regime was interested only in marketing production of the commercial farmers; only with independence were roads in remote areas improved and depots established. That lesson needs to be learned by Tanzania where inefficient marketing and extremely poor roads discourage the most industrious peasants so much so that they grow either only for consumption . . . or in order to smuggle produce across borders into Kenya, Burundi or Rwanda.

The early 1980s drought also emphasised the need for co-ordination in food aid so that neighbours would not compete with each other for international assistance. In 1984 they presented joint proposals to the international community, particularly important as it exposed members' relative needs in comparison to others in the region. Although all suffered from the drought, Botswana's food production was down to five percent of consumption. Over 100,000 in Mozambique actually starved to death, not only because of the drought, but because food aid caravans were attacked by the South Africa-backed MNR. In contrast, Zimbabwe had hungry people and provided food for work projects, but no one starved.

## Agro-Industry

In the industrial sector, co-ordinated by Tanzania, SADCC designated production for basic needs as the priority: food, clothing, housing. Agricultural implements, fertilisers, chemicals for cotton textiles, are the first projects. Even agricultural hand tools, like the hoe, are in short supply. Planners found that hand tools produced by local artisans spent one-tenth the foreign exchange as an imported one. Now artisans in each country are encouraged to produce hand tools.

This choice also raises the question of appropriate technology. Many peasants even in Zimbabwe have little draught power and scotch carts are in short supply. Local workshops are being established to train artisans in metal and woodwork, to build tools and to repair them. Tractors – from the US, Britain, USSR – have a long history of failure in Africa because of the extremely hard soil and harsh climate. The laterite soil breaks up the blades of a plough, not the reverse; such harsh conditions cause engine problems. SADCC, therefore, is interested in developing tractors for local conditions, promoting complementarity of production in Swaziland and Tanzania. Turnpan of Lonrho in Zimbabwe, however, has developed a 'people' s tractor' of 45 hp (only engine parts imported) but quite separate from SADCC planning. If the Lonrho tractor becomes practical, perhaps it could be adopted in SADCC. If not, it will remain a private endeavour, separate from SADCC auspices and competitive with SADCC production.

The area in which growth could occur most quickly is food processing. In 1985 only 10–20 percent of food raw material was processed in Africa; for developed countries in the West, 80–85 percent of farm-produced raw materials is processed before reaching the consumer.[26] Estimates are that the African percentage will increase dramatically in the next ten years. A SADCC study found that 'it is by no means an exaggeration to state that the entire technical historical spectra of cereal processing and meat processing are to be found within the region: cereals are processed by simple grinding stones, or in large mechanised mills and bakeries; meat is processed by sun drying (biltong) and also by modern freezing and canning technologies.'[27]

SADCC is trying to plan growth in processing to aid all involved. Again, priority will be with basic foods, not exotic artichokes or olives. Here too complementarity of production will be important so that several countries can have processing firms. Finally, attempts will be made to locate some plants in order to create jobs away from overcrowded cities. In its planning SADCC has to confront the fact that Zimbabwe, Malawi and Swaziland have already advanced food processing plants, most under foreign ownership. In Zimbabwe, for example, four of the top five firms in terms of assets and earnings are foreign owned corporations with food processing as a major sector of their production (Delta, National Foods, TA Holdings, Hippo).[28] Cairns, under partial South African ownership, is the largest and most diversified food and beverage processor in Zimbabwe.[29] Anglo-American Corporation of South Africa controls much of the citrus fruit and sugar industries. Delta, then fully a South African subsidiary, in its 1985 annual report indicated it had set up a separate division 'encompassing food and industrial operations....Through this division Delta will be developing its role as a processor of Zimbabwe' s vast agricultural potential. The Food and Industrial division is unique in the SADCC region....'[30]

Large transnationals usually do not prefer planned production, even if a good profit is built in. SADCC is interested not only in food production but in getting it on the table so it is unlikely the governments will leave these foreign firms totally without supervision or control. At independence Duncan Clarke described Zimbabwe' s food industry as follows: 'Transnational corporate investment in agro-allied industries represents a major element of control over food output, foreign exchange, employment, and agrarian investment.'[31] Since then state-owned corporations in Zimbabwe have taken control of 25 percent of the food marketing, including beef and pork, milk and dairy, and grains. In 1990 the government had to purchase Super Canners, which processes meats, for the corporation was involved in transfer pricing; the owner ran up a debt and then left for overseas.

## Institutional Development and the Business Community

Probably more than anywhere in the Third World, basic needs of the region have been systematically and exhaustively studied under SADCC direction. A major accomplishment in the first decade, most of the sectoral units have dramatically increased their knowledge of the region through multiple feasibility studies, especially in transport and communications (Mozambique), energy (Angola), agriculture (Botswana and Zimbabwe) and industry (Tanzania). The region is learning to set its own priorities.

Yet the major weakness of SADCC emerges from this very strength. Its decentralised model of sectoral units has deterred the development of new institutions. Only SACCAR and SATCC (Southern African Transport and Communications Commission run by Mozambique) are legal entities able to enter into contracts. A study by the Organisation for Economic Co-operation and Development (OECD) on SADCC' s structures has noted that such a lack of institutional direction means that the terms and implementation of projects for similar tasks, like cowpea or bean research, differ according to the host government and the co-operating partner (donor). Allowing for flexibility in the early stages, this approach creates much confusion as projects multiply. Lack of institutional clarity in defining relationships also leaves SADCC more vulnerable to competing interests. As the OECD review concluded, there is '...a need to clarify exactly where, within SADCC' s sectoral structures, responsibility lies for monitoring the components of the sectoral programmes especially in terms of decisions with policy or strategy implications.' [33]

The sorghum/millet research project – a research success – demonstrates the institutional frailties of SADCC. Expatriate agricultural economists with USAID and ICRISAT wrote the project design, consulting neither with the SADCC Secretariat nor the Botswanan Director of Agricultural Research (SACCAR was not yet in existence). The Zimbabwe food security unit was informed, but no other national agricultural experts or officials in all of SADCC participated in designing the project.

The first scientists hired for the project were all from outside the region, recruited by ICRISAT, not SADCC.[34] They were employed on international terms, at salaries substantially above any in SADCC. The program included a major training component for advanced postgraduate studies, but to have no SADCC scientist involved in the initial stages is not conducive to training SADCC nationals. Not wanting to hire scientists needed in their national posts, the sorghum/millet program became more an ICRISAT project than a SADCC one. Finally, financial accountability for the project was from ICRISAT to the donors. There was no financial accountability in the first instance in the region.

Only after two years did SADCC challenge this organisational control, even though the initial project funding had elicited much protest from member states. The funding from USAID explicitly stated, 'None of the grant funds will be used to fill gaps in the national research systems of Angola, Mozambique, and Tanzania unless AID agrees in writing.'[35] These restrictions applied to two budget items and were based on political sanctions imposed by the US against Angola (no diplomatic recognition) and Mozambique (CIA officials had just been expelled from Mozambique). The exclusion of Tanzania was related to its ineligibility for US aid because it was in arrears in debt repayments. As the SADCC consultant report concluded, 'while the restrictions were not as great as had been suggested by some outside commentators, they were invidious at the level of principle and understandably gave rise to strong objections by SADCC.'[36] With the full operation of SACCAR, some of the above problems have been mitigated, although ICRISAT remains very much the 'executing agency'. A review in 1988 of the first five years of operation complimented the research progress achieved, especially the extensive out-station observations and adaptations which strengthen national programs. Problems still remain although institutional development in this sector is now well established; for other SADCC sectors, however, the institutional paucity remains serious.

With SADCC emphasising the role of the state in planning both production and distribution and seeking to evolve its own model, the business sector was ignored until 1987. Since then SADCC has begun discussions with the 'enterprise sector': transnational corporations, private local corporations, parastatals and co-operatives.

Like the donors, businesses found the decentralised model difficult to relate to, especially as each sector unit seemed to operate differently. In spite of SADCC's emphasis on production, there was no legal network for cross-border investment, and banking and insurance facilities were insufficient and inefficient. These obstacles were largely the product of South Africa's economic domination of the region: it owned most of what banks and insurance companies there were in the region; at independence, some national financial institutions were established, but they were fragile entities, in some cases more symbolic of sovereignty than real competitors with the foreign institutions.

What business leaders wanted first was trade facilities to boost their regional sales before embarking upon further investment. SADCC responded slowly and deliberately with feasibility studies for a revolving fund and export credit facilities. Part of the deliberation was SADCC's priority to promote production; although trade and production are obviously linked, SADCC officials wanted co-ordination in production to remain the leading edge.[37] Further, the membership was not ready for one fund, for national conditions vary greatly; the eligibility and terms for the pre-financing of exports had to be defined differently in each economy. By 1989 each member set up a Pre-Financing and Revolving Fund (EPRF), based on models already established by Zimbabwe and Tanzania, to loan foreign exchange to businesses who would in turn earn foreign exchange from exports. Along with the Export Credit Facility (ECF), these moves represented the beginning of a financial base for increased trade. A cross-border investment facility will take longer to establish, for investment codes and incentives vary widely in the region.

This cautious approach is dictated by political considerations – suspicion, derived from the colonial experience of foreign capital. As shown in the food-processing industry, 'private' production often meant foreign control. Only a handful of Africans benefited from 'growth' or 'development'. To a number of SADCC states, 'free enterprise' is only a label to mask markets created and maintained by coercion.

Some experiences since independence have also not encouraged trust, e.g., corporate sabotage by the Portuguese of the new state of Mozambique, by way of the destruction of infrastructure in general, and the flight of capital and skilled personnel. In 1986 the Zimbabwean medical profession raised an outcry that critical pharmaceuticals were not available because of foreign exchange shortages. The government responded by raising the allocation for chemicals. One pharmaceutical corporation was nationalised (from South Africa with compensation) at independence but the others remain private. The government soon found that the private pharmaceutical companies were using the increased import of chemical compounds to increase production of cosmetics from those compounds. Cosmetics provide a very high profit margin, especially in relation to the controlled prices of drugs. Therefore, even with higher foreign exchange allocations, the drugs were still not available.

And SADCC has done its homework. Not only are they suspicious of customs unions as entities to help the strongest, the members know the role of private enterprise in other regional economic groups in the Third World. Experiences of other regional co-operation organisations with transnational corporations has increased this wariness:

> Every empirical study done on the subject of transnational corporations in the regional integration of the least developed countries has confirmed that the transnational enterprises have dominated, or been the major beneficiaries of, regional integration processes among the least developed countries.... local private groups are progressively displaced or co-opted by the transnational corporations. [38]

The United Nations study especially cites negative experiences in the Central American Common Market (CACM), the Latin American Free Trade Area (LAFTA) and the Andean Pact. In fact, research shows that during crises in regional co-ordination, transnational corporations follow a policy of 'divide and rule' to play one country off against another. With more than a bit of bravado but indicative of the attitude taken, a representative of Chrysler declared, 'We were able to block the whole Andean Pact integration scheme.'[39]Based on research for the Andean Pact and the CACM, however, 'divide and rule' has been at least partially effective.[40]

Despite the above, SADCC is obviously not anti-capital as an engine of growth. Understanding that provision must be made for sufficient profit for corporations as well as for development concerns such as increased employment and training, SADCC is just not yet sure of the formula. What it is clear about is that the corporations do not enter the region alone, but come with powerful international financial agencies (IMF, banks, government loans) behind them, and hence SADCC insists on more state involvement than that preferred by the private interests.These considerations have delayed the building of institutions to facilitate capital movement. In 1987 SADCC proposed the setting up of national business councils to comprise collectively a SADCC Regional Business Council. The national business council in Zimbabwe was one of the first to be constituted but immediately clashed with the government. Imbued with their own importance, business leaders demanded that the Minister of Finance represent the government on the council; the government responded by appointing a deputy secretary with little authority to negotiate.

The SADCC Regional Business Council met in April 1989 in Harare, with all but Swaziland attending. The first tentative discussions examined how to exchange information and increase trade and investment and participate in SADCC projects. In regard to the latter goal, it decided to avoid projects in food processing and agriculture manufacturing (equipment, fertiliser, etc.) and to concentrate on the area of transport. The Beira Corridor Authority (BCA) was identified as offering an innovative institutional way to combine private and public capital under the direction of a SADCC project.

Needing financing to refurbish the life-line of rail, road and port for Zimbabwe (and oil pipeline), Zambia, Malawi and northern Mozambique, the members set up the BCA under SATCC. Private capital, both national and international, have invested, following SATCC's priorities and schedule of return on investment. The Zimbabwean government has contributed over $5 million in investment (as well as providing troops to protect the rail line from MNR sabotage).

To respond to this initiative, the Beira Corridor Group (BCG) in Zimbabwe organised businessmen to invest in the corridor. Private capital, both national and international, have joined the BCG, pursuing BCA' s priorities and ostensibly accepting the BCA's schedule of return on investment. The group of businessmen (BCG) have worked to increase the use of the corridor by Zimbabwean and Zambian exporters who prefer to ship through South Africa, citing 'efficiency' as their reason; the Beira Corridor's lower cost is now attracting more traffic. It increased its capacity to 2.2 million metric tons by 1988, saving Zimbabwe, for example, $690 per container of tea shipped to Beira instead of Durban, South Africa and $450 per container of tobacco. Traffic in the first half of 1988 increased 16 percent over the same period in 1987. Container capacity rose to 30,000 by 1990. The BCG has, however, also been criticised for not investing in the corridor. To 1989, they had only assisted the BCA and SADCC in promoting use of the corridor. Encouraging local producers to use SADCC routes is important enough for Malawi to form a group, called the Malawi Import and Export Routes Ltd., complementary to the BCG.

Similar plans for private involvement are under discussion for the Limpopo corridor from Zimbabwe to Maputo in Mozambique and for the Benguela railroad in Angola. Rehabilitation of the Limpopo Corridor will cost an estimated $154 million, with Britain, the US, Canada, Portugal and others expressing interest in the funding. Security will be provided by the joint Zimbabwe–Mozambican forces.

SADCC members worked several years before they could establish their own shipping and forwarding company, Mozima. Owned jointly by Navinter of Mozambique, Meridian Shipping of Zimbabwe and Skycargo of Malawi, it will be a major competitor to South African shipping firms, which encouraged everyone to ship via South African ports and discouraged overseas lines from stopping at Mozambican ports. Mozima will now be able to co-ordinate forwarding services for all three Mozambican ports.

In the first decade of its existence, SADCC has been successful in promoting the region, both locally and internationally. Studies and debates continually review the projects which increase regional interaction and promote production. Based on the successful innovations, the

1990s for SADCC will probably be a decade of establishing more institutional linkages to formalise and regularise their co-ordination as they persevere in redefining the region. However, even after the wars are over and the fires burning crops are put out, and even with a free South Africa, powerful interests will continue to promote their own definitions and their own economic 'restructuring' against SADCC.

# NOTES

1   SADCC, *Workshop on Rehabilitation and Upgradation of Priority Industries in the SADCC Region–Objectives, Rationale, Approach.* Arusha, Tanzania, 27–29 August 1988, pp. 42–4, 81–2, 91–2.

2   As stated in Chapter 1, the Central African Federation was created in 1953 to integrate the economies of Southern and Northern Rhodesia (Zimbabwe and Zambia) and Nyasaland (Malawi). In reality, the federation subordinated Northern Rhodesia and Nyasaland to the industrialisation of Southern Rhodesia; they became mineral and raw material suppliers to nascent Southern Rhodesian industry. The East African Community also followed the colonial pattern of subordinating the weaker Tanzanian and Ugandan economies to the benefit of the stronger – Kenya. Disputes arose even over the allocation of locomotives and other transport equipment among the three. When it broke up in 1977, Tanzania closed its border to Kenya in protest over equipment confiscated by Kenya.

The Southern African Customs Union (SACU) still exists, comprising South Africa, Namibia, Botswana, Lesotho and Swaziland (BLS). Receiving preferential prices for their goods, it is supposed to be a help to the poorer economies. In fact, delays of payments are so long that benefits are often negligible, wiped out by inflation or currency devaluation (which South Africa does without consultation of the others).

For the BLS the customs union means revenue; for South Africa it provides protectionism, markets, and industrial dominance. Joseph Hanlon reports that the World Bank and the Ford Foundation, a 'respected body not given to starry-eyed nationalist economics,' conclude that even Lesotho would benefit from leaving SACU: '...membership of SACU is impeding development in Lesotho and has exacerbated dependence....Lesotho should accordingly take active steps toward disengaging from the customs union.' Joseph Hanlon, *Beggar Your Neighbours,* Bloomington: Indiana University Press, 1986, p. 88.

3   SADCC. Record of annual conference, Blantyre, Malawi, 19–20 November 1981, p. 28, quoted in Layi Abregunrin, 'Southern African Development Co-ordination Conference (SADCC): Towards Regional Integration of Southern Africa for Liberation,' *Current Bibliography on African Affairs.* 17:4 (1984–85): 375.

4   Colin Stoneman. 'An Indicative Regional Plan for the Industrial Development of SADCC, 1987–2000,' Preliminary Report, Commonwealth, January 1987, p. 9.

5   SADCC. *Industry,* sector report presented at annual conference. Harare, Zimbabwe, 30–31 January 1986, pp. 21–3.

6   Carl Eicher. 'Agricultural Research for African Development: Problems and Priorities for 1985–2000,' paper presented at the World Bank Conference on Research Priorities for Sub-Saharan Africa, Bellagio, 1985, p. 16.

7   Raisuddin Ahmed and Narendra Rustagi. 'Agricultural Marketing and Price Incentives: A Comparative Study of African and Asian Countries,' Washington, DC: International Food Policy Research Institute, 1985, p. 25.

8   David S. Kingsbury. 'Potential Incentive Effects of Pricing Policy on Agricultural Trade in Several SADCC Countries: Preliminary Results,' paper presented for conference on Food Security Research in Southern Africa, Harare, 1988, p. 7.

9   Michael Bratton. 'Farmer Organizations in the Communal Areas of Zimbabwe,' *Working Paper 1/84*, Department of Land Management, University of Zimbabwe, 1984.

10  Economist Intelligence Unit, *Botswana, Lesotho, Swaziland, 1988–89*, London: EIU, 1989.

11  John H. Mellor. 'The Changing World Food Situation – A CGIAR Perspective,' *Annual Report 1984*. Washington: IFPRI.

12  Interview with Louis Mazhani, Plant Breeder, Government of Botswana, 12 June 1985.

13  Sam Moyo, Nelson Moyo and Rene Lowenson. 'The Root Causes of Hunger in Zimbabwe,' paper presented to conference on Churches Drought Action in Africa, Geneva, September 1985, p. 7. It is instructive to note that at a time when Zimbabwe was producing 109 percent of its per capita food requirements, upwards of 20 percent of children under 5 years were malnourished and nearly 39 percent were stunted. A. Berg. 'Malnutrition in Zimbabwe,' World Bank, 1982, quoted in *ibid.*, p 20.

14  For an analysis of Swazi ruling class interests, see John Daniel and Johnson Vilane. 'The Crisis of Political Legitimacy in Swaziland,' *Review of African Political Economy*, no. 35 (May 1986): 54–67.

15  Relying solely on the perspective of agricultural economists (not the agronomists, plant breeders, agricultural extension experts, etc. who were in the consultative technical committees–CTCs), this reorganization was written and strongly promoted by the US Agency for International Development. Interview with John Dhliwayo, head of SADCC Food Security Technical and Administrative Unit in Zimbabwe, 14 July 1988.

16  This decentralized and consensual process also allows national governments to enter into regional projects on a bilateral basis, ignoring SADCC structures. Zambia proceeded with grain reserve discussions with the EEC while SADCC was trying to initiate a regional project with EEC assistance. In the transport sector, which also requires various committees to review a project, Malawi contracted with the World Bank for a northern road to connect with the Tazara rail line in Tanzania, without informing SADCC. For these, both Malawi and the World Bank came under severe SADCC criticism, one result of which is that the World Bank now has an officer in Washington, DC assigned solely to SADCC. Ephraim Kaunga and Tore Rose. 'Case Study on SADCC Project 3.7.1. Development of Navigation on Lake Niassa/Nyasa/Malawi.' OECD Development Centre/SADCC Secretariat Joint Research Report (20 March 1987).

17  Interviews with John Samki, October 31, 1985; with Michael Walsh, April 30, 1986; Records of Fourth Joint Meeting of SADCC CTCs, June 11–14, 1985, Harare.

18  SADCC. 'Agricultural Research and Training,' *Food, Agriculture, and Natural Resources*, sector report for annual conference, Luanda, People's Republic of Angola, 1–3 February 1989, p. 2.

19  A.C. Mosha. 'Sorghum and Sorghum Products for Better Food Security and Income,' *SADCC Post Production Systems Newsletter,* no. 10 (October 1988):16–23.

20  *Financial Gazette*, 19 September 1986. The UN Food and Agriculture Organisation seems to think that international constraints on transnational corporate control of seed are sufficient. See FAO, Committee on World Food Security, 'Transnational Corporations in Food and Agriculture, Forestry and Fishery Sectors in Developing Countries,' CFS: 87/6, February 1987, pp. 6–7.

21  *African Business* (October 1988): 39.

22  Ian Robertson, 'Biotechnology: Its Potential Impact on Food Security in Southern Africa,' paper presented at conference on Food Security Research in Southern Africa, Harare, 31 October – 3 November 1988, p. 2.

23  *Herald* (Harare), 20 April 1987. See also Frederick H. Buttel. 'Biotechnology and Agricultural Development in the Third World,' in Henry Bernstein, *et al.*, eds. *The Food Question–Profits versus People?* New York: Monthly Review Press, 1990: 163–80.

24  'SADCC Genebank: Prospects and Problems,' SADCC–NGO Newsletter, International Coalition for Development Action, Brussels, April 1989, p. 7. 'Era of Biotech Abounding in Uncertainty over Potential Benefits?' *Financial Gazette* (Harare), 17 February 1989.

25  Discussion based on interviews with team officials including Victor Kachoka, October 5, 1985 and June 25, 1988.

26  Barbara Dinham and Colin Hines. *Agribusiness in Africa*. London: Earth Resources, Ltd., 1983, p. 43.

27  SADCC. 'Report and Recommendations on SADCC Regional Food Security. Projects 6 and 7 [Post Harvest Loss and Food Processing].' International Development Research Center, Ottawa, consultant. January 1982, p. 22.

28  *Financial Gazette*, 23 August 1985.

29  *Herald* (Harare), 22 April 1986.

30  Delta Corporation, *Annual Report 1985*, (1 April 1984–31 March 1985), p. 10.

31  D.G. Clarke, *Foreign Companies and International Investment in Zimbabwe*. London: Catholic Institute for International Relations, March 1980, p. 58.

32  Robin Cohen. *The New Helots: Migrants in the International Division of Labour*. Hants: Gower, 1987, p. 173.

33  Organisation for Economic Cooperation and Development (OECD) Development Centre and the Southern African Development Coordination Conference (SADCC) Secretariat. 'Joint Study of Structures and Procedures in Development Co-operation,' March 1987, p. 9. This discussion is also based on interviews with several consultants to SADCC, including David Anderson, 28 January 1986, and several with Tim Sheehy and with Reginold Green.

34  This discussion is from the following: Interview with Dale Pfeiffer, USAID, Harare, Zimbabwe, March 25, 1985. Interviews at the Matopos Sorghum/Millet Research Station in Zimbabwe, May 2, 1985. Sam Montsi and Brian

van Arkadie. 'Case Study on SADCC Project 3.0.2 – The Sorghum-Millet Improvement Programme,' OECD Development Centre/SADCC Secretariat Joint Research Study, March 1987.

35  *Ibid.*, p. 14.

36  *Ibid.* Attending the January 1984 SADCC annual meeting in Lusaka, Zambia, when the conditional restriction first became public, this author disagrees with the OECD report that 'restrictions were not ...great.' SADCC officials spent three hours in a Council of Ministers meeting debating the restrictions, which totally disrupted their important agenda in the midst of a severe drought in the region. They agreed not to accept the restrictions, and the project only received approval after USAID found funding from other donors to cover the exclusions.

37  SADCC's attention to trade is either complicated or facilitated, depending on one's analysis, by the existence of the Preferential Trade Agreement of Eastern and Southern Africa (PTA) which promotes trade among 16 members* by lowering tariffs for selected goods on a common list. At first only five members of SADCC joined. Tanzania was hesitant for fear of losing out competitively to more powerful Kenya. Angola and Mozambique were not exporting much in the midst of full scale war and were not sure they wanted to join such a capitalist enterprise. Botswana suggested that membership would affect its relations within the Southern African Customs Union, although Swaziland and Lesotho were members of both SACU and PTA. More likely, Botswana, with a strong economy, felt it had little to gain from the PTA. Tanzania, Mozambique (after receiving a preferential rate) and Angola have now joined, leaving only Botswana out.

The PTA has made progress in issuing PTA traveller's cheques, a common customs form which greatly reduces time and trouble in crossing borders, and an insurance policy. The clearing house, central to the agreement, to maintain exchange balances among the trading countries has been more controversial. Gradually, it is being used more, but the endemic problem of some countries always having a surplus and others a deficit is not resolved. Zimbabwe, especially, has been under repeated attack for restricting imports from the area, while pushing its own exports.

Most criticized by fellow SADCC members is Zimbabwe's insistence on reducing drastically, or even curtailing, the PTA's requirements for locally produced goods to be put on the common list. First, Zimbabwe (and Kenya) successfully fought the requirement that a firm had to have 50 percent ownership and 50 percent local management for its goods to be listed. Zimbabwe, still with much foreign capital in 'Zimbabwean' firms, would have found many of its goods ineligible for the tariff reductions. Second, Zimbabwean business opposed the value-added provision, requiring local manufacturing to have done more than assemble the product in order to call it 'national.'

The PTA also tries to improve transport routes, like the road which runs from Botswana to Kenya. In these projects, there has been some disagreement with SADCC's transport sector. A PTA-SADCC Liaison Committee has been formed to discuss the differences.

Many analysts think the PTA and SADCC can be complementary not competitive. Others disagree and point out their fundamental political differences expressed in their different priorities. Another approach urges all SADCC members to support SADCC's proposals as a bloc within the

PTA. However, business has a significant voice in the PTA because it is a trading organization, and the reality is that 'Zimbabwean' business interests (not necessarily government) find they often share goals with their counterparts in Kenya, more than with their immediate neighbours.

\* Members of the PTA include Angola, Djibouti, Ethiopia, Somalia, Kenya, Uganda, Rwanda, Burundi, Tanzania, Comoros, Mauritius, Mozambique, Malawi, Zambia, Zimbabwe, Swaziland, Lesotho.

See Carol B. Thompson. 'Zimbabwe in SADCC: A Question of Dominance?' *Zimbabwe's Prospects.* Colin Stoneman, ed. London: Macmillan, 1988, pp. 238–56. Interviews with Keith Atkinson, Confederation of Zimbabwe Industries (CZI), 13 and 31 May 1985; with Richard Hess, Imani Consultants, 7 July 1988.

38 United Nations Centre on Transnational Corporations. *Measures Strengthening the Negotiating Capacity of Governments in their Relations with Transnational Corporations: Regional Integration cum/versus Corporate Integration.* (ST/CTC/10) New York: United Nations, 1982, pp. 42 and 53.

39 Constantine Vaitsos, 'Crisis in Regional Economic Cooperation (Integration) among Developing Countries: A Survey,' *World Development* 6: (June 1978). Reprinted in *Recent Issues In World Development: A Collection of Survey Articles,* Paul Streeten and Richard Jolly, eds. New York: Pergamon Press, 1981, p. 304.

40 United Nations Industrial Development Organisation (UNIDO). *Regional Co-operation: Experience and Perspective of ASEAN and the Andean Pact.* Vienna: UNIDO, 1986, p. 60.

# 5.

# Forces of Food and Finance: The United States in Southern Africa

We do not intend to be perpetual suppliers of raw materials. We intend to develop our industry and agriculture. *We intend to participate in the international division of labour in a position of equality.*

Samora Machel
President, Mozambique
(1975–1986)

Although discussion of the failure of African agriculture spans more than a decade, the prolonged drought throughout Southern Africa in 1982–84 underlined the urgency of the problems. Emphasis on grain production emerged with the first SADCC documents in 1979 but the drought forestalled solutions as governments hurried to keep people alive with emergency food supplies. By 1984, however, SADCC members had submitted joint proposals for relief and rehabilitation to the international community.

As shown in the chapter on policy, admitting errors and organising to prevent their repetition have been a strength of SADCC; collectively, SADCC has discussed failures on the part of governments and examined possible solutions from within the region. This regional approach to solving problems became evident at the 1986 United Nations symposium on the African economic crisis. Here African governments agreed to structural adjustment policies for their economies, including higher prices for food producers and a greater share of government revenue for agricultural development.

What has not been so evident is admission of error by international aid and finance agencies, for if African agriculture is the total failure everyone accuses, then international agencies, which have been involved in African agriculture for over 20 years must share the blame. A bit like an abandoned field with junk car parts, the African landscape is strewn with failed projects, broken-down inappropriate technology, salinated soil from improper irrigation, stunted hybrids that did not receive timely inputs – all sad monuments to expensive international consultancies and aid programmes.

A Tanzanian minister, for example, expressed frustration that the World Bank had promoted, established, and monitored programmes which it now condemns as serious Tanzanian mistakes, such as the highly centralised marketing board for grain (National Milling Corporation). The World Bank fully or partially funded experiments in the production of flue-cured tobacco (1971), smallholder tea (1972), cotton and cashew (1974), maize (1976), and smallholder pyrethrum (1980), all of which it now criticises. In addition, it had promoted estate farming of sugar (1963) and of dairy (1976) and invested in the Tanzania Development Finance Co. (private farmers) and the Tanzania Rural Development Bank (co-operatives).[1] A 1987 World Bank discussion paper, which audited the rates of return on 10 Tanzanian World Bank projects, found that seven had negative results and concluded Tanzania would have been better off if it had not borrowed capital to fund them.[2]

Two particular schemes reveal some of the reasons for the World Bank's failures. In the 1971 tobacco project, Tanzanian and World Bank officials, reminiscent of colonial ways of controlling labour production, decided every detail for the peasant – how, when and how much land to plant, timetables for weeding, fertilising, harvesting, curing. The peasants only provided their labour power, and so not surprisingly, participated in the project without enthusiasm or any sense of involvement or ultimate responsibility. It failed.

In the 'Western Cotton Zone' in Tanzania, also established by the World Bank, people were traditionally semi-agricultural and semi-nomadic. The government's villagisation programme in the mid-1970s consolidated the people into permanent villages and broke down many of the communal ties that bound peasants. This transformation of life style – settled mainly to produce a cash crop – resulted in violence among competing clans and in cattle rustling. Eventually, killings became the order of the day. Because the security forces found they could not control the situation, in 1982 the government officially recognised peasant militia (*sungusungu*) as the only way to arrest the violence, an admission that state forces could not resolve the social conflicts unleashed by villagisation and the emphasis on cash crops.[3]

Examples such as these could be cited for most countries of SADCC, and the rest of Africa as well. International aid agencies have been fully involved, as agricultural production in Southern Africa deteriorated in the 1970s. They pursue their own interests and agendas in allocating assistance: often the motive is to create a demand for its own products, and the US is no exception. As analysed in many studies,[4] eliminating hunger in Third World countries is not the major goal of US aid programmes. To justify aid to the American taxpayer, members of Congress regularly cite that for every $1 of aid the US receives $10 in return through sales of American products or savings for low cost materials. A US

General Accounting Office (GAO) report compares the US Congress appropriation of $1.54 billion for six international organisations which loan money to poor countries with the World Bank spending $1.59 billion in the US alone to supply its development projects.[5]

A primary goal of aid is to create markets for US goods, in turn creating American jobs. One well-known mechanism is to require recipient governments to use the cash provided to buy US products and ship them in US vessels. In this way, 'foreign aid' purchases quickly become 'domestic subsidies' for US corporations. The policy is so well established that Teresa Hayter has suggested 'aid' should be renamed 'public subsidy for private profit.'[6] By loaning or donating funds which must be spent in the US, overseas markets are guaranteed, even for American corporations which may be less competitive in a free market.

Foreign aid also creates a climate for US investment. Loans for the infrastructural development of roads or dams reduce transport or water costs for manufacturing. Major aid packages are not often given to governments which refuse to offer lucrative investment incentives, such as long tax holidays, and liberal terms for remittance of profits back to the US, as well as a 'controlled' (i.e., repressed) labour force. In addition, the distinction between investment and loans has become blurred, for the corporations building the factories borrow from the banks to finance investments, the interest of which must be paid in foreign exchange earned by production in the new factory.

Finally, aid also provides access to cheaper raw materials – mineral or agricultural. Encouraging production of cash crops like cotton or coffee allows them to be purchased at minimal prices on the international markets. Although aid is most often tied to conditions or contracts, such as requiring the recipient to buy inputs (e.g., seed, fertiliser, spare parts, irrigation pumps, tractors) from the donor, the donor is rarely, if ever, required to offer a guaranteed market for the output produced. Once the cotton is grown or the sugar harvested, it enters the international market where it is vulnerable to the fluctuations of the market and where prices can drop below the costs of production.

Aid is in many respects something of a misnomer because larger and larger proportions are now loans, not grants, and add to the Third World's debt burden. Only a few countries have written off government loans; the Scandinavian countries and the Netherlands have been the most generous in this respect in Southern Africa.[7] The US has been reluctant to write off loans, and US Treasury Secretary James A. Baker repeatedly refused to convert loans to grants for the poorest countries.[8] Where a country is not in the best of relations with the US, arrears on repayment results in the recipient being cut off from further assistance. The distinction between rewriting a loan or cutting off funds is made on a political, not economic, basis. Countries like Zaire receive repeated extensions, while others like Tanzania are cut off. Furthermore, aid is used as an ideological tool to promote capitalism, by assisting private over public capital, as was done in Tanzania and Mozambique.

The creation of markets and investment opportunities and access to cheap raw materials are the main economic goals of aid. Often as important is the political goal of 'buying' friendship or support. The US mission at the UN keeps a computer tally of voting records in the UN General Assembly. If an aid recipient does not vote with the US on key issues, it can jeopardise its next aid allocation. The vote count is often used against Southern African countries and was one reason for stopping aid to Zimbabwe in 1986. Just before he stepped down as President of Tanzania in 1985, Julius Nyerere criticised such attempts to create acquiescent puppets; at an address at the UN he stated Tanzania would like to document which countries have voted against issues crucial to Tanzania's interests and proceeded to condemn US positions on many issues dear to Africans.

In forums where rich and poor have an equal voice, the US often downgrades its delegation 'to show contempt,' as one official declared at the July 1987 UN Conference for Trade and Development (UNCTAD) meeting. The head of the US delegation, Deputy Assistant Secretary of State for International Organisations, Dennis Goodman, described himself as a 'traveling insult,' for the delegation did not have the authority to negotiate commodity prices or the debt.[9]

The politics of aid is an old story. What is new is the impact on the developing world of the US' own economic crisis. Michel Camdessus, Managing Director of the IMF, has cited 'the US budget deficit as the *single largest contributing factor* to global economic imbalances...of interest rates, balance of trade, credibility of efforts to stabilise the dollar and on allocations of savings around the world.'[10] Since 1985 more capital flowed into the United States than to all the Third World combined. The American monetary policy of high interest rates and the created strength of the dollar to finance its deficit encouraged investors and speculators alike to send capital to the US, not only from Japan and Europe but also from Latin America. The unprecedented deficit financed by foreign funds has led more than one analyst to conclude 'that the US has been guilty of the most irresponsible fiscal behaviour in its history during the last seven years [1980–87].'[11] The US pushed the world economy into deep recession through a tight money policy, combined with the high interest rates (which drove up Third World debt servicing). It drove down commodity prices and preached austerity while spending wildly on Star Wars.[12]

The US is not alone as a source of diminishing capital for investment. Net non-concessional receipts from the Organisation for Economic Co-operation and Development (OECD) to SADCC fell 70 percent between 1981–84 from $1.183 billion to $381 million. As SADCC summarised, 'improved profit margins are either being paid out as dividends, or being used to finance the bout of acquisition and take-overs which have become a common feature in all major international markets.' [13] In short, providing an open economy for investors, as the US and international agencies required, did not attract capital to the developing economies, for the US government also pursued a contradictory policy which made sure any available capital would be invested in the US.

The US government also does not act alone in its aid/loan policies. As the major donor to the IMF and the World Bank, the US often leads and determines policy for both. By the early 1980s, the 'sister' institutions had similar policies and their earlier distinction as international banker (IMF) versus project grantor (Bank) had become blurred. Both attached conditionality to loans – currency devaluations, reduction of government subsidies to consumers on staples, reduction of expenditure on education and health care, reduced state ownership in production and marketing, etc. These conditions were offered so uniformly to African countries that a Nigerian government minister observed: 'What would you say about a doctor who prescribed the same remedy no matter what the disease or relative health of the patient?'

Other arguments question the categories and definitions of the IMF and World Bank. Central to their conditionality for loans is a reduction of government expenditure, and the primary targets for cuts are invariably education and health care, high cost items on almost any budget. The two view such expenditures as consumption items which must be reduced until production increases to provide the revenue to enable governments to meet the bills. Yet many now question this approach as myopic. Production is not simply dependent on machinery and capital but needs labour – healthy, skilled labour. K. A. Malima, Vice-Chair of Tanzania's Economic Planning Commission, asked 'What sort of government is it that is spending less on education than it did 30 years ago?' When good health care increases labour capacity or when imparting educational skills increases productivity, should spending on health or education be classified as '*consumption*' rather than '*investment*?' Why indeed wouldn't a government increase that investment for a more stable economic future? As Malima concluded, 'You can't starve the cow that you are later going to milk.' [14]

In Southern Africa, Tanzania resisted IMF conditionality for six years, arguing that the remedy was worse than the disease. It is widely agreed that Tanzania acquired its debt through a combination of financing unilaterally the war to rid Uganda of the Amin regime's tyranny, the severe drought of the early 1980s, declining world commodity prices for its tea and coffee, and government mismanagement particularly in the areas of pricing and marketing. Even though the government gradually devalued the shilling to encourage exports, it pointed out that there was just so much international demand for Tanzanian coffee, cashews, tea and cotton. Those commodities, in a saturated international market, are not really price elastic. At the same time, higher prices of imports destroyed the ability of industry to buy spare parts and necessary raw materials; because Tanzania already imported very few luxury products, higher prices affected production more than consumption.

Tanzania refused to cut expenditures on education and health care to the levels demanded by the IMF. One of the poorest of the poor countries, Tanzania has the highest literacy rate in Africa (including wealthier Kenya) and refused to curtail its successful programmes. Because Tanzania refused IMF terms, however, other lenders also withheld capital. In 1986, the IMF compromised on some of its terms, but Tanzania still had to devalue the shilling drastically, cut production subsidies and permit a free flow of prices (which all immediately soared upwards) for most goods.

Since 1975, when the price of Zambia's one major export (copper) plummeted, the government has complied with IMF terms. In fact, Zambia almost destroyed the Frontline States' alliance in the war against Southern Rhodesia when it unilaterally opened its southern border (closed to respect sanctions against Southern Rhodesia) in 1978 so that fertiliser could be imported in time for planting. The opening was encouraged by the IMF before it would extend a further loan.[15]

Throughout the next decade, Zambia tried to implement IMF terms. In 1985 Zambia even agreed to experiment with a weekly foreign currency auction to bring the price of the kwacha in line with demand, ultimately devaluing the kwacha by 725 percent. The government also curtailed expenditures and privatised some, admittedly inefficient, state industries and honoured debt repayments to the extent that some 26 percent of its export earnings were taken to service the IMF debt;[16] total repayment obligations, including all debts, took over 60 percent of export earnings. When the Zambian government complied with yet another IMF demand to cancel the subsidy for maize meal in November 1986, the worst riots in independent Zambia's history broke out, with at least 15 people killed. It was on this occasion when the national flag was pulled down by people outside a grocery store in Kitwe, and in its place they hoisted 'our own flag,' an empty polythene bag for maize meal.[17]

The government restored the subsidy. On 1 May 1987 President Kaunda announced that Zambia would no longer hold the currency auction nor follow IMF recommendations. The economy was in a shambles, mainly because of the fall of the copper price, failures in agricultural policies, and war for majority rule in Zimbabwe and South Africa; however, over 12 years of IMF 'remedies' had also not helped. In four years of the previous IMF programmes to stabilise the economy, annual per capita income dropped from $600 in 1981 to $400.[18] He explained his actions as follows:

We joined the programme in the firm belief that it would help us out of those problems. But after 11 or 12 years we've discovered that this was not to be.... The best I can hope for is that the death of 15 of our people will lead the IMF, and all of us who belong to the IMF group, to think again about this approach.... It actually reduces the ability of a nation to grow economically. I can only hope and pray that the blood spilled in Zambia was not in vain.[19]

Donors responded to Zambia's attempt to avoid stringent IMF conditionality by withholding funds, including the usually more sympathetic Sweden and the Netherlands. In spite of several measures by the government to stabilise the economy, inflation rose to 100 percent in 1989 and bad weather reduced the maize crop. External debt became one of the highest per capita in the world, although the cause was not simply mismanagement; a Commonwealth study estimated the cost of destabilisation and of efforts to reduce dependence on South Africa at $7 billion, about the same as the debt. Nevertheless, Zambia renegotiated with the IMF by 1990 and food subsidies were once again cut drastically. A new condition was added: IMF official Jacques Brussières of Canada became the new head of the central bank. A coup attempt in June 1990 was almost successful as citizens protested the economic deprivation and repression of voices of discontent. Kaunda finally agreed to a multi-party election in October 1991, but the economy did not quickly recover; as one Zambian economist concluded, 'despite strict adherence to the medicine prescribed, the Zambian economy slipped into a coma.'

An IMF study in the early 1980s showed that IMF targets had been met in less than half of the 23 African countries; of 92 programmes in Africa from 1980–86, 83 were suspended or fundamentally altered in the demands for adjustment made to the recipient.[20] By the mid-1980s, the situation had deteriorated severely. Even after the Structural Adjustment Facility was created in 1986 (with easy terms of 10 year loans at only 0.5% interest rate), 'between 1986 and February 1987, African countries transferred, on a net basis, *three and a half times* as much money to the Fund as they received from it in 1985.' [21] IMF remedies had a high failure rate even when they originally provided a net transfer of capital, because repayment requirements later reversed the capital flow, and African governments still could not pay because the fundamental reasons for their economic crises had not been altered.[22] Given these very high failure rates over almost two decades, it is no wonder African governments recoil at the continuing financial leverage the IMF has over their economies. Ex-President of Tanzania, Julius Nyerere, called it the 'International Ministry of Finance'; US presidential candidate Jesse Jackson was even more graphic: the 'Infant Mortality Foundation.'

The human reality behind the macro-economic statistics is grim indeed, resulting not infrequently in deaths in food riots where subsidies are cut or eliminated; or from malnutrition-related diseases. As serious is the political impact of conditionality. The IMF not only dictates fiscal and monetary policies but often requires that IMF personnel supervise African ministries. Many analysts have referred to this penetration of finance, trade, industrial and agricultural ministries as the 'recolonisation' of Africa:

> Such international co-ordination and degree of takeover – recolonisation – was imagined by only the most paranoid radical critics of ten years ago. Today this constitutes an observable reality noted in mundane language in press description and by non-radical establishment government figures in African states.[23]

In this way, the state in Africa has lost control of basic economic decisions, which determine the livelihood, the education and health of its citizens. Reduced to accumulating revenue from its citizens by IMF conditionality, the state has little say in the distribution of capital. Eliminating the distribution role of the state can create a crisis of legitimacy, for the government should provide services to the people, e.g., subsidised food, water, education, health care, roads, garbage collection. Consequently, political repression increases to maintain 'economic stability.' State intervention has *not* diminished but has changed from one of distribution of goods and services to repression.

The common call of US aid and other international agencies is for the privatisation of production. Based on the analysis that state production has been highly inefficient and expensive, the government is directed to turn over distribution and production to the private sector. Recognising that state enterprises have often been inefficient, overstaffed – crowded with underemployed bureaucrats, and sometimes corrupt, many African governments have moved to tighten budgets and clarify channels of responsibility. However, most SADCC members do not agree that full-scale privatisation is the major or best remedy. State intervention often occurred in the first place because private enterprise was only interested in those few sectors with substantial profit margins. The Zimbabwe government, for example, has opened its economy considerably but remains concerned because its most profitable sectors are not agriculture or small manufactures but real estate speculation and tourism. Additionally, foreign investors often expatriated all or most profit and were reluctant to reinvest in the host country; transfer pricing also took money out of their countries. And certainly, corruption is as probable in the private sector as the public. Government participation in key industries deterred some of these practices.

SADCC notices that the West does not always follow its own advice. Few SADCC countries have as much government intervention in farming as the US or European Economic Community (EEC) member states do. These so-called 'private enterprise' economies have farming systems which are almost totally dependent on government subsidies and government-assisted export marketing. In 1986, the US government spent $11.9 billion in price support for maize alone or the same as the combined budgets of the State, Justice and Interior Departments.[24] Direct farm subsidies in the US in 1987 reached $70 million per day, and from 1983–87, price-support programmes increased more rapidly than any other budget item, including defence. One Texas farm owned by International Paper Company and the Crown Prince of Liechtenstein received $2.2 million in subsidies from American taxpayers. J.G. Boswell Co. in San Joaquin Valley, California, collected $20 million. Government subsidies to farms have become a welfare system that helps two percent of the population, and not the needy two percent. [25] During the debate between the US and the EEC over reducing subsidies, an agricultural counsellor for the EEC pointed to the difference between US admonishments and practice: 'I don't see much reliance being put on the market by the United States. Think of the deficiency payments, target prices, loan rates, sugar import quotes...the tobacco programme and so on. I don't find much evidence of market forces.'[26]

By 1990 the Congress cut the farm programme by 25 percent or $13.6 billion, to be phased over a period of five years. Subsidies remain to support 5–15 percent of the land lying fallow.

In Japan rice farmers receive three times the world price but then the rice is dumped on the world market at half the world market price as animal feed.[27] Such fundamental governmental intervention within developed capitalist countries undercuts international market prices. Zimbabwe would have earned about $25 million over three seasons from maize exports alone, if developed nations' agricultural subsidies had not lowered world prices.[28] These practices make it hard for African nations to accept the demand for less government control or intervention. A double standard seems at work.

When challenged about such extensive state intervention in farming, the US argues that it is a 'strategic' sector. SADCC members concur and will thus maintain some government intervention in the production, pricing and marketing of agriculture, in spite of criticism from aid agencies because:

> It is now widely recognised, even in the neoclassical tradition, that in developing countries the inefficiency or absence of well-organised commodity, factor, and capital markets reduces considerably the ability of the free market economic system to carry out the functions of resource accumulation, allocation, and management optimally. Consequently, government intervention in the economy through development planning has now come to be accepted as an essential and pivotal means of steering and accelerating balanced economic growth in developing countries. [29]

Another favourite refrain of US and international agencies over the last three decades has been for trade liberalisation to reduce trade barriers and promote export-led growth. This advice is once again receiving new interest. An assessment at the end of 1987 of four years of trade liberalisation in Tanzania revealed that the shops were full but the houses empty. Chocolate bars, previously unavailable in Tanzania because they were banned as a luxury import, sat on the shelves in abundance – for $5 each. More critically, imported synthetic-blend trousers cost about 3000/– (Tanzania shillings), while the minimum monthly wage stood at 1300/–. The fact is that whereas consumers lack the cash to buy expensive imports, shopkeepers seem to have unlimited foreign exchange. One report on trade also noted that rhinoceros and elephant poaching had trebled since the introduction of trade liberalisation (one rhino horn is worth $20,000 – hard currency – in the Middle East).[30] It seems that poached ivory brings foreign exchange so candy bars and synthetic material can be put on the shelves for the rich. Trade liberalisation also frequently destroys the nascent, but local, manufacturing of shoes, clothes, or processed foods. As they fail to compete with foreign goods in price or quality, small businesses find the marketing of foreign goods more lucrative, and domestic production declines. For example, Tanzania used to have a growing cotton textile industry. Many Tanzanians continue to criticise trade liberalisation, for it seems to benefit mainly the small elite of currency speculators.

Zimbabwe also resisted trade (import) liberalisation, but finally complied to it as a condition exacted by the World Bank for further funds. Zimbabwe's manufacturing sector, accounting for about 25 percent of GNP, is based on processing of goods from the primary sector. Import liberalisation could threaten local manufacturing, which integrates agricultural and mining production through processing, and could result in the 'deindustrialisation' of the economy. When Zimbabwe raised the level at which an import licence was needed from Z$500 to Z$5000, imports of video recorders and televisions increased much more drastically than of spare parts. The government was also reluctant because the policy ignores the regional context of trade: opening the economy even more to South African goods, liberalisation could affect current efforts to reduce Zimbabwean dependence on South Africa, even a free South Africa. Colin Stoneman has pointed out:

> There is scarcely a successful country in the world which did not use protection as a means of building up industry; we can go back to Germany in the early part of the 19th century, to France, Italy and Japan a bit later, or to the 1960s and South Korea and Taiwan. In all these cases (and many others) the state played a strategic, stimulating role, helping to 'pick winners' and supporting them, sometimes investing itself.... it should be noted that the latter two countries are liberalising their foreign exchange controls only this year [1990], as is Italy, and many are aware of the important role of trade barriers (mainly non-tariff) in Japan.[31]

Obviously, one way to earn foreign exchange is to export goods; however, there are many problems with that simple formula, problems well documented from previous 'export-led growth' attempts. First, the economy orients production not around the needs of its people but around the capricious demand of wealthy overseas consumers. Thus, food importer Lesotho exports artichokes to Europe. Under this policy, land has been consolidated for export crops, with fewer peasants able to retain land or grow staples; unemployment and malnutrition increase. Second, export crops are vulnerable to an erratic international market so that a bumper crop often means lower prices because of oversupply problems. The terms of trade for agricultural exports have declined drastically. World Bank data reveals that all major categories of agroexports suffered real price declines from 1950–84.[32] From 1980–86, commodity prices fell 35 percent in real terms, striking their lowest since the depression of the 1930s.[33] The net effect has been that SADCC members must export more and more of their commodities just to buy the same tractor.

Table 5.1: *Terms of Trade*

|  | (1975=100) | | (1980=100) | | | |
|---|---|---|---|---|---|---|
|  | 1970 | 1979 | 1982 | 1983 | 1984 | 1985 |
| Angola | 68 | 113 | | | | |
| Malawi | 99 | 85 | 109 | 113 | 137 | 101 |
| Mozambique | 88 | 75 | | | | |
| Tanzania | 103 | 102 | 88 | 91 | 94 | 94 |
| Zambia | 227 | 100 | 72 | 78 | 74 | 72 |
| Zimbabwe | | | | 95 | | 89 |

NB: Botswana, Lesotho and Swaziland are still members of the Southern African Customs Union, and figures are not computed separately for them.
*Source:* World Bank, *Development Report.* 1983, 1986, 1987, New York: Oxford University Press; 1983: Annex Table 13, 1986, p. 196, 1987: p. 220.

A third problem with trade liberalisation is encountered when primary producers attempt to process their main export products: tariff and other trade barriers of the developed economies. Tanzania found its high grade coffee beans sold well on the London coffee exchange, but when processed into instant or ground coffee for export with Tanzanian labels, it could not compete with the larger corporations and secure a sufficient market niche. The recent focus on export-led growth also comes at a time when protectionism is increasing among Western economies. Simultaneous with encouraging developing economies to export, Western countries have closed their domestic markets to new producers. President Reagan, the apostle of the free market, introduced more import restrictions than the previous six presidents combined. The percentage of total imports subjected to restrictions under his presidency rose from 12 to 24 percent.[34]

Basing growth on commodity exports, therefore, really delimits growth, for it does not encourage increased manufacturing which, in turn, creates jobs and capital. It perpetuates the developing country as only a primary commodity producer, with little or no diversification of production. As one SADCC consultant has noted: 'Internal development of the region would be subservient to the demands of the world market, so that regions or countries without the endowments necessary to cater for this market would stagnate relative to more-favoured regions.'[35]

Privatisation, trade liberalisation, and export-led growth, therefore, have not been generally successful in promoting development. SADCC remains skeptical of the prescription especially because the developed nations have not met their part of the bargain. The United Nations recovery programme, which pledged all of Africa to a combination of the three policies (along with currency devaluation for most) reports that international economic conditions, beyond the control of Africa, have not improved. The terms of trade for all of Africa fell by 32 percent in 1986 alone, giving the sharpest fall in export revenue since 1950. In 1986, the developed countries agreed that $23.7 billion was necessary to finance the basics of the programme and instead, Africa lost $19 billion in foreign exchange earnings. Export credits to encourage exports ceased altogether in 1987. In contrast, the UN found that African nations had an impressive record of implementing economic reforms as their share of responsibility to reverse historic economic decline. [36]

As the table on p.114 illustrates, SADCC has concluded that Malawi, Mozambique, Tanzania and Zambia are simply unable to meet their debt service obligations in the near to middle term and has called for frank discussions with its co-operating partners about the debt burden. It welcomes dialogue about the problems 'provided such consultation does not entail conditionality, avoids ideological economic prescription and takes into account the peculiar circumstances of each member state.' [37]

Yet the developed world has no answers. The debt-for-bonds 'solution' of Morgan Guaranty Trust and the US Treasury for Mexico is not under discussion for small countries with small gross debts. One of many reasons why the Mexico option is not for Southern Africa is the fact that Mexico has foreign reserves with which to buy the discounted bonds of $2 billion; Southern African governments would have to borrow more to purchase the bonds, continuing the now familiar perversion of going further into debt to pay debt.

As stated earlier, US Secretary of Treasury Baker refused to convert loans to grants even for the most destitute nations. His famous 'Baker Plan' to help the poorest debtor nations was never a serious programme

*Table 5.2: SADCC Members' Debt Service as a Percentage of Exports of Goods and Services*

| | 1980 | 1986 | 1988 |
|---|---|---|---|
| Angola[a] | .5 | 31.1 | 7.5 |
| Botswana | 1.7 | 4.3 | 4.0 |
| Lesotho | 21.8 | 4.2 | 5.2 |
| Malawi | 20.3[b] | 40.1 | 17.2 |
| Mozambique | | 275.0[c] | 7.8 |
| Nambia[d] | 1.3 (1982) | | 5.2 (1989) |
| Swaziland[e] | 2.8 | 7.1 | 5.2 |
| Tanzania | 8.4 | 15.3 | 17.1 |
| Zambia | 18.2 | 16.8 | 14.2 |
| Zimbabwe | 2.6 | 22.3 | 24.8 |

a) The IMF notes that if all Angolan debt service obligations had been met in 1988, the debt service ratio would have been 46 percent. Rescheduling and arrears reduced it to 7.5 percent. Over half the debt ($3.34 bn) is owed to the USSR. Source for Angola: The Economist Intelligence Unit, *Angola, 1987–88*, pp. 37–8; 1988–89, p. 41; 1990, No. 3, p. 20 and No. 4, p. 23.

b) Economist Intelligence Unit, *Zimbabwe, Malawi*, 1988, No. 4, p. 35.

c) Mozambique had this debt service rescheduled to 'unprecedented' terms of 20 years with low interest, after a 10-year grace period. The USSR cancelled all interest payments. Economist Intelligence Unit, *Mozambique*, 1988–89, p. 35.

d) Economist Intelligence Unit, *Namibia, Botswana, Lesotho, Swaziland*, 1990, No. 4., p. 28. The Namibia service ratio rose to 7.9 percent in 1990.

e) By March 1990, Swaziland had repaid its foreign debt. Data from Economic Intelligence Unit, *Botswana, Lesotho, Swaziland*, 1988–89, p. 90 and *Namibia, Botswana, Lesotho, Swaziland*, No. 1, 1990, p. 46; No. 2, p. 54.

*Source (unless otherwise indicated):* World Bank, *World Development Reports*, New York: Oxford University Press, 1985: p. 181; 1987: p. 238; 1988: p. 258; 1990: pp. 224–25.

according to Robin Broad, a former Treasury official who helped to write the Baker Plan:

> ... the Baker Plan was primarily rhetoric – a good speech, but without follow-through. It called for substantial new lending to the 15 most troubled debtors between 1986 and 1988...but no one even asked the private banks if they were willing to increase lending to the Third World. And the other creditor nations of Western Europe and Japan ... weren't even consulted.... in fact, the plan was pasted together quickly in breakfast meetings between the Treasury Secretary, James A. Baker, 3d and Paul A. Volcker, then chairman of the Federal Reserve Board. It was simply an attempt to steal the thunder from the newly inaugurated Peruvian President Alan Garcia who had the gall to unilaterally implement his own formula for cutting back Peru's unsustainable debt service without consulting the US. Mr. Baker's speech was calculated to regain the initiative.[38]

And the plan failed. Fatal flaws were that it left out IMF loans, depended on voluntary participation by the banks and never admitted the vast capital needs. In fact, net capital flows from official sources to the highly indebted (the 15 selected countries) actually fell, from $9 billion annually in 1983–85 to $5 billion annually in 1986–88. In early 1989, after food riots broke out in Venezuela in response to an IMF-imposed cut in subsidies – with the police shooting several hundred women and children robbing grocery stores – US officials began to talk of 'political fatigue.' The new US Secretary of Treasury, Nicolas Brady, finally proposed 'debt reduction,' but the Brady plan presented many of the same problems as the Baker plan: voluntary participation by the banks in debt forgiveness and new lending; underfinancing by addressing less than six percent of the outstanding debt. Even more consistent, US Treasury official Charles Dallara explicitly admitted that early beneficiaries would be countries 'of particular strategic and political interest to the US.'[39] To attract banks to participate, the proposal suggests that the IMF and World Bank underwrite interest guarantees for new loans as well as the debt for bond exchanges. In short, the taxpayers in developed countries will help cover some of the banks' losses. The small American farmer, run out of business by debt, might ask just why his taxes should bail out BankAmerica or Citibank for their insolvency.

The programme speaks not at all to Africa, for it involves only the debt financed by commercial banks. African debt is 87 percent held by governments and international agencies. What the plan could represent is a precedent for debt reduction, for it is the first time that the US agreed to that principle.

The developed world – both governments and international agencies – has no real solution to the debt problem because the primary objective has been to protect the short-term profitability of the banks. The Mexican debt-for-bonds deal was not agreed until the banks had assured their equity and could write off some of the bad loans. In announcing his plan, one of the major points Brady emphasised was, '...we must maintain the important role of the international financial institutions and preserve their financial integrity.' In 1982 Third World debt was three times stockholder equity in the big banks or enough to wipe them out three times over. By 1989, the debt-to-equity ratio was about 100 percent. Of the American banks, J.P. Morgan was safe, but BankAmerica, Manufacturers Hanover and Chemical Bank were not, which is why they demanded guarantees from the IMF and World Bank.[40]

Protecting equity and the viability of international banks seems necessary to keep the present international economic system functioning, but what developing countries like those in SADCC are arguing is that this system must be transformed. In contemporary capitalism, risk appears to be mainly socialised for the rich – as banks are rescued with public funds but small farmers go out of business and poor peasants starve. African governments have admitted errors – devastating ones which have caused death and environmental destruction; what is not yet forthcoming is admission by the rich that they are not only partners in this degradation, but that the international economic system must also be restructured, perhaps more severely than the African economies.

The burden for the errors has fallen on the most vulnerable: women, children, landless and unemployed. When drought compounds the errors, people already living on the margin die. In Southern Africa, they die within a few hundred kilometres of stored grain, because war has prevented delivery of the grain. Aid agencies send in more emergency food, but the banks and Western governments refuse to transform the conditions which cause the starvation:

> Passing on the burdens of recession to those who have the least political muscle to resist the blow, and the least economic fat to absorb it, is not only unjust and inhuman – it also undermines the health and growth of the poorest children and so copes with the crisis of today only by guaranteeing more crises tomorrow.[41]

In 1988 the IMF undertook its own study which came to many of the same conclusions as its critics. Even with the careful bureaucratic language, the implications are clear:

i)  ...policies aimed at restructuring production aggravated the plight of some vulnerable groups in the short run and did not help to alleviate the poverty of some groups in the longer run....

ii) Devaluation in countries with large urban poverty groups imposed immediate costs on the urban poor...and was ineffective in improving the short-run position of those poor farmers whose short-run supply elasticities were small....

iii) Cuts in health and education expenditures accruing to the poor adversely affected poverty groups, in both the short and the long run....In the long run, they may have hurt the productive capacity of the poor.

iv) Sharp cuts in capital expenditures may have hurt the poor both in the short and the long run.[42]

Yet the developed countries have not helped to stabilise prices for commodity exports, for they have fallen still further; trade credits have diminished; investment has slowed to a trickle as available capital flows to speculative deals in the US; private lending has almost stopped altogether and development aid from the US has decreased.

Furthermore, the West is indifferent to the pain of the poor countries. The Mozambican government has been praised again and again by international agencies for organising the delivery of food and medicine to areas most under siege by the MNR. Yet in late 1987 the international community only delivered half the food they had pledged and remained largely silent about the cause of the suffering – aggression by South Africa. In 1989 Western donors pledged a mere $251 million out of $383 million requested for emergency assistance; disappointed by the poor response, Mozambique requested only $136 million in 1990, a strict minimum necessary to keep alive 1.5 million totally dependent Mozambicans. The government chose to be realistic and did not hide the fact that it had deliberately left 400,000 underprivileged people out of the estimates because it did not have the logistical means to reach them. The pledges were such that the government could count on only one-third of the amount requested.[43] Instead, the IMF sets up new austerity plans for the Mozambican economy, and the World Bank writes studies praising the free market system. No mention is made that free markets do not work at all when goods cannot move. Historically, wars call for increased government spending, not less. This response deviates greatly from SADCC's request of 'no conditionality, no ideological prescriptions' and the need to recognise the 'peculiar circumstances of each economy.'

## US Policy Toward SADCC Agriculture

In addition to its various degrees of involvement in military destabilisation and in economic restructuring of the Southern African region, the US government has tried directly to alter SADCC's fundamental policies. At the 1987 annual conference of SADCC in Gaborone, the head of the US delegation, M. Peter MacPherson stated that South Africa would maintain its economic superiority over the region even after majority rule. Ignoring SADCC's repeated calls for sanctions against South Africa and ignoring the non-racial nature of all the SADCC governments, he also asserted, 'It is important that trade linkages between the SADCC states and the emerging black business community in South Africa be strengthened whenever possible.'[44] Another USAID official in Harare was more explicit, saying the members would not have to grow much maize after South Africa was free because it alone could take care of the demand. When questioned about the fact that a new government would try to feed malnourished South Africans first before exporting grain and would have to redistribute land which would affect production, she simply replied, 'Well, the US has hungry people and we still export much grain.' The *assumption* of USAID with regard to a free South Africa is that production relations will be maintained as they are inside South Africa and that the economy will outperform SADCC in almost every sector.[45]

'An Initiative for Economic Progress in Southern Africa,' presented to Congress by President Reagan as a 'comprehensive multi-year programme designed to promote economic reform and development in the black ruled states of southern Africa,' called for one-third of aid allocated to SADCC to be for policy reforms such as the ones discussed above – currency stabilisation, price adjustments, privatisation.[46] Many in Southern Africa agree with the need for policy reforms to achieve fiscal and monetary stability. However, SADCC has explicitly and repeatedly stated that it cannot make such policy; it is the purview of each sovereign state to determine its fiscal and monetary policy. Decentralised and operating by consensus, SADCC is a co-ordinating, not a supranational, organisation. If the US administration desires to pursue policy reforms, it is only appropriate on a bilateral basis with each government.[47] To demand policy reforms from SADCC is to misunderstand its structure, its power and its goals.

US government advice on agriculture has been quite consistent since the 1960s and the themes are continued by USAID in Southern Africa. This section will analyse four such themes in the context of Southern African production and SADCC priorities: 1) the creation of master farmers 2) specialisation of production 3) the promotion of cash crops and 4) the promotion of hybrid research. A new theme, still under debate within USAID, is the use of triangular exchanges to promote US grain exports while aiding food deficit countries.

What is different – and somewhat alarming – is that SADCC's documents on food and agriculture began to echo parts of USAID policy in 1987, repeating exact words and expressions used by USAID. USAID has been the major financier of the SADCC administrative unit for agriculture and food security in Zimbabwe over the last several years and has provided a multi-million dollar grant to the Department of Agriculture at the University of Zimbabwe. Pamela Hussey, Director of USAID in Harare, pointed out that the university and the SADCC unit 'have worked in tandem to help develop the research and policy agenda for food security and to formulate the food, agriculture and natural resources strategy for the SADCC region.'[48] She failed to mention that USAID recommendations and training are integral to the university programme. One of the Americans in the USAID programme boasted that 'proposals start here and SADCC reacts.' Further, regular seminars are held for USAID experts to share their expertise with Zimbabwean officials working in the Ministry of Agriculture. By 1987, US influence was shining through the pages of SADCC planning documents, especially in areas 2–4 cited above.[49]

## Master Farmers

US policy defines efficiency in agricultural production as yield per acre, not per cost input, perhaps because US agriculture is the most efficient in the world only in terms of yield per acre. The means by which to increase yields has historically been consolidation of land under large holdings to make high levels of mechanisation cost effective and to develop high-yielding hybrids, sustained with fertilisers and pesticides. This formula increases grain availability but not accessibility as small farmers are pushed off the land, often to become unemployed in urban areas.[50] They can no longer grow food and often cannot afford to buy it. More food is produced, but the policy can create a whole sub-class of marginal people – those with skills to grow food yet with no land or jobs. By 1978 in the US, five percent of the landowners owned 75 percent of the 1.3 billion acres (over 500 million hectares) of land in private hands. From the passage of the 1985 farm bill to 1988, a farm went out of business every four to seven minutes of every hour. They were mostly family farmers.[51]

To increase food production in Africa, USAID has first encouraged making new inputs and information available to the master or emergent farmers, ones who can benefit most readily from the inputs. Rarely, if ever, does USAID mention land reform to increase production – redistribution of land to the poor who will grow food first, not exotic cash crops. A prominent USAID consultant to SADCC, Carl Eicher, conveniently defined it out of the agenda: 'If food security researchers define their research agenda as broadly as agricultural development, they will become bogged down with research on credit, land tenure, processing, etc. In sum, the food security research agenda should be restricted to a limited number of key policy questions and focus on both...food availability and access to food.'[52] Yet land reform increases production more immediately than hybrids. It stabilises the labour force (which puts more food on tables), and innovative techniques can be adopted, although not large scale ones.

SADCC is on record that land reform is important to increased production in Zimbabwe and Swaziland.[53] Other documents speak of the danger of large numbers of unemployed in such countries as Zimbabwe or even Botswana; the USAID solution is greater birth control, not land redistribution to maintain people on their land. In fact, master farmers are only more productive if they have tracts sufficient for high-tech production so that creation of master farmers, as defined by USAID, is antithetical to land redistribution.[54] However, more than one programme has shown that peasants can grow food crops quite efficiently on only one acre and increase production to satisfy food needs. Intensive labour inputs make up for what is lost in size of plots.

Southern Africa does not have foreign exchange to purchase or to distribute highly technical inputs to farming. What they do have is adequate and skilled labour. Peasants have shown they are receptive to innovations that can be sustained after the field representative leaves or the outside funds dry up. One key to accepting innovation is stability of land tenure. USAID points this out but calls for private ownership of communally held land. The conventional wisdom still promoted is that people do not invest for the future unless they feel secure about tenure of the land and that the 'problem of the commons' (overgrazing and no protection from stock destroying maize or other crops) deters rational animal husbandry.

Rights to land utilisation are not really insecure in African traditions, for they often extend through generations. One survey designed a crude indicator of security of tenure by asking Zimbabwean peasants on communal land if they were willing to plant trees or build a fence on the land they were using; they replied positively. The conclusion from this and other studies for Zimbabwe was that 'there does not seem to be any overpowering argument that part of the communal system that governs people's access to arable land has to be changed as the prerequisite for any improvement.'[55] Other programmes promoting private, individual tenure of African land, such as in Kenya, have not promoted production or removed poverty: those who have the land use the title to borrow for every purpose other than agricultural production and those on the land have no title or credit.

The debate extends to the South African discussion on the future of the bantustans. Several now argue against the idea that individual tenure in the reserves would increase their agricultural production. D.R. Tapson argues against the 'freehold option' as a 'blind alley' because the permanent alienation of land into private ownership would lead to land being acquired and controlled by the wealthy and powerful elite. More important to increased productivity than individual tenure are price incentives and government expenditure on inputs like irrigation or roads.[56]

The historical experience of the foremost promoter of individual tenure is also informative. During American colonial times in New England, the farmers lived clustered in villages, with their fields scattered over hills, following the terrain, rivers, and forests. As Native American land was stolen, and therefore acquired by the government as 'public domain,' the government decided to survey the land in squares of 640-acre sections, down to the famous 160-acre quarter sections, ignoring any natural terrain, the flow of rivers or soil type. This policy was very conducive to land speculation, allowing land to be sold as squares on a piece of paper. With tantalising profits, the rich rushed to purchase and resell large, nicely geometric, blocks of surveyed land.[57] Private tenure of the public domain endowed the gentry and turned US land policy into one of selling to the highest bidder:

> To discard the feudal land system, despite its European universality, was easy; to devise a fresh alternative taxed the inventive powers of Congress. Strong arguments can be made, from the perspective of two hundred years, that Congress failed. It faced enormous pressure for outright sale to the

highest bidder. In the process it lost opportunities to devise a national commons, invent long-term leasing, and offer tracts more adapted to terrain, climate and soil conditions.[58]

What is needed is not privatisation of land (often given to cabinet ministers and friends) but rights to land utilisation for the women who cultivate the land. The instability of tenure stems from the inferior legal status in most African societies of women who do not have access in their own right or the right to retain production off the land; both are given to the husband, brother-in-law or son. If a widowed or divorced female knew she could retain rights to land or if a married woman knew she had control over an equal share of family production, food production could take off in Southern Africa. In Zimbabwe the succession law now gives women the right to inheritance, but the ability of women to exercise that right in the face of traditional family customs is limited. Their own rights to land use and to the fruits of their production are only the first steps for women, however; access to innovative techniques, credit, and inputs have to follow.

SADCC does discuss redistribution and security of land tenure, but most member states do not yet recognise the role of women in food production in the concrete way of female rights to land use. USAID will continue promoting its land consolidation programme, under the private ownership of upper class males. Production may increase but at a high cost of inputs and with a large increase in the number of unemployed.

## Specialisation of Production

Comparative advantage has from the outset been the ideological foundation of US policy toward the Third World. USAID policy, therefore, counsels each to produce what it is most efficient in producing. For example, Botswana should minimise maize production as the 'maize belt' across Zambia, Zimbabwe and Malawi will take care of Botswana's needs.[59] This policy could provide Botswana with more maize for less cost in good years but when drought hits, would Botswana still acquire a percentage of scarce Zimbabwean grain, forcing Zimbabwe into importing maize? Or would Botswana then have to purchase grain on the open market at the seller's price? In fact, Botswana did not have long to wait to be proven correct in its hesitancy to depend totally on neighbours. In late 1987, Zimbabwe stopped all maize exports because the drought that year had reduced grain reserves, and Zimbabwean domestic consumption took priority.

SADCC has accepted the logic of comparative advantage only for certain items, and only after much study. As discussed under industry, to take a policy of comparative advantage to its logical conclusion would mean that Zimbabwe would produce most items, with the others remaining raw material providers to Zimbabwe, or in the case of a free

South Africa, all would be providing inputs to South Africa. After much careful consideration, SADCC has opted to have each member produce grain as a strategic need reserving 'comparative advantage' to more marginal items, such as sugar or pineapples.

## Cash Crops

USAID forcefully promotes the growing of cash crops as a major foreign exchange earner. Another reason, not often expressed, is that this complements well with the master farmer goal; according to an American advisor: 'Growing sorghum and maize is never going to make anyone rich.'[60] Relatively better off peasants can take advantage of the incentives for cash crops and 'become rich.' Until 1987 SADCC focused only on food crops. In the annual sector report for agriculture presented to the 1987 Gaborone conference, there was the first mention of cash crops as a SADCC priority. Perhaps in this area, SADCC has followed USAID's admonishments. Diverting the focus, cash crops are receiving more attention. Such advice has been bad policy in the past as countries such as Tanzania paid more attention to tobacco and cotton than maize and then had to import grain at high prices. African history, from Kenya and the Sudan to Liberia, is replete with policy failures of growing cash crops in order to buy 'cheaper' grain from the developed countries.

By focusing on cash crops, SADCC could in theory plan which ones to grow where, but it is doubtful that SADCC has the infrastructure or funds to concern itself with cash crops until its proposed projects for food crops are implemented. Optimally, of course, the countries should plan for both and strive for diversification. In that way, they could provide food from both local production and from purchases overseas paid for by sales of cash crops. The problem with this approach in the SADCC arena is one of priority; neither weather nor external markets have been favourable to regional food security. Overcoming the vagaries of Southern African weather (through early warning systems, development of stable producers, etc.) seems more feasible for SADCC than trying to outguess capricious international demand for flowers, tea, coffee, or artichokes. National policies will co-ordinate both cash and food crop production. However, that cash crops appear on the regional agenda when reducing constraints on food production is so overwhelming, yet vital, seems to be the result of external policy interventions.

## Hybrid Research

The promotion of hybrids in Africa by USAID seems to be done with no regard to the equity problems which emerged out of the green revolution in Asia. Hybrids greatly increased yields in Asian rice and wheat but also greatly consolidated land under larger landowners who could afford the necessary fertilisers and pesticides and buy access to irrigation. In short, the hybrids helped the policy of creating master farmers. Now countries like India produce record amounts of grain and have larger absolute numbers of hungry people.

Recent SADCC documents have referred more favourably to hybrid development, such as maize SR–52. Individual SADCC officials speak highly of developing hybrids but do not see them as a panacea. As stated earlier, there is much interest in developing stable producers which will increase yields, yet not be as vulnerable to variations in inputs as the hybrids. If USAID influence is delimited, the green revolution as defined by SADCC, will be a combination of the development of both hybrids and stable producers in traditional peasant food crops such as sorghum and millet. SADCC accepts assistance in developing hybrids but will also spend time and funds on protecting indigenous seeds and new strains of stable producers.

## Triangular Transactions

Since 1984 SADCC has promoted a promising new policy – triangular exchange – to benefit food-deficit and food-surplus countries alike, but the US has not supported it. The intention is that a country with a surplus in some grains, but a deficit in others purchases the shortfall in grain from the US and pays for it by shipping its own surplus grains to a food-deficit country; that latter transaction becomes food aid from the US. For example, Zimbabwe needs to import wheat so purchases it from the US, and pays for it by shipping its own surplus maize to neighbouring Mozambique. That exchange becomes US food aid to Mozambique. Such triangular exchanges have occurred in Southern Africa mainly with Malawi and Zimbabwe as the middle country and Mozambique, Zambia and Botswana as the food aid recipients.

SADCC strongly supports such triangular deals, for it rewards those countries able to produce surplus grains by assisting them to sell it. In addition, the deficit countries receive grains from neighbours more quickly and at lower transport and handling costs. SADCC also expected donor countries to be delighted with the trade, for it is the result of 'export-led growth' of the grain surplus countries. However, very small amounts of grain have actually been involved in triangular transactions. The largest participant is the World Food Programme which started the policy in Southern Africa, using donations to purchase needed grain from surplus neighbours. In 1986–87, however, only 141,000 tonnes of over two million tonnes available for export by Zimbabwe were involved in a triangular deal; Malawi fared better with 28,000 of 104,000 tonnes available taken in triangular transactions.[61]

Initially the US Department of Agriculture (USDA) resisted the triangular deals arguing that Mozambicans should receive surplus American maize. When reminded that Mozambicans prefer white Zimbabwean maize to yellow maize, which they usually feed to animals, the USDA responded that aid recipients should not complain, but must accept what is sent. It argued that over time Mozambicans would begin to change their tastes for yellow maize, thereby creating a market for US maize.[62]

After nine months of internal US government discussions, it was finally agreed to ship 9600 tonnes of wheat to Zimbabwe for 7000 tonnes of Zimbabwean white maize to Mozambique. An additional 3000 tonnes would be shipped by Malawi. (The original triangular request from USAID in Maputo was for 40,000 tonnes from Zimbabwe.) The papers were signed on 13 June 1986 and the Zimbabwean Grain Marketing Board began deliveries six days later. Zimbabwe also contributed about $175,000 in local currency to help cover delivery costs. Such a rapid response by Zimbabwe and the willingness to help with local costs revealed the enthusiasm of the government for the programme and its willingness to assist a SADCC neighbour.

The US government, however, tried to keep triangular deals to a minimum and began shipping maize (22,000 tonnes) from Kenya to Mozambique, instead of from Zimbabwe. One reason given was that transport costs would be lower to ship from Mombasa to Maputo – questionable even if the grain stayed near Maputo. For almost any other destination in the rural areas, Zimbabwe and Malawi would have much greater proximity. Consultants for the World Food Programme analysed that a strict cost-benefit analysis of export prices gave only a partial picture: some inland districts in war-ravaged Mozambique could be reached only from Zimbabwe; reconsigning large shiploads to small lorries for inland districts raised costs; use of the Beira Corridor in time of emergency had 'regional political significance'.[63] The consultants to USAID noted that the inclusion of Kenya in the triangular exchange occurred at the time when the President of Kenya was about to visit the US and when US–Zimbabwe relations were strained. In addition, 'quite a bit of baldly political pressure was exerted from time to time....cost and timeliness alone were certainly not the only criteria involved in the eventual selection of Kenya over Zimbabwe.'[64]

US agricultural policy promotes specialisation in production and export-led growth. However, when a country does succeed in producing surplus in one or two grains and is needing to export it to reduce storage costs, US policy hesitates to facilitate such trade through triangular deals. Further, an ally closer to the US, but further in distance from the recipient country, becomes the one able to ship its surplus grain through US assistance. The consultancy report states that triangular transactions do not adversely affect international market prices; the World Food Programme goes further: 'These purchases have been a small but highly positive counter-weight to the competition of subsidised exports and import restrictions of developed countries faced by developing country exporters. Shipments of grain between land-locked countries in Southern Africa and purchases of pulses [legumes] might be singled out as being particularly cost effective.'[65] Further, the exchange could create a market for US wheat in Zimbabwe (or Malawi and Kenya) while the market for yellow maize would only be temporary, until Mozambicans could obtain white maize again. Both the consultants recommended more triangular trade. However, it appears that the US continues to prefer bilateral aid assistance, one which uses surplus American grain; in 1988 there were no US–Zimbabwe–Mozambique triangular transactions at all[66] even though Zimbabwe had surplus maize and Mozambique was still in dire need; instead, surplus American yellow maize was shipped to Mozambique.

Pursuit of national self-interest by the US continued to subvert regional exchange in 1989. The Commercial Grain Producers of Zimbabwe asked the US to stop dumping maize into Malawi because it would adversely affect maize farmers in the region. In a meeting, USAID assured the organisation that it was only contemplating shipping maize for relief in Mozambique. Shortly thereafter, a lorry on its way to Malawi, involved in an accident, spilled American yellow maize all over the road; another 17000 tonnes were still off the coast of South Africa to be shipped in. Not only ignoring SADCC rail lines, the US was also dismissing any idea of purchasing Zimbabwe maize from a stock pile of 1.54 million tonnes, which it needed to sell to reduce the costs of storage.[67]

Triangular transactions are one way by which SADCC would like to build regional grain reserves, but the storage project has been deferred and debated for years; it also exposes other donor attempts to control SADCC policy, and manipulate its fragility. An EEC-funded study in 1982 to establish a SADCC food reserve policy recommended the construction of silos at a cost of $322 million, with annual maintenance and storage costs at $35 million. Too grandiose, SADCC and the EEC both rejected it. The General Manager of the Grain Marketing Board of Zimbabwe designated another reason, in that 85 percent of the materials needed for the construction programme was available in Zimbabwe and would not have to be purchased in the donor country.[68]

In proceeding with another study, the EEC began having second thoughts. In a project study that was principally intended to lay out the options for a food reserve, the document instead proposed fundamental policy changes. The study concluded that storage was adequate and the lack of foreign exchange was the only deterrent to regional food exchanges. Because of this proposal, the European consultants then raised questions about national production policies; ignoring SADCC's very essence, they tried to use a regional project to demand changes in national pricing policies.

SADCC responded by noting that such recommendations addressed neither food security nor food storage priorities. SADCC expressed concern for storage in vulnerable Lesotho, blockaded by South Africa to the extent that food became scarce. It pointed out that 'adequate' storage facilities were open to different interpretations; new storage was proposed in 1987 by the Non-Aligned Movement and targeted for the Frontline States in a direct response to South African threats of sanctions and the actual embargo against Lesotho.

The SADCC Agricultural Ministers endorsed the proposal to store 365,000 tonnes, costing $200 million for three years in July 1986, without accepting the pricing conditionality. They waited in vain for meetings with the EEC to discuss how to raise funds. Britain argued that the fund was unfeasible. Meanwhile, the donors continued with their bilateral food aid, with Canada joining the US in rejecting triangular transactions; in contrast, the EEC was quite receptive to triangular exchanges, with 30–40 percent of its food aid disbursed in that way.

By mid-1988, donor requirements had become more stringent. For example, they stipulated that 1) prices for grain purchases in the region had to reflect world market prices; 2) consultation with donors was required for the allocation of food aid to deficit areas in the region; 3) a 'visible contribution to the cost' of the project had to come from SADCC. SADCC officials were furious. They argued that world 'market' prices did not reflect a free market at all, but rather highly subsidised grains for sale under oligopoly conditions. As noted earlier, all the major food surplus countries heavily subsidise their grain production and then argue that the price reflects the actual cost. Five grain corporations control the international grain trade and very much affect the 'market' price of grain. Most important of all, the world market price for maize is for yellow maize no.2, while Southern Africa is exchanging white maize. Why should one type of maize, traded regionally, have to match the price of a totally different strain set on the Chicago Board of Trade?

Agreeing with the third condition about SADCC responsibility, the head of FSTAU, John Dhilwayo, stated,'We should demonstrate our commitment to the project, but we cannot allow foreigners to administer our food aid programme [condition two]. Major food donors are creating employment for their own people besides using food aid as a weapon to influence policies of governments.' SADCC officials also warned against changing tastes to new food types which are not economically sustainable in the region, e.g. wheat.

At the annual meeting in Luanda in 1989, the project was 'ready for implementation;' SADCC seemed to have won the round of negotiations. A Food Reserve Board, constituted only of one representative each from SADCC members, would direct and monitor the project. The reserve would rely on food sources from surplus producers in the region, only going outside if the supply falls short. The target was to raise resources to acquire up to 356,000 tonnes of white maize (not yellow maize or

wheat). Financed initially from donors, SADCC members would pro-
gressively take over the funding. However, pledges for the requisite $220
million were modest (although Argentina sent 1500 tonnes of wheat). As
one report concluded, 'Some donors are believed not to be keen on the
project as they feel that the creation of the fund would mean that some
developed countries would lose markets if SADCC governments step up
the process of buying in the region.'[69]

This project reveals efforts by donors to write policy demands in what
was supposed to be a technical feasibility study. The EEC offered only a
list of four potential consultants for the 1982 and the 1984 studies, an
insufficient choice for SADCC; from outside the region, the selected
consultants demonstrated their lack of knowledge of regional problems
and concerns. As the project delayed, the donors did not try to interface
their bilateral food aid to the region with the regional plans; the EEC
mainly communicated with the Harare office, letting others pursue
national programmes uninformed about the continuing discussions.
When SADCC refused the policy interventions, the donors made them a
prerequisite for financing and added the demand that donors help decide
allocation. Further, some donors still refuse to participate in the major
mechanism proposed, triangular transactions, to finance the reserve.

SADCC was wrong in first accepting the short list of consultants which
included no one from the region. This mistake was probably made
because the SADCC side of the negotiations were handled mainly by
Zimbabwe, without the expected consultation with other members. The
continuing bilateral talks could also have been questioned by SADCC,
but although this project represents one which will benefit the whole
region, SADCC national interests are competing in the short term. The
decision-making process within SADCC was slow and unclear about
who had the authority at what stage of the deliberations; the overworked
Zimbabwe staff in the FSTAU office could not direct enough attention to
the various inflections coming from the donors. Finally, the reserve
represents a major financing allocation by the members for maintenance
of the reserve, which requires long term commitment.

The question remains whether aid will address the food production
and distribution problems in SADCC and whether SADCC can select its
own programme. In summary, USAID is promoting the technology in
which the US excels: high tech farming with hybrids, large machinery,
chemical pesticides, etc. Such technical advice creates business for
American firms. USAID is also promoting the class relations inside
SADCC which it prefers. To do so, USAID analyses the advantages of the
master farmers, motivated by high profits, in increasing production. It
does not ignore unemployment problems; it simply discusses those quite
separately from its agricultural analyses. A class of master farmers will
demand privatisation of land, use high tech inputs and prove that

capitalist farming relations increase production. Revealing a contradiction of capitalism, when countries do follow USAID advice, such as production for export in commodities favoured by comparative advantage (e.g. Zimbabwe export of maize), the US competes with such trade rather than facilitating it. Finally, donor policy demands to restructure prices and fundamentally alter the agricultural economy show up in technical feasibility studies.

USAID is also clear about what country will continue to dominate relations in Southern Africa. The programmes assume that a free South Africa will remain the breadbasket (based on the present large commercial farms) and works to guarantee that by calling for SADCC planning to be based on comparative advantage. When South Africa becomes free, it could step into the plans with the greatest comparative advantage in almost all food production; this scenario is exactly what SADCC is organising to recast.

# Notes

1  Interviews with Kighoma Malima, Minister of State in the President's Office, Tanzania, January 25, 1986 and A.Sangu, Ministry of Economic Planning, Tanzania, November 6, 1985. Marjorie Mbilinyi. 'Agribusiness and Structural Adjustment in Tanzania: Struggles over the Labour of Women Peasants and Farm Workers,' draft paper, 1988, p. 17. See Marjorie Mbilinyi. 'Structural Adjustment, Agribusiness and Rural Women in Tanzania,' *The Food Question–Profits versus People?* Henry Bernstein *et al.* New York: Monthly Review Press, 1990, p. 111–24.
2  *Wall Street Journal*, 13 April 1988.
3  Henry Mapolu, 'The State and Peasantry,' *The State and Working People in Tanzania*. Issa Shivji, ed. Dakar: Codesria, 1985, pp. 121–122 and 131.
4  See, for example, Kevin Danaher, Phillip Berryman, and Medea Benjamin. *Help or Hindrance? United States Economic Aid in Central America*. San Francisco: Institute for Food and Development, 1987. Susan George. *Ill Fares the Land*. Washington, DC: Institute for Policy Studies, 1984. Teresa Hayter and Catharine Watson. *AID: Rhetoric and Reality*. London: Pluto Press, 1985. Denny Kalyalya, *et al*, (eds.) *Aid and Development in Southern Africa*. Trenton, NJ: Africa World Press, 1988. Francis Moore Lappé, Joseph Collins and David Kinley. *Aid As Obstacle*. San Francisco: Institute for Food and Development, 1980. J.R. Parkinson (ed.) *Poverty and Aid*. London: Basil Blackwell, 1983. Roger C. Riddell. *Foreign Aid Reconsidered*. Baltimore: Johns Hopkins Press, 1987.
5  *Herald* (Harare), 5 May 1987.
6  Teresa Hayter and Catharine Watson. *op. cit.*, p. 2.
7  In May 1987 when President Chissano visited England, the Thatcher government wrote off all loan repayments for Mozambique. Canada has also dismissed loan repayments.

8   *New York Times,* 9 September 1987 and 12 April 1988. Only in 1989 did the US begin to consider writing off government loans for very few.
9   *New York Times,* 9 July 1987.
10  *New York Times,* 30 September 1987.
11  Felix Rohatyn. 'On the Brink,' *The New York Review,* 11 June l987, p. 3.
12  Jerry W. Sanders and Sherle L. Schwenninger. 'A New Grand Strategy: U.S. Policy toward the Third World,' *Post–Reagan America,* Archibald L. Gillies *et al.,* eds. New York: World Policy Institute, 1987, pp. 102–3, 106.
13  SADCC. *Investment in Production.* Gaborone: SADCC, 1987, p. 17.
14  UNICEF. *State of the World's Children 1986.* Oxford: Oxford University Press, 1985, p. 71. Quotes of K. A. Malima from Colleen Lowe Morna. 'Tanzania's New P-SAP Strategy: Will it Work?' *African Business* (August 1990): 12.
15  Carol B. Thompson. *op. cit.* pp. 62–3, 82–3, 119–20.
16  Neva Seidman Makgetla. 'Theoretical and Practical Implications of IMF Conditionality in Zambia,' J*ournal of Modern African Studies* 24:2 (1986).
17  John Mukela. 'Food and Flames,' *The New Internationalist,* no. 189 (November 1988): 21.
18  *South,* July 1987, pp. 32–4.
19  *Ibid.*
20  Isebill V. Gruhn, 'The Recolonization of Africa: International Organizations on the March,' *Africa Today,* 4th quarter (1983): 41. International Coalition for Development Action. *SADCC-EC Briefing,* no. 1, May–June 1988.
21  Report of the Secretary-General. 'Critical Economic Situation in Africa: United Nation's Programme of Action for African Economic Recovery and Development 1986–1990,' United Nations General Assembly, 42nd Session, A/42/560, 1 October 1987, p. 15. When one compares total indebtedness with compassionate emergency aid, the picture is not brighter. The worldwide private generosity to the African famine emergency amounted to less than $300 million. The amount pledged in extra aid by governments is about $3 billion, and the amount Africa paid to the industrialized world in debt and interest repayments during 1985 alone was over $7 billion. UNICEF, *op. cit.* pp. 77 and 79.
22  In April 1988 meetings, the IMF agreed to provide more funds to the Compensatory Financing Facility; however, the funds would only be available to countries following rigorous adjustment policies, even if the conditions causing the debt were originally beyond control (e.g. drought) of the debtor. *New York Times,* 12 April 1988.
23  Gruhn, *op. cit.,* p. 41.
24  *New York Times,* 23 January 1990.
25  *New York Times,* 11 November 1986 and 10 December 1986.
26  *New York Times,* 5 March 1989.
27  *The Times* (London), 8 July 1986.
28  Australian High Commissioner to Zimbabwe, Alan Edwards, *Herald* (Harare), 14 September 1987.
29  A. Tibaijuka. 'Planning for Agriculture,' *Macro-Economic Survey,* Report on the Lilongwe Workshop, SADCC, 25–27August 1987, p. 35.
30  *Daily News* (Dar es Salaam), 10 December 1987.
31  Colin Stoneman. 'The Impending Failure of Structural Adjustment: Lessons from Zimbabwe,' paper presented at Canadian Association of African

Studies, Dalhousie University, 11 May 1990, pp. 4–5.

32 Kevin Danaher *et. al., op. cit.*, p. 55.

33 Bernard Chidzero, Finance Minister, Zimbabwe, speech at SADCC conference, reported in *Financial Gazette* (Harare), 12 February 1988.

34 Noam Chomsky, 'The Tasks Ahead', *Zeta (*May 1989): 3.

35 Colin Stoneman. 'An Indicative Regional Plan for the Industrial Development of SADCC, 1987–2000,' Preliminary Report, January 1987, p. 6.

36 Report to Secretary General, *op. cit.*, pp. 11–13. *Africa News* 30:5 (5 September 1988): 2–3.

37 SADCC. *Annual Progress Report,* July 1985–August 1986, p. 8.

38 Robin Broad, 'How About a Real Solution to Third World Debt?' *New York Times,* 28 September 1987.

39 The plan ostensibly sought voluntary reduction of 20 percent of the foreign debt of 39 nations within three years. J.P. Morgan rejected both the voluntary debt write-off and new lending provisions by increasing its reserve level to 100 percent of its exposure. Fully covered, it could then do what it wanted without pressure to grant new loans and found ways to write-off old ones at steep discounts. *Financial Gazette* (Harare), 12 May 1989. *Guardian* (New York), 17 May 1989. *New York Times,* 24 September 1989.

40 'Loan Sharks'. *Nation,* 15 May 1989.

41 UNICEF, *op. cit.*, p. 75.

42 Peter S. Heller, *et al.* 'The Implications of Fund-Supported Adjustment Programs for Poverty–Experiences in Selected Countries.' Occasional Paper 58. Washington, DC: International Monetary Fund, 1988, p. 33.

43 ' "Aid Fatigue" threatens Budget Support,' *African Business* (September 1990): 40. *The Manchester Guardian Weekly* (January 13, 1991).

44 M. Peter MacPherson, speech at SADCC annual meeting, Gaborone, Botswana, February 5–6, 1987.

45 Interview with Janet Schulman, Project Development Officer for Agriculture in the SADCC region, USAID, Harare, 12 March 1986 and with Roy Stacey, US Department of State, 16 March 1987. See also USAID's overall plan in Carl Eicher and Mandivamba Rukuni, (eds.) *Food Security for Southern Africa.* Harare: University of Zimbabwe/Michigan State University, February 1987. A University of Stellenbosch survey in 1977 stated over 2.9 million children were malnourished in South Africa, but that one-third of the maize crop had been exported for foreign exchange earnings. Robert Henderson. 'The Food Weapon in Southern Africa,' paper presented at the Congress on Development and Destabilization in Southern Africa, National University of Lesotho, 1983, p. 9.

More recent estimates state that between 30–50 percent of all children in South Africa die before the age of five, not due to war, but to malnutrition-related diseases. About three million Blacks (includes Africans, 'Coloureds' and Asians) under the age of 15 suffer from malnutrition. Ernest Harsch. *Apartheid's Great Land Theft: The Struggle for the Right to Farm in South Africa.* New York: Pathfinder Press, 1986, p. 28. See also Francis Wilson and Mamphela Ramphele. *Uprooting Poverty: The South African Challenge.* New York: W.W. Norton and Company, 1989. Francis Wilson and Hoosen M. Coovadia. 'Children in South Africa,' *Children on the Front Line.* New York: UNICEF, 1989.

46 United States Department of State. 'An Initiative for Economic Progress in

Southern Africa', 29 January 1987.

47 The policy reforms will remain national decisions, but SADCC very much advocates that the international agencies take into consideration the regional context when calling for currency devaluations or other national reforms which do impact the neighbours.

48 *Financial Gazette*, 13 November 1987, p. 6.

49 See especially, SADCC, *Food, Agriculture and Natural Resources*, sector report for annual conference, Gaborone, Botswana, 5–6 February 1987, pp. 5–23.

50 The myth of the yeoman farmer is only partially a myth, for the individual, tenacious and resourceful yeoman did open up new lands and improve them. However, even the legendary Homestead Act of 1862, providing anyone with 160 acres simply for farming them for five years, allocated paltry amounts of land, relative to what was made available to the railroads and speculators. Further, even in the better land areas, not all could maintain the farms. From 1880–85, only 50 percent could retain title in lush Michigan, 63 percent in Wisconsin and only 46 percent in Missouri. John Opie. *The Law of the Land: Two Hundred Years of American Farmland Policy.* Omaha: University of Nebraska Press, 1988, p. 65–6.

51 David L. Ostendorf, 'Who Will Control Rural America?' *Christianity and Crisis* (2 May 1988): 156, 158. A report commissioned by the US Secretary of Agriculture in 1981 concluded that US policy – mainly taxes, farm commodity and credit systems, and the marketing system – are all 'biased toward the larger farmers and wealthy investors.' United States Department of Agriculture, *A Time to Choose: Summary Report on the Structure of Agriculture.* Washington, D.C.: USDA, January 1981, pp. 142–43. The decline in US farm income was so drastic that by 1982, the US Department of Agriculture simply stopped publishing its routine estimates of net farm income. Congressional Quarterly, *Farm Policy: The Politics of Soil, Surpluses, and Subsidies.* Washington, DC: Congressional Quarterly, 1984, p. 17.

52 Mandivamba Rukuni and Carl Eicher. 'The Food Security Equation in Southern Africa,' *MSU International Development Papers,* reprint no. 5, 1987, p. 14.

53 SADCC. *Macro-Economic Survey 1986.* Gaborone: SADCC, September 1985, p. 139.

54 This policy of commercialisation of large farming tracts also happens to coincide with current South African policy. White farms range in size from 200 to 1800 hectares, with some as large as 15,000 hectares. The Ministry of Agriculture found those under 200 hectares to be 'sub-economic.' Ernest Harsch, *op. cit.*, p. 14. Consolidation of land is also recent: between 1960 and 1975, the average farm size increased from 867 ha. to 1102 ha. (27 percent). Even more recently, in the maize farming region of western Transvaal, the average size of farms increased from 664 ha. in 1968 to 1155 ha. in 1981 (by 75 percent). Although estimates vary, few would argue that there are important economies of scale over 300 ha. And research in South Africa reports more arable land is left fallow each year on the white commercial farms. Francis Wilson and Mamphela Ramphele, *op. cit.*, pp. 40–1, 310–11. Land distribution will be a priority in a free South Africa. A combination of lease-held land, smaller private farms, large private and

government estates, as well as co-operatives, will probably emerge and co-exist.

55 FAO, 'Policy Options Paper for Agrarian Reform in Zimbabwe,' 1985, p. 34.

56 D.R. Tapson. 'Freehold Title: Blind Alley in the Homelands,' quoted in Francis Wilson and Mamphela Ramphele, *op. cit.*, pp. 311–12.

57 George Washington himself searched for advantageous deals, even at times of national crisis; unemotional as a war hero and president, he became visibly agitated over a good land deal and would ride out to see some new offering. By 1796, he held 32,373 acres (13,000 hectares) in the Ohio country, drawing criticism from Thomas Jefferson. John Opie, *op. cit.*, p. 6

58 *Ibid.*, p. 7.

59 This 'maize belt' reference is one frequently used by USAID to push comparative advantage, and the term showed up in SADCC, 1987, *op. cit.*, p. 8.

60 Richard Bernstein, University of Zimbabwe Food Security Programme, 29 June 1988.

61 RONCO Consulting Corporation. 'Study of Trilateral Food Aid Transactions,' report to USAID, 28 April 1987, Table I.

62 Several discussions with USAID officials in Harare, October 1985, over this USDA interpretation that they were opposing. Interview with Janet Schulman, *op.cit.*

63 Relief and Development Institute (London). 'A Study of Triangular Transactions and Local Purchases in Food Aid,' *World Food Programme Occasional Papers,* no. 11, July 1987, p. 20.

64 RONCO Consulting Corporation, *op. cit.*, p. 42.

65 Relief and Development Institute, *op. cit.*, p. 45.

66 Interview with Joshua Mushali, Agriculture sector, USAID office, Harare, Zimbabwe, 22 July 1988.

67 *Financial Gazette* (Harare), 20 October 1989.

68 *Herald* (Harare), 26 April 1985.

69 *Financial Gazette* (Harare), 27 January 1989.

# 6.

# Lessons for
# Regional Co-operation

Post-apartheid debates are attracting international attention, for the stakes are high for this potentially wealthy region. National, perhaps collective, fortunes are to be made. Most of the discussions focus on the structural constraints against economic transformation, such as the colonial legacy and the dominant international economic relations, reinforced by IMF and World Bank requirements.[1] However, few analyses have addressed the policies already in place as a deterrent or impediment to plans for transformation. Even fewer have acknowledged that the Southern African nations have their own plans for their region.

By 1990 it was clear that the apartheid regime and its international allies were moving toward accepting the need for negotiations for majority rule, while trying to control and manipulate the transitional process. What is suggested by this specific analysis of agriculture is that policies throughout the 1980s of such agencies as USAID were laying the groundwork for the maintenance of South African regional dominance. More than just pursuing policies which promote American markets, US feasibility studies and recommendations for SADCC agriculture assumed continued post-apartheid South African economic dominion over the region subordinating SADCC to the 'grain basket' of South Africa. In short, what could not be achieved by the grandiose plan for a 'constellation of states', may more modestly be achieved in agriculture by SADCC following the logic and advice of USAID and its international economic partners.

The unrelenting advocacy of comparative advantage in grain production implied that food deficit countries would rely on imports from South Africa (and the US). As discussed earlier, the US has counselled SADCC members to grow cash crops in areas where grain is less feasible in order to earn foreign exchange to buy grain on the international market. Such a policy totally ignores SADCC emphasis on national production of grains for food security. SADCC policy promotes national specialisation of production in other crops than grain, but the members resist dependence on the purchase of foreign grain to feed their people.

The policy for master farmers, with highly technical inputs and less

133

labour-intensive production, is also advocated for free South Africa. Large commercial farms in Southern Africa will provide surplus production, without worrying about distribution or consumption. As elsewhere in the region in the 1980s, there will be no call by the US for post-apartheid South Africa to redistribute land; 'efficiency' in grain production will legitimise continuing control by the few. Whether inside South Africa or in the region, jobs for displaced families, pushed off their land by 'marginal' production, must be sought in the cities. In order for jobs to be available, the economies must be open to all investors and the market open to foreign goods. The capital most ready to take advantage of new investment and of new trade opportunities in the region would be South African.

What remains to be seen is whether this agricultural policy, advocated by the US but thoroughly exposed by the early 1970s for its waste, pollution, and concentration of control, can endure for the 1990s.[2] It has endured up to now because grain production has, in fact, increased and risen to surplus levels. That surplus in the US has been used as a foreign-policy weapon, benefiting the farm sector and those in government who support their needs. This strong class alliance ignores 22 million Americans who are hungry because they cannot afford the 'surplus.' It looks the other way and is slow to react to the starving in developing countries, created by their governments' following the advice to grow cash crops to buy grain, advice which assumes stable or rising commodity prices and declining grain prices. Such a buyer loses either way: if international (subsidised) grain prices remain low, then local food production declines from the competition of grain prices below the cost of local production. If prices spiral because of declining supply or increased demand, the buyer can no longer afford sufficient food for subsistence consumption.

International grain prices are controlled through government subsidies in the North (US, EEC, Japan) and the ability of private grain oligopolies to manage supply; prices of cash crops are only partially stabilised through international commodity agreements, which, however, can be sabotaged by the monopsony of Northern buyers, and for some commodities like coffee or sugar, the US alone can alter the price agreements.[3]

SADCC is challenging the assumptions behind this dominant agricultural policy and, therefore, has to confront the terms of various recommendations, feasibility studies, and cash grants. As shown in this study, the SADCC record is mixed in this regard, sometimes succumbing to expediency in order to implement a project, or following the lead of class fractions allied with master-farmer, high-tech, specialised farming. Other times SADCC has resisted (e.g., grain storage scheme) the requirements which could subvert the real goals. This policy debate reflects the more fundamental struggle over property relations and market control within the Southern African region, one that intensifies each day as the region advances toward 'post-apartheid.'

In addition to the policy compulsion, Western modernisation theories of growth and of regional co-ordination have become irrelevant. By the 1990s, the condition of African economies should on their own be a decisive refutation of the validity of the assumptions behind structural adjustment policies. Instead of discrediting structural adjustment, IMF's failures have ironically served only to increase its control over national policies. However, the recipients of structural adjustment have begun to challenge the validity of the theories. Showing the failures as quite separate from any occasional mistake or misjudgment, the United Nations Economic Commission for Africa (ECA) has given an item-by-item refutation of the orthodox economic assumptions which must be in place for structural adjustment theories to be operative: few if any of the assumptions apply to Africa. The ECA has shown that these failures are not deficiencies of policy implementation but of theory. Tampering with a little bit more devaluation here, or a little less state intervention there, will not sustain growth.

Questioning the argument that growth is best pursued by the free play of market forces and that prices are the most effective instruments for efficient allocation of resources, the ECA points out the assumptions:

> The argument is based on the assumption that economic structures are time invariant and sufficiently flexible so that demand and supply changes respond promptly to market signals. Another important aspect of the theoretical basis derives from a strong belief in the efficacy of monetary instruments, in particular the belief that ... the price level can be regulated by controlling the supply of money and that socio-political forces ... play a negligible role.[4]

The ECA discusses how the African farmer cannot respond to price incentives without assured supplies of inputs and how IMF credit recommendations lead to 'output contraction and the acceleration of the inflationary pressure and, while it might succeed in improving the current account, it leads to a reduction in investment.' As important, the priorities are wrong: 'What is worse is the substitution of the profitability criterion for the social welfare criterion in vital areas such as water supply in a continent where the majority of the population have no access to potable water.'[5]

When the structural adjustment policies have failed so badly in so many settings (as shown in Chapter 5), their perpetuation becomes a question of control and power, and their 'theoretical' tenets ideology. As Claude Ake has noted: 'It was bad enough that what was to guide development in the Third World was purely derivative from mainstream Western social science, and routinely applied: even worse was that its application was not adaptive.'[6]

Equally spurious are the general theories of economic co-ordination:

> To put it bluntly, the economic integration failures of the underdeveloped countries are an impressive monument to the professional arrogance of

most 'conventional wisdom' economists from the industrially advanced North, the intellectual sheepiness [sic] of the flock of their unconditional followers in the underdeveloped areas both on technical and policy-making levels, and the inability of the states and dominant political structures to work out any sort of longer-term development policies which the present-day advanced societies had never faced, even at the beginning of the first industrial revolution in the eighteenth century.[7]

Theories in the neo-classical economic tradition often assume that customs unions are the model for economic co-ordination:

... the basic economic theory on this subject could be characterised as thought diverting and, to a large extent, irrelevant. The traditional theory of international economics and international trade as applied to LDC's [less developed countries] economic integration appeared to be, at best, sterile, ...simply rationalising normative positions and external interests. In fact, the postulates drawn from traditional theory lead to the conclusion that developing countries 'ought to form customs unions, if at all, with some of the industrialised countries.'[8]

The theories do not address equity or distribution concerns. Further, the transition from functional co-ordination (transport, communication, cultural events, etc.) to co-ordination of production is often treated as unproblematic, as if the exchange of national dance troupes or table tennis teams is the same as the co-ordination of steel production.

Invalid theories of regional co-ordination are not, however, the preserve of Western orthodox models, for theories from the socialist East have been equally deleterious. The assumption behind many Soviet or East European theories is that the economies which want to co-ordinate must, as a precondition, have the same economic systems: economic integration 'can only happen within the framework of one social and economic system.'[9] Such an assumption condemns most areas of the Third World as inappropriate for regional co-ordination.

By now, for the 1990s, Western and Eastern theorists should consider serious scientific theoretical formulations from analysis of concrete actions and experience in Southern Africa.[10] Put simply, SADCC practice is ahead of theory; SADCC is writing theory. It is turning regional co-operation theory on its head and it is beginning modestly to restructure the region. SADCC is not just debating plans for the post-apartheid era, it is implementing them – in spite of South African aggression and in spite of donor policies adverse to their goals. The theories are not fully developed and may not work; the policies are not guaranteed. Serious contradictions discussed in the previous chapters could overwhelm SADCC tomorrow but what SADCC has already shown in its first 11 years is that policies for growth, or of economic co-ordination, not grounded in their regional realities will fail not only the masses of the people, but those with controlling interests.

# Summary of SADCC Food Policy

A summary of SADCC's food policy concretely illustrates the argument about assumptions and theories. In Southern Africa, as in many developing economies, the ability to grow or purchase grain sufficient for subsistence is more fundamental to 'security' than weaponry. It is only when an adversary plants land mines in fields and sets fire to crops that weaponry becomes equally important. Food security is a precondition for economic self-determination and political sovereignty.

According to SADCC, therefore, food production is too vital and basic to be left solely to the profit motive. Simply offering incentives for production might be fine for batteries or shoes, but not for food. Policy must carefully decide such questions as incentives for whom? The answer will determine the whole fabric of the economy – as well as who becomes satiated and who dies from malnutrition. In some developing countries the answer has created a generation of children with unusually high numbers of mentally retarded; in many developed countries, it has turned control over to a few powerful food conglomerates, which determine foreign policies and engender trade wars.[11]

The members of SADCC have been acting together to formulate agricultural priorities, but they are not acting in unison. Botswana would be vulnerable to outside market forces without the available food supply from SADCC neighbours. In spite of this availability, Botswana will continue to find ways to increase grain production as part of its national plan. Continuing to import the majority of its grain, the Botswana government wants to reduce drastically the ratio of imported to domestic grains. Zimbabwe, already self-sufficient, would also be more vulnerable without the region as customers for its surplus grain. Zambia has learned the costly lesson of depending on its copper revenue to buy 'cheaper' grain from overseas than it can produce at home or purchase from next door. If Zambia had in 1981 imported surplus grain from Zimbabwe, instead of buying it on the world market, it would have saved $14.5 million. And this cost does not take into account the preference for white maize.[12] SADCC, therefore, is working toward regional 'collective-reliance' in grain production, by assisting each member in promoting national production.

To fulfil this seemingly contradictory goal of promoting regional 'collective-reliance' through national production, SADCC members act together to reduce obstacles to national food production, allowing each member to decide how to implement the new technology, distribute new data or seeds, and assign new technicians to rural areas. They all agree to state planning in agricultural production, but not to one regional plan. Such a plan would require some to forego basic food production, in order to grow or manufacture what it can produce more easily. Each country regards the basic grains as too vital – to individual livelihood, to the economy and to a stable government – to depend mainly on their import.

SADCC's approach to food security avoids separating agricultural policy from general economic decisions. Adequate food production requires efficient marketing as well as basic manufactures. A much more difficult task – food on the table for all – requires distribution of land, jobs and income to insure that no one is malnourished. No single, isolated decision, such as raising producer prices, suffices. Agricultural policies, therefore, must be integrated into general economic planning.

In order to pursue this multi-leveled policy of 1) regional collective-reliance in grains, 2) regional efforts to remove obstacles to national food production, and 3) integration of food policy into overall economic planning, SADCC has devised a new model for economic co-ordination. The model and its relation to food policy offer many lessons for other developing countries.

## Turning Economic Co-ordination on Its Head

Challenging orthodox theories of regional co-operation, SADCC has turned economic co-ordination on its head, in several ways. First, after rejecting centralisation as unworkable within the diversity of the economies, members chose a highly decentralised model for co-ordination. With each country executing projects in a sector, participation and exchange among the members increase. Accountability is clearer. If a project falters, it is the sector co-ordinator which must investigate and report.

Second, SADCC has reversed priorities of regional co-ordination by promoting production before trade. The goal has been for each member to increase production – under constraints of inadequate foreign exchange, inadequate machinery and repair capabilities, and limited numbers of technicians – according to sector priorities in basic needs industries (e.g. food processing, textiles, farm tools) as determined by consensus decisions. If only trade were co-ordinated, foreign firms would come in to take advantage of the market, but their production might have little to do with local economic priorities. Co-ordinating production allows members to plan growth and equity, and increased production will generate trade.

Third, the equitable distribution of benefits from co-ordination has been made a priority, not an afterthought nor left to chance ('trickle-down'). Dominant theories in advanced capitalist countries, especially but certainly not limited to the monetarists, discuss distribution as a side-effect of growth. The popular adage of the theories is that one has to have production (growth) to share before it can be distributed. SADCC does not dispute the obvious, but points out that growth in most developing countries has benefited the very few, while the masses are impoverished, not elevated to the middle class, as the theorists suppose. Production priorities, therefore, do propose and try to follow a 'basic needs' agenda. SADCC is also committed to policies which reduce the inequities among their economies, because it is recognised that the strongest cannot grow without ready supplies from, and markets within, their neighbours. Zimbabwe needs its neighbours not as labour reserve areas, but as suppliers and customers.[13]

For some national ruling classes in Southern Africa, this equity priority reflects a concern for social justice as well as the self-interest of an economy with much to gain from regional co-ordination. For others, including the most capitalist (Swaziland, Malawi), the goal of economic growth with distribution exposes the contradiction inherent in their revenue bases. They remain dependent on the revenue and taxes generated by transnational corporations, not on a substantial tax base among their own people. Economic growth (based either on import substitution or export growth), therefore, can actually increase the economy's and the state's vulnerability to the vagaries of the international economy: commodity price changes, currency fluctuations, decreased demand for exports, etc. But if production is oriented not only to export markets but is turned more to domestic consumption, then the tax base of the state can become more diverse and more localised. Because of the economic diversity of SADCC, it cannot dictate policy to individual members about domestic equity or distribution, even though regional equity is central to the SADCC agenda.

After the fragmentation caused by colonial rule, SADCC has set out to reunite the regional economy. To this end it has stood regional co-ordination on its head in a fourth way, by affirming that co-operation strengthens, not delimits, national power. As shown in the early chapters, shared raw materials, shared skills, and co-ordinated production will enable a national economy to grow more easily than individual state efforts. In contrast to most theories of co-ordination, therefore, SADCC members see their insistence on consensus to preserve sovereignty not as a detriment, but as an impetus, for development. Co-ordination, based on consensus, will encourage joint efforts and reduce competition; no one project can be accepted at the expense or displeasure of a member.[14] It must reflect an overlap of national interests. Not a perfect congruence, it is one which recognises that an arena for extensive co-ordination exists:

> People have failed to see the difference between SADCC and everything else that has failed. It is essentially a project for co-operation and the main aim is to identify projects of *national interest*. Nothing like this has been attempted before in which each of the nine states can bring something toward regional development without sinking *national interests*.[15]

The co-ordination began, therefore, with lists of short-term development projects; any project which benefited more than one member could be accepted as a regional one. Five years into SADCC, each sector devised a five-year plan to co-ordinate and strategise regional projects. No longer on a 'wish list,' the projects had to be relevant to these development plans. Officials state that this approach has overcome fears that national sovereignty would be curtailed and has facilitated increased partici-pation.[16] SADCC, therefore, has a sector plan for agriculture, which only addresses problems of removing obstacles to *national* production. It is not a regional plan designating who grows what; decisions remain national.

## Restructuring the Region?

This co-operative process is the means for the attainment of the funda-mental goal of SADCC: restructuring the region. First on the agenda is reduction of their dependence on apartheid. Some must, and others choose to, exchange with South Africa, but all reject the racism of apart-heid. Even those that trade the most with South Africa (Swaziland and Lesotho) have joined SADCC to seek alternative economic links in the region. United in poverty under apartheid dominance, SADCC envisions multiple economic relations among states where all participate in choices about trade and investment.

At Lusaka in 1980, SADCC members emphasised their development goals while speaking of reduced dependence on apartheid. Now, after a decade of apartheid aggression, they stress that their development cannot occur without the eradication of apartheid, for the regime has literally set fire to many of their fields. As Peter Mmusi, President of the Council of Ministers of SADCC and Vice-President of Botswana, stated in Harare in 1986: 'The abolition of apartheid will be the greatest single contri-bution which could be made in the economic development of this region.' By 1988, SADCC was negotiating security aid along with project aid, for investment in many projects is useless without their being defended from apartheid's surrogate forces. Namibia joining SADCC in 1990 was the fulfilment of the goal of freedom from apartheid rule, yet apartheid aggression continues in Angola and Mozambique, with hints of possible escalation in free Namibia, also through the use of surrogate forces.

South Africa is the short-term adversary, for the apartheid state is under siege. The longer term adversaries are those interests which try to maintain the Southern African economies as subordinate primary commodity producers. SADCC's political consensus, therefore, is much broader than simple anti-apartheid sentiments. The present configuration of power and dominance is seen as the result of colonialism and there is a desire to alter the region's position in the international division of labour. This goal underlines the congruity of interest among the states. Not similar in economic choices about the relations of production, they all agree on a need for greater domestic control over their national economies.

It is a nationalist response, but one in which national interests overlap and reinforce each other. SADCC, for example, cannot alter international commodity prices for its exports – minerals, coffee, tea, cotton, beef, sugar – but it can try to reduce the impact of fluctuating prices on their economies by the diversification of production and by joint marketing efforts, such as the Botswana/Zimbabwe consortium for selling beef to the EEC. Instead of receiving food aid from the US under the dictates of whatever administration ('sign Nkomati Accord before food will arrive' ... 'we will give you only yellow maize not white,' etc.), SADCC wants to be able to produce or buy food, and failing that in the medium-term, remain politically non-aligned so it can accept aid from whomever.

These goals, although modest and logical when viewed historically, are a major challenge to the international economic status quo. SADCC is not rejecting free enterprise; it seeks the creativity and ingenuity which that engenders. However, it rejects a totally free-market economy; such an economy provides an arena where small enterprises often become victims of 'take-overs' by large foreign-owned corporations. SADCC accepts the virtues of competition in promoting innovation, but only under the auspices of national and regional planning. From their colonial experiences, Southern Africans know a larger pie is not a guarantee of wider distribution of the pieces. Executive Secretary of SADCC, Simba Makoni, admonishes, 'There is now, I think, a consensus that the market is a good servant, although quite clearly a bad master.'[17]

Private enterprise will endure in each SADCC economy, but not free of all constraints, because these economies do not generate sufficient surplus to allow imports for just any production. In some, almost every import decision, down to the smallest screw, must be planned. Misuse and waste means shortages in another sector. Competition within SADCC will engender innovation and growth but within the context of sector plans and priorities, like clothing production. Market mechanisms which elevate whiskey and perfume to greater importance (i.e. profit) than sorghum or medicine remain suspect. Protection of a basic needs programme and development of an economic base which can reduce over-dependence on exports of primary products are still seen as depending on state initiative and the protection of selected industries. Those who insist on open investment and market strategies are seen as the privileged who gained their wealth from the status quo, based on the export of primary products.

Planning also is not a panacea, but a pragmatic attempt to regulate the economy so it can buffet the storms engendered by the international economy. The state is vulnerable to corruption but so is private business.[18] SADCC regards the state as an arbiter among conflicting interests, not a neutral one, but one which must consider multiple interests and provide political mediation. The state must pay regard to both profit and political stability; the latter does not materialise if only a few benefit from economic growth. SADCC's view, therefore, is state intervention is a necessary but not sufficient condition for the realisation of equity in the economy.

If SADCC is serious about challenging either apartheid or its own position in the international division of labour, then each member has to be serious about helping 'small producers.' When they can become more efficient, with appropriate seeds and inputs, then food distribution, along with availability, will increase. If female producers can be given security of land tenure (i.e., control over land use, not necessarily private ownership) and access to basic inputs, again both production and distribution will increase. And a small farmer strategy cannot be conceptualised outside the context of the relationship of the peasant class to state power.

If government officials, instead, use SADCC's research and expertise primarily for master farmers or the commercial estates (as Malawi is presently doing), then neither the food distribution agenda, nor the lessening of dependence on apartheid, nor the restructuring of international economic relations will be achieved. Food production may increase dramatically, but under the old patterns of local and international dominance. Issa Shivji has summarised the problem as follows:

> In our countries experience has shown that economic privatisation does not necessarily produce political liberalisation. More often than not, the contrary is true. This is because the private comprador bourgeoisie will not be able to deliver even some basic needs of the popular masses. And lacking in any political legitimacy, it will inevitably resort to naked force to subjugate the people.[19]

As analysed in the previous chapters, the attack on property relations in SADCC has been comprehensive. In calling for the privatisation of land, production and marketing, international agencies are not just advocating another 'policy for growth;' rather, they are requiring structural transformation (not 'adjustment') of production relations. It would require a fundamental and radical change in class relations within each state. SADCC, as a decentralised and consensual organisation, will not direct these national class struggles; it can provide, however, a new regional context which will influence social relations.[20]

In fact, too preoccupied with top-down coordinating, the states ignored non-governmental organisations (NGOs) in the first years of SADCC. Auspicious for the future, it was the NGOs which took advantage of new telecommunication and transport links and began to compare national policies and experiences. As early as 1985, co-operatives from Mozambique, Tanzania and Zimbabwe met together to discuss their problems and analyse possible solutions; they argued over the advantages of marketing versus producer cooperatives. Women in the Mozambican delegation admonished the other two for not electing women to positions of responsibility in the co-operatives. They learned from each other how to minimise state bureaucratic obstacles. Women's groups have also met across national boundaries, sharing techniques of how to overcome state refusal to extend them credit by setting up their own credit schemes. These regional groups are modest endeavours to change conditions of production, but SADCC – by focusing on appropriate technology, on the small producer, by improving transport and communications – facilitates these exchanges. What could happen is that these interests will attain their own dynamism from mobilisation within the region which will, in turn, profoundly alter the regional context for the states. The relationship is dialectic. SADCC projects can alter the terrain of the class struggle – creating conditions which facilitate organisation and production by local groups across national boundaries. These groups, through their own mobilisation, can in turn profoundly affect the policies and directions of SADCC projects – and their class base. They remind each SADCC sector that co-ordination among non-state actors (NGOs, business councils, journalists, universities) may determine the nature of regional co-operation as much as anything SADCC does. Such tendencies will require close scrutiny and analysis to understand the next decade of SADCC.

Reconstituting a regional economy means that multiple, sometimes experimental, economic relations are established. The immediate successes of SADCC show that theories of regional co-ordination are at least partially correct; the easiest and most expeditious way to co-operate is to build infrastructures which benefit all. SATCC (Southern African Transport and Communications Commission) has been the most successful sector in planning 201 projects with 40 percent secured funding, accounting for over two-thirds of all SADCC funding.[21] Rehabilitating or building rail, port, road, telecommunications links, and electricity grids can benefit all.[22] This functional co-ordination has also established new regional institutions and encouraged experimentation with institutional formats. Even if SADCC disintegrated tomorrow, both SATCC and SACCAR (Southern African Centre for Co-operation in Agricultural Research) would likely continue, for they meet tangible and non-competitive needs for each economy.

The Beira Corridor Authority is also an experiment in regional institution-building, a model to bring governments and private capital together in a regional joint venture. SADCC cannot yet agree to a unified policy toward foreign or national capital; instead of breaking apart over this problem, SADCC agreed to co-ordination of investment in one project, namely, the Beira Corridor (port, rail, road). Co-ordinating investment in the corridor from foreign governments, international capital, private regional capital, and national governments in the region, SADCC has attracted capital and met the deadlines of each stage of the plan. Learning from this practical experience, the next occasion to co-ordinate investment will be easier and more extensive. These practical solutions coincide with the structure of SADCC as previously described:

SADCC have viewed institutions [e.g. Beira Corridor Authority, SACCAR, SATCC] as *facilitating and consequential rather than causative forces* or ends in themselves. Therefore, it has consistently sought to develop concrete areas of activity and to identify their actual servicing requirements first and only then to create institutional structures.[23] [emphasis added]

Functional co-ordination (rails, roads, research, etc.) does not in itself transform economies but it is a necessary building of networks for restructuring production in the region. Further, during this early and easier stage of co-ordination, SADCC has built new institutions, a more contentious task, yet fundamental to the investment of capital, its ownership and control for long-term projects. New institutions initiating new interaction among capital interests can begin economic restructuring. Such regional restructuring is fundamental because separately, 'none of the [members] has a large enough market, a sufficiently diversified economy or command of an adequate range of resources to underpin the development of a modern industrial economy.'[24]

## Region-to-Region Co-operation

Inter-regional co-operation is another means used by SADCC to gain recognition for the redefinition of Southern Africa and to solicit assistance in regional restructuring. Needing international capital but remaining vulnerable to it, SADCC signed two region-to-region accords in 1986, with the Nordics and with the EEC. For both, it was the first region-to-region agreement with developing countries. They have agreed to relate to SADCC members as a region: even when negotiating bilateral projects or joint ventures, the regional impact is to be taken into consideration and efforts made to shift from mainly bilateral terms to regional projects benefiting more than one country.

The region-to-region accord with the EEC was the first of its kind with any ACP (African-Caribbean-Pacific) region under the Lomé Convention. Although the EEC had increased its multilateral aid and investment to SADCC, bilateral state relations were the norm. Of about $1 billion available to the region under Lomé III (1985–89), 78 percent was assigned to national indicative plans.[25] Regional projects, such as the Nacala rail corridor, were funded as national programmes, contributing to unco-ordinated decision-making and disarticulated projects. Further, increased trade, not investment, remains the preoccupation of the accord. The EEC surprised SADCC at the end of 1990 by setting the regional allocation for Lomé IV at 121 million ECU, reduced 20 million ECU from Lomé III. SADCC quickly pointed out this reduction did not take into consideration the expanded SADCC Programme of Action, the entry of Namibia into SADCC, nor inflation. More pernicious, the EEC announced that SADCC will now have to compete with the PTA (Preferential Trade Agreement of Eastern and Southern Africa) for the regional allocation, although the region-to-region accord was signed only between the EEC and SADCC and the PTA includes all of eastern Africa. Therefore, the EEC, not too dissimilar from the US, promotes policies which contradict SADCC goals. One SADCC member is not included in the Lomé definition of 'Southern Africa,' for after 11 years, Tanzania is still seen by the EEC as 'eastern Africa.' Because of EEC subsidies in 1983, 7.5 million tonnes of grain and 1 million tonnes of butter were in storage in Europe; in spite of this exorbitant policy, the EEC as a donor acts as an expert to dictate the conditions of storage and allocation of SADCC grain (see Chapter 5).

One area of EEC agricultural policy does seem to offer alternatives. Citing problems with capital-intensive agriculture, 'opinion is gathering among scientists and the public to mitigate such problems by maintaining smaller farms that absorb more labour....'[26] This re-thinking may facilitate exchanges following SADCC production and equity priorities, not just European trade goals.

The more comprehensive and innovative accord was signed with the Nordic countries (Denmark, Finland, Iceland, Norway and Sweden). Individual members of SADCC have long and special relations with individual Nordic countries.[27] Tanzania, which has consistently been the largest recipient of Swedish, Danish Norwegian, and Finnish aid, received from 40 to 60 percent of each country's total bilateral aid for the period 1980–85.[28] Tanzania, Mozambique and others saw the Nordics as offering alternatives to large and dominant capital interests; Nordic aid and investments simply had not been as manipulative as, say, British Lonrho (expelled from Tanzania over Lonrho's complicity with the white Rhodesian regime) or as threatening as South African interests.[29] With small populations (SADCC has over three times the combined population of the Nordics), the Nordic countries have successfully developed and pursued democratic socialism; therefore they were not as adverse to the idea of state intervention and joint ventures as larger capitalist countries. They have also periodically written off debts owed to them by the poorer countries. The Nordics constitute by far SADCC's most important donor. The US and the Federal Republic of Germany have been large bilateral donors but do not support regional projects at nearly the same level as the Nordics which is equivalent to the combined total of such major donors as the EEC, Canada, France, Italy, US and the World Bank. For bilateral aid, from 1981–86, the combined Nordic bilateral disbursement in constant dollars increased by 136 percent, or three times the rate of increase of those in the Development Assistance Committee of the OECD (Organisation for Economic Co-operation).[30] Because of the long-term Nordic commitment to SATCC in Mozambique (three-quarters of Nordic aid has been to SATCC), Nordic aid to SADCC transport priorities is even more impressive. At the end of 1987, the Nordics had provided 19 percent of all funds secured for the Beira Corridor and 38 percent of funds secured for the Dar es Salaam Corridor.[31] By that year, however, the US had designated the Dar Corridor as its major recipient and allocated $45.9 million mainly for locomotives. Another $10.5 million was given by the US to upgrade lake facilities to transport Malawian goods to Tazara for the port of Dar es Salaam.

Supporting the Frontline States in their efforts to topple white minority rule in the region since the early 1970s, the Nordics adopted a common programme to isolate South Africa in 1978. With a few exceptions,[32] Denmark, Finland, Norway and Sweden have implemented a general trade boycott of apartheid South Africa and prohibited any new investments, credit guarantees and the sale of krugerrands.

From their perspective, the Nordics promoted the accord because they approved of SADCC development goals which included equity and poverty concerns. Responding to needs in the region, they pointed out that four SADCC states belong in the group of least developed countries and six are landlocked. Supporting the region's efforts to reduce its vulnerability to apartheid aggression, in 1988 the Nordics began to offer security protection for projects they were helping to finance in Mozambique.

The political affinity between the Nordics and SADCC also reflects the fact that the Nordics, forming their organisation in 1952 (Finland joining in 1955), understand the importance as well as the problems of co-ordinating smaller economic powers. thus they regularly consult among themselves before attending international meetings in order to present a united Nordic position on various issues. In relation to building regional infrastructure, co-ordination of electricity grids facilitated its quick diversion to deficit areas. Workers seeking jobs can cross national boundaries of the Nordic countries and retain social security benefits. Yet the limitations on this small region are equally manifest. Nordic tariff reductions must parallel closely that of the EEC; one devalued its currency against the deutschmark and the others had to follow. And it all takes time. A Norwegian delegate in 1979 pointed out that some 60 items on the agenda had been coming up for discussion in one forum or another for more than 50 years.[33] Such experience engenders patience and understanding about SADCC's precarious progress as well as its desire to protect sovereignty.

The Nordic/SADCC initiative emphasises several areas for co-operation:

- increased Nordic support for intra-regional co-operation in priority areas established by SADCC;
- increased technical assistance;
- support to build up, maintain and rehabilitate SADCC productive capacity;
- promotion of trade;
- promotion of contacts between the commercial, industrial and financial sectors in the two regions;
- promotion of cultural co-operation.[34]

The accord promises new co-operation in joint ventures, transfer of technology, finance, trade and cultural exchanges, offering a comprehensive approach to development. Such studies as a review of the Nordic export and investment guarantee institutions, the analysis of SADCC export commodities, the evaluation of SADCC science and technology capabilities and of potential firm-to-firm training programmes have contributed to the implementation of the exchange. Appropriate technology for labour-intensive production is central to the exchange, based on success stories like the replacement of tractors for oxen in northern Zambia, 'one of the reasons behind the dramatic increase in maize production in the area.'[35]

In January 1988, the Norsad Fund was proposed to guarantee availability of convertible currency for operations of joint ventures between SADCC and the Nordics. The Fund is dedicated to increased production, not trade. Some Nordic NGOs argued that the Norsad Fund should support basic need production for local markets; however, as most national currencies in SADCC are overvalued, the Nordic governments decided that Norsad should finance export production. By alleviating the foreign exchange constraints for those able to export, officials hope the fund will encourage the establishment of at least 40 joint ventures, viewed as the best way of transferring skills and technology. Although the amount of capital available in the Norsad Fund ($32 million in 1989) is less than that which might be available from larger capitalist economies, SADCC views it as a viable alternative to those larger capital interests which might be tempted to undermine regional priorities in order to pursue their own corporate development plans. By early 1991, it was not as clear whether Nordic corporations viewed it as an opportunity, however, for few had yet to try the Fund.

One of the many successes of a joint venture, which demonstrates what is possible, dates from 1980 in Tanzania when EB National Transformer (Norway) joined the government in a 20:80 joint venture to manufacture transformers. In 1982 a locally built unit still cost 60 percent more than one imported from Norway; by 1989, however, it cost 40 percent less and was selling in Malawi, Mozambique, Zambia and other African countries.[36] A newer joint venture reduces Zimbabwe's vulnerability to South African destabilisation tactics. South African capital is a major shareholder in nitrogen and phosphate manufacturers in Zimbabwe. In early 1989, Norsk Hydro (51 percent state owned) joined two Zimbabwean enterprises, TA Holdings and the Industrial Development Corporation, to buy out Chemplex, owned by African Explosives and Chemical Industries (AECI) of South Africa. Chemplex owned 50 percent of Zimbabwe Fertiliser Company (ZFC) and Zimbabwe Phosphate Industries (Zimphos), as well as a transport company, Shamwari Explosives and Dorowa Minerals.[37] This joint venture therefore loosened South

Africa's strangle-hold grip on Zimbabwean fertiliser production.

In interviews in 1988 in Zimbabwe and Mozambique, Zimbabwean businessmen and US government representatives referred to 'Nordic imperialism' gaining in the region, which could mean that the business-men and others were feeling competition from the Nordic plans. No SADCC official expressed such a complaint. What does seem to be clear is that the self-interests of the Nordics appear less threatening to SADCC than those of the more powerful.

Trade is one reflection of these interests. In contrast with the EEC, Nordic trade with SADCC is small and maintains a trade deficit for SADCC. In 1986 the Nordic trade surplus with SADCC (excluding Lesotho) was $85 million and climbed to $157 million in 1987.[38] What little the Nordics do import is unprocessed raw materials (ores and metals), not even attaining the same processing level as EEC imports from SADCC.[39] Long term solutions offered have included barter trade, a joint Nordic import guarantee, and some version of a Nordic Stabex scheme.[40]

In 1984 at the height of a severe Southern African drought, the Nordics echoed US, FAO, and World Bank agricultural policy recommendations. The US used the congruence to legitimise the policy, emphasising that diverse interests (American, Nordic, international organisations) were advocating the same policy changes. SADCC recognised the gravity of the drought and errors in agricultural policy, but carefully and firmly rejected many of the policy recommendations. Interviews of SADCC food security officials revealed their surprise that the Nordics had joined the others in what was viewed as a policy slanted toward very narrow interests. In the 'Response by SADCC Agricultural Ministers to Nordic and FAO Papers,' SADCC replied to the critique of SADCC priorities for small producers, and the admonition to 'not exclude large-scale farmers' from government assistance, by affirming that it tries to promote policies that 'strike an appropriate balance.' In the call by the Nordics for pricing policy reforms, SADCC responded, 'It is not only SADCC pricing policies that need improvement but also that the international pricing mechanisms may need to be changed since they may also have adverse effects on the domestic policies which, in turn, will affect the local farming community.'[41] Reacting to the demand that policy adjustments were urgent, SADCC reminded the Nordics that adjustments can only be implemented by individual member states and more important, that conditions in each state needed close examination, not imposition of a general policy. Not focusing much on the agriculture sector at the time, the Nordics allied with the very interests SADCC was opposing; the crisis of the drought intensified the disagree-ments as SADCC was desperate to receive aid with no policy strings attached. A Danish expert is now assigned to the SADCC food security office in Harare; it will be interesting to see if Nordic agricultural advice still echoes that of USAID, a prominent voice in the Harare office.

Although the Nordic/SADCC accord is an attempt to expand investment, fundamental change will take time to alter current interests; investments remain linked to less serious items such as Danish beer. Swedish
firms, ranked higher in capital assets and still operating in South Africa
(only new investment was banned), have not found it attractive to move
into the SADCC arena. Complaints range from the instability caused by
apartheid aggression to problems with earnings in non-convertible
currencies and the large financial commitments necessary to launch new
enterprises. Discussions among various Nordic research institutes suggest
that the impressive Nordic aid must be restructured to underwrite risk
capital for new investments in Southern Africa. Then the question arises
whether Nordic taxpayers, supportive of aid for development co-operation, would approve of subsidising profit-making by Nordic enterprises.
One report concludes that no other alternatives exist to motivate investment interests to the degree needed by SADCC.[42]

SADCC has no doubt the Nordics will pursue their self-interest in
increasing investment opportunities and building a market for Nordic
goods. Given that basic reality, however, from the increasing aid of the
Nordics to SADCC, their vital assistance in the transport and communication systems, their offer of non-lethal aid to protect development projects
from South African assault, and their willingness to transfer technology
and skills while providing foreign exchange, it appears that the Nordic-
SADCC agreements are very close to the kind of extra-regional co-operation that SADCC desires. Indeed, experiences of individual countries over
the last decades have shown that the smaller capital interests and more
appropriate technology of the Nordics assist their development needs more
than larger capital powers. The accord is comprehensive but puts production as central, with the goal of changing the structures of the SADCC
economies. As a 1988 SADCC document stresses: 'The Nordic/ SADCC
Initiative currently provides the only vehicle outside the [SADCC] annual
consultative conference for formal consultations between SADCC and a
group of its co-operating partners on matters specific to investment, production and trade. It is hoped that this kind of forum will be broadened...'[43]

SADCC officials analyse that co-ordination reduces the influence of
individual transnational enterprises in any one of their countries. Similar
to the Beira Corridor Authority, the region-to-region accords provide
alternatives to individual capital enterprises or even individual donor
countries and increase SADCC's bargaining power. The accords are a
means for SADCC to encourage outsiders to recognise its role and goals.
They encourage the practice of outsiders to view the economies as a
*region,* not as separate and competitive markets.

## SADCC and a Free South Africa?

National restructuring of economies will probably be more affected by a free South Africa than by SADCC, but SADCC will remain an important actor in post-apartheid Southern Africa. To create habits of co-operation, SADCC includes the African National Congress and Pan Africanist Congress in its meetings. South Africans have begun to discuss the problems of regional planning, and how planning could bring more for less. By far the strongest economy, South Africa is still very open, dependent on foreign trade. A free South Africa could provide jobs for the millions of unemployed only with an expanding economy, and a regional market is key to that expansion. Blockages to South African development, like shortages of water or the lack of petroleum, can also be met by the region, in a co-ordinated and planned manner.

A free South Africa will bring to SADCC all the negative aspects of large-scale commercial agriculture: one of the most inequitable distributions of land in the world; landless, malnourished and illiterate farmworkers; high cost capital intensive production; an emphasis on cash crops, with neglect of traditional crops. Any new government in South Africa (left, right or centre) will have to undertake a redistribution of the 87 percent of the land reserved for whites only. The new government will also have to pay more attention to questions of availability and distribution of food to the millions of malnourished inside South Africa, rather than to the present preoccupation with crop exports.

SADCC has ready lessons for a free South Africa. The success of Zimbabwe in providing agricultural inputs (seed, etc.) and rural transport depots to small producers could be a model for South Africa to consider. The training and promotion of agricultural extension workers (many female) and the attention to seeds that are 'stable producers' as well as hybrids offer suggestions to a free South Africa. Regional institutions, such as SACCAR, would welcome South African expertise and share its findings about sorghum, millet, and the legumes. Water from South Africa's neighbours could perhaps provide irrigation for the more arid areas. Working together, the whole region could quickly become a breadbasket, able to share its bounty with less endowed areas of Africa.

Negative examples are also important, as South Africans watch and learn from the slow and overly deliberate land redistribution in Zimbabwe. As more detailed data is available about increased peasant production in Zimbabwe, South Africans may find that the Zimbabwe policy favoured only a few better-off peasants and could participate in SADCC to discuss how best to help the poorest of the poor producers.

At another level, Tanzania, Zimbabwe and Mozambique have different but important models for public health care which emphasise preventive, not curative medicine. Rural health centres in all three countries have educated millions about primary health care, from the dangers of bilharzia in irrigated fields in Zimbabwe to education about the benefits of a nutrition-balanced diet. Because more than half of the infant and child mortality (in peace time) results from a combination of preventable communicable diseases and malnutrition, health workers discuss the benefits of vegetable gardens and crop variation for each village.[44] SADCC can assist a free South Africa with these urgent issues.

How to educate the millions of South Africa who have been subjected to inferior education under apartheid will also be a priority. Again, new methods have been developed by its neighbours which could be adapted and improved upon by the new South African government. Mozambique, before the MNR atrocities, established literacy classes in many work places – both rural and urban – and male and female workers were given time off work at mid-day or in the late afternoon to participate. University students were sent to the rural areas to collect oral histories before their elders died without passing on the traditions. Newly-graduated doctors were required to spend time in rural clinics.

Zimbabwe educated more at the primary and secondary school level in the first five years of independence than the Southern Rhodesian government did in 90 years of white minority rule. This success has created new problems of 'too many' students qualified for the university (8000 in 1990 for only 2000 places for the first year), a 'problem' many South Africans would love to have. Zimbabwe and Botswana have also implemented experimental programmes of 'education with production,' to combine practical skills with liberal arts education. These and other experiments abound in the region for South Africans to critique and adapt to their own needs.

The most important lesson from all of SADCC to South Africa is reconciliation. Zimbabwe and Namibia are the most recent examples, but Botswana, Tanzania and Zambia have also shown various but successful paths for national unification across ethnic and colour lines. A free South Africa will not be a Zimbabwe or Zambia or Mozambique, socially or politically, but SADCC provides practical lessons and a ready forum for debates to occur at the regional level.

The peoples of SADCC are not content, however, with their successful achievement of reconciliation. They agree with South Africans that a free South Africa cannot simply replace black faces for white, in the same relations of dominance and exploitation; the eradication of apartheid means the transformation of economic as well as political relations to provide land, employment and a decent quality of life for the majority. Only a decade old, SADCC is also making a statement that a free South Africa cannot simply substitute black faces for white in their dominance over the Southern African region. SADCC calls for a transformation of economic relations in which a free South Africa becomes a co-operating partner in an economically liberated Southern Africa.

# NOTES

1. P. I. Berger and B. Godsell, eds. *A Future South Africa – Visions, Strategies, and Realities*. Pretoria: Human & Rousseau and Tafelberg Publishers, 1988. This study was funded by major US and South African companies. Roger Southall. 'Post-Apartheid South Africa. Constraints on Socialism.' *Journal of Modern African Studies* 25:2 (1987): 354–74. John Suckling and Landeg White. eds. *After Apartheid: Renewal of the South African Economy*. London: James Currey, 1988. Special 'After Apartheid' Issue. *Third World Quarterly* 9:2 (1987). One conference which did focus on SADCC's role in post-apartheid Southern Africa was the SIAS/SADRA conference, 'Regional Cooperation in Post-Apartheid Southern Africa,' Harare, September 1988. Papers are published in Bertil Oden and Haroub Othman, eds. *Regional Cooperation in Southern Africa: A Post-apartheid Perspective*. Uppsala: Scandinavian Institute of African Studies, 1989.

2. Conservative estimates calculate US top soil loss at 2 billion tons per year; soil erosion rates are now higher than at the time of the Dust Bowl in the 1930s. Since 1970, pesticide use has increased 140 percent, but crop losses to insects have also increased 40 percent. A 1984–88 study reported that methods using little or no chemicals on crops yielded the same as pesticide and fertiliser use. There are also growing financial costs to America's allegedly cheap food. In 1986, US taxpayers spent $26 billion in farm subsidies, more than $433 per family of four, up from $70 per family in 1981. Kevin Danaher. 'US Agricultural Policies: Costly at Home, Bad News for Other Countries.' *Financial Gazette,* 23 June 1989 (extracts from a forthcoming book by Global Exchange, San Francisco). Report of the National Academy of Sciences on chemical use, *New York Times,* 8 September 1989.

3. At the very time that President Bush was asking Colombian President Barco to spend money to fight the cocaine growers and dealers, the US demanded two conditions which suspended the price-support agreement for coffee, Columbia's largest export earner. (The estimates are that Columbia earned $1.7 billion from coffee in 1988 compared to $1.5 billion from cocaine.) The US wanted more flexibility in quotas so it could buy a greater percentage of top-quality coffee grades and wanted to end sales to Eastern Europe at prices far below those in the agreement. President Barco sent a frank letter to President Bush: 'The [price-support] agreement was not extended due to the lack of political willingness on the part of the United States.' Before the pact was suspended, coffee sold for $1.45 per pound; two months later, the price was 85 cents, less than it costs Columbians to grow and ship the coffee. 'Coffee Impasse Imperils Columbia's Drug Fight,' *New York Times,* 24 September 1989.

     In 1985, bio-tech production of 4.5 million tons of sugar from maize starch in the US and Japan oversupplied the world sugar market and deterred exports of sugar from developing countries. Folker Frobel, Jurgen Heinrichs, and Otto Kreye. 'Changing Patterns of World Market Integration in Third World Countries,' paper presented at Conference on Economic Policies under Crisis Conditions, University of Zimbabwe, September 1985, p. 21.

4. United Nations Economic Commission for Africa. 'African Alternative Framework to Structural Adjustment Programmes for Socio-Economic Recovery and Transformation,' E/ECA/CM.15/6/Rev.3, 21 June 1989. See especially pp.

18–20 and 37–43. The document also echoes the Lagos Plan of Action (1980) in calling for 'regional collective self-reliance' and acknowledges that 'in line with the objective of establishing a human-centred development, the first priority area for collective self-reliance is that of *regional food security.*' p. 14.

5   *Ibid.*, pp. 18–19.

6   Claude Ake. 'The Political Economy of Development: Does It Have A Future?' *International Social Science Journal*, No. 118 (November 1988): 485.

7   Miguel Wionczek. 'Can Humpty-Dumpty Be Put Together Again and By Whom? Comments on the Vaitsos Survey,' *World Development* 6: 6 (June 1978): 781.

8   Constantine Vaitsos. 'Crisis in Regional Economic Cooperation (Integration) among Developing Countries: A Survey,' *World Development* 6: 6 (June 1978): 310. At the end, the author is quoting Peter Robson. *Economic Integration in Africa.* London: Allen and Unwin, 1968, pp.32–3.

9   Soltan S. Dzarasov. 'Socio-Political Aspects of the Rise of Different Types of Integration,' in *Economic Integration: Concepts, Theories and Problems*, Mihaly Simai and Katalin Garam, eds. Budapest: Akademiai Kisado, 1977, p. 109. See the same interpretation in Gert Kuck. 'Economic Co-Operation and Integration: The Case of the Developing Countries,' *ibid.* For a contrasting interpretation, see Helmut Faulwetter. 'The Concept of Increased Economic Relations among Developing Countries.' *Marxist Views on the Transformation of the International Economic Order. Asia, Africa, Latin America,* special issue 11. Helmut Faulwetter and Peter Stier, eds. Berlin: Akademie-Verlag, 1983.

10  'In the neo-classical tradition, indeed in the entire mainstream Western social science, there is hardly any serious scientific theory developed specifically from concrete concern with Third World conditions. This is certainly true of economics. The Third World has not engaged the great minds of the West and concern with it has not yielded any scientific breakthroughs....' Claude Ake, *op. cit.*

11  Martha Hamilton. *The Great Grain Robbery and Other Stories.* Washington, DC: Agribusiness Accountability Project, 1972. Jim Hightower. *Eat Your Heart Out: How Food Profiteers Victimize the Consumer.* New York: Crown, 1975. Dan Morgan. *Merchants of Grain.* New York: Viking, 1979. North American Congress on Latin America (NACLA). 'U.S. Grain Arsenal,' *Latin America and Empire Report* 9:7 (October 1975). NACLA, 'Bitter Fruits,' *Latin America and Empire Report* (September 1976).

12  Ulrich Koester. 'Regional Co-operation to Improve Food Security in Southern and Eastern African Countries,' Research Report no. 53, International Food Policy Research Institute (IFPRI), July 1986, p. 10.

13  Large enterprises in apartheid South Africa also began to realise in the 1980s that the South African economy needed its neighbours more as customers than as labour supply areas. However, the smaller businessmen and farmers, the core supporters of apartheid, disagree. The small businesses do not need the regional market, for the South African market of 33 million people is adequate, especially as the black standard of living is raised. The farmers fear competition of their grain on the regional market by surplus grain producers in Zimbabwe.

14  In this sense, the SADCC model is similar to ASEAN (Association of South East Asian Nations) and further underlines the equity priority:

    ASEAN has given no official provision for special treatment of any member country, but it does not follow that the issue of distributive gains is not important in the ASEAN context of co-operation. The problem is indirectly tackled under the consensus mechanism; in reaching a consensus, no member country could take undue advantage of others....The negotiators would commit themselves to projects only if they could perceive prospective gains or expect the gains to be equitably distributed. In short, ASEAN has not left out the distributive issue but has instead handled it in a rather time-consuming manner.

United Nations Industrial Development Organization (UNIDO). *Regional Co-operation: Experience and Perspective of ASEAN and the Andean Pact.* Vienna: UNIDO, 1986, p. 85.

15 *New African* (London), No. 174 (November 1981): 74.
16 Interviews with W.L. Nyachia, Ministry of Industry and Trade, Tanzania, 4 November 1985; David Anderson and Reginold Green, SADCC Liaison Committee, 28 January 1986.
17 *Financial Gazette* (Harare), 6 March 1987.
18 Dare one even mention the US arms for drugs deals in the Iran-contra scandal, the S&L scandal, or corporate abuse of the Department of Housing and Urban Development (HUD) subsidies? Most private enterprise economies have an equally tainted list of profit-motive adventures.
19 Issa G. Shivji. 'Introduction: The Transformation of the State and the Working People' in *The State and the Working People in Tanzania.* Issa G. Shivji, ed., Dakar: Codesria, 1985, p. 13.
20 Carol B. Thompson. 'Zimbabwe in SADCC: A Question of Dominance?' *Zimbabwe's Prospects.* Colin Stoneman (ed.), London: Macmillan, 1988.
21 SADCC *Annual Progress Report* (July 1988–September 1989).
22 One energy scheme has caused considerable acrimony. Electricity was the single largest import ($29 million) by Zimbabwe from Zambia in 1981. Zimbabwe developed its Hwange power station, based on thermo (coal) energy, at the encouragement of the Anglo-American Corporation (part-owner of the coal fields) and the World Bank. By July 1987 Zimbabwe had ceased importing hydro-electric power from Zambia, and Zambia was demanding compensation from Zimbabwe for breaking an agreement to import surplus power from their joint supply at Kariba Dam. Further, Zambia is now in perpetual trade deficit with Zimbabwe. By 1989, in the light of conflicting feasibility studies because of variable water flows on the Zambezi in years of drought, President Mugabe personally delayed plans for the Kariba South expansion project. The consensus seemed to be emerging that Zimbabwe will shortly (1993) need the full capacity of its own production (thermo and hydro) as well as Zambian and Mozambican (Cahora Bassa) electricity.

E.D.D. Cohcrane, Dan Ndlela, Roger Riddell. *Study of the Manufacturing Sector in Zimbabwe,* Main Report, Vol. II, DP/ZIM/84/ 018, prepared for the Zimbabwe Government by UNIDO, 12 September 1985, p. 287. *Financial Gazette* (Harare), 17 and 24 July 1987. *Africa Economic Digest,* 19 June 1989, p. 14.
23 SADCC. *From Dependence and Poverty Toward Economic Liberation,* Blantyre: SADCC, 1981, p. 16.
24 SADCC, *SADCC: Investment in Production,* report presented at annual conference, Gaborone, Botswana, 5–6 February 1987, p. 7.
25 AWEPAA and CIIR. 'Southern Africa's Future: Europe's Role,' Background Papers for European Parliamentarians' Working Seminar on Support for SADCC, 13–15 May 1987, p. 30.
26 Food and Agriculture Organisation. *The State of Food and Agriculture 1984.* Rome: FAO, 1985, pp. 38–39.

27 Tor Sellstrom. 'Some Factors behind Nordic Relations with Southern Africa,' in Bertil Oden and Haroub Othman, eds. *Regional Cooperation in Southern Africa: A Post-apartheid Perspective*. Uppsala: Scandinavian Institute of African Studies, 1989, pp. 13–46.

28 Tom Ostergaard. 'Aiming Beyond Conventional Development Assistance: An Analysis of Nordic Aid to the SADCC Region.' CDR Working Paper 88.1, July 1988, pp. 13–14.

29 In more than one visit to factories in Mozambique, this author witnessed the result of direct sabotage by foreign corporations against Mozambique: a shipment of German cloth for a textile mill with crates full of shredded cloth and rocks (1979), and factories that had equipment 'repaired' by South African electricians or mechanics but when the machinery was run for a short time, the engines burned up or circuits destroyed (1986, 1988). At independence in 1975, the Boror Corporation loaded its full copra crop on four ships and simply sailed away with two million pounds sterling worth of harvest. Sena Sugar Estates (British) was only taken over by the Mozambican government in 1978 after it ran production down to one-third of pre-independence levels, owed 25 million pounds sterling to the Bank of Mozambique and two million pounds to foreigners. Unfortunately, examples like these abound in Southern African history. Joseph Hanlon. *Mozambique – The Revolution under Fire*. London: Zed Books, 1984, pp. 48, 65. See Dan Morgan, *op.cit.*, for how US grain corporations regularly cheat Third World countries which do not have the equipment to weigh the shipments received.

30 Tom Ostergaard, *op. cit.*, pp. 9, 71. DAC would include some non-Nordic countries in Western Europe and US.

31 SADCC. *Annual Progress Report*, July 1986–August 1987, pp. 110–12.

32 'Summary of Measures Implemented by the Nordic Countries against South Africa,' mimeo, January 1988. Trade with South Africa fell 75 percent in 1988; only Norway's imports were sustained because of purchases of South African manganese ore by the metal firm Elke, whose dispensation to continue trading extends to 1991. *Africa Economic Digest*, 5 June 1989, p. 16.

33 Barry Turner. *The Other European Community: Integration and Cooperation in Nordic Europe*. London: Weidenfeld and Nicolson, 1982, p. 173.

34 Joint Declaration on Expanded Economic and Cultural Cooperation between the Nordic Countries and the SADCC Member States, 29 January 1986.

35 *Africa Economic Digest*, 27 May 1988, p. 17.

36 *Africa Economic Digest*, 5 June 1989, p. 18.

37 *Financial Gazette*, 3 March 1989.

38 Calculated from trade table *Africa Economic Digest*, May 27, 1988, p. 19.

39 Helge Hveem. 'If Not Global, then (Inter-)Regional: The Mini-NIEO Alternative,' mimeo, March 1988, p. 9.

40 Kimmo Kiljunen. 'Nordic-SADCC Cooperation.' *Cooperation and Conflict* 22 (1987): 165.

41 SADDC. 'Response by SADCC Agricultural Ministers to Nordic and FAO Papers and other Donor Statements,' September 1984, pp. 1–2.

42 Hans Abrahamsson. 'Transport Structures and Dependency Relations in Southern Africa – The Need for a Reorientation of Nordic Aid.' Padrigu Papers, Gothenburg University, 1988, p. 29.

43 SADCC, *Industry and Trade, Mining, Tourism*, sector report for the annual conference, Arusha, Tanzania, 28–29 January 1988, p. 2.

44 Dr. G. Monekosso, Regional Director for Africa of WHO (World Health Organisation) has reported a reappearance of nutritional deficiency disorders, TB, meningitis, malaria, and yellow fever on the continent. *Herald* (Harare), 4 August 1987.

# Bibliography

Abrahamsson, Hans. 'Transport Structures and Dependency Relations in Southern Africa – The Need for a Reorientation of Nordic Aid.' Padrigu Papers, Gothenburg University, 1988.

Abregunrin, Olayiwola. 'Southern African Development Coordination Conference (SADCC): Towards Regional Integration of Southern Africa for Liberation,' *Current Bibliography on African Affairs.* 17:4 (1984–85): 363–384.

—— *Economic Dependence and Regional Cooperation in Southern Africa: SADCC and South Africa in Confrontation.* Lewiston: Edwin Mellen Press, 1990.

Adams, James. *The Unnatural Alliance: Israel and South Africa.* London: Quartet Books, 1984.

African Centre for Applied Research and Training in Social Development (ACARTSOD). *Understanding Africa's Food Problems: Social Policy Perspectives.* London: Hans Zell, 1990.

Ahmed, Raisuddin and Rustagi, Narendra. 'Agricultural Marketing and Price Incentives: A Comparative Study of African and Asian Countries,' Washington, DC: International Food Policy Research Institute, March 1985.

Ake, Claude. 'The Political Economy of Development: Does It Have A Future?' *International Social Science Journal*, no. 118 (November 1988): 485–97.

Allen, Mike and Goodison, Paul. 'British and European Aid to the Southern African Development Coordination Conference,' paper presented to conference on Peace and Development in the Front Line States, London, June 9, 1988.

Amin, Samir; Chitala, Derrick and Mandaza, Ibbo, eds. *SADCC: Prospects for Disengagement and Development in Southern Africa.* London: ZED Books, 1987.

Arrighi, Giovanni. 'Labour Supplies in Historical Perspective: A Study of the Proletarianization of the African Peasantry in Rhodesia,' *The Journal of Development Studies* 6:3 (April 1970): 197–234.

Association of West European Parliamentarians for Action against Apartheid (AWEPAA). 'SADCC and Its Partners – an Overview,' paper presented at conference on Southern Africa's Future: Europe's Role, Lusaka– Harare, March 23–30, 1988.

—— and CIIR. 'Southern Africa's Future: Europe's Role,' Background Papers for European Parliamentarians' Working Seminar on Support for SADCC, May 13–15, 1987.

Axline, W. Andrew. 'Underdevelopment, Dependence and Integration: the Politics of Regionalism in the Third World,' *International Organization* 31:1 (Winter 1977): 83–105.

Barry, Tom. *Roots of Rebellion: Land and Hunger in Central America.* Boston: South End Press, 1987.

Beinart, William. *The Political Economy of Pondoland 1860–1930.* Cambridge: Cambridge University Press, 1982.

Beit–Hallahmi, Benjamin. *The Israeli Connection – Who Israel Arms and Why.* New York: Pantheon, 1987.

Bender, Gerald J. 'Washington's Quest for Enemies in Angola.' *Regional Conflict and U.S. Policy: Angola and Mozambique.* Richard J. Bloomfield, ed. Algonac, Michigan: Reference Publications, Inc., 1988.

Berger, P. I. and Godsell, B. eds. *A Future South Africa – Visions, Strategies, and Realities*. Pretoria: Human & Rousseau and Tafelberg Publishers, 1988.

Bernstein, Henry; Crow, Ben; Mackintosh, Maureen; Martin, Charlotte, eds. *The Food Question – Profits versus People?* New York: Monthly Review Press, 1990.

Biermann, Werner and Wagao, Jumanne. 'The Quest for Adjustment: Tanzania and the IMF, 1980–1986,' *African Studies Review* 29:4 (December 1986): 89–103.

Blanpied, Nancy A., ed. *Farm Policy: The Politics of Soil, Surpluses, and Subsidies*. Washington, D.C.: Congressional Quarterly, Inc., 1984.

Bloomfield, Richard J. *Regional Conflict and U.S. Policy: Angola and Mozambique*. Algonac, Michigan: Reference Publications, 1988.

Boesen, Jannik *et al*, eds. *Tanzania: Crisis and Struggle for Survival*. Uppsala: Scandinavian Institute of African Studies, 1986.

Booth, Alan R. *Swaziland: Tradition and Change in A Southern African Kingdom*. Boulder: Westview, 1983.

Bonner, Philip L. 'Classes, the Mode of Production and the State in Pre-Colonial Swaziland.' *Economy and Society in Pre-Industrial South Africa*. Anthony Atmore and Shula Marks, eds. London: Longman, 1980.

Botswana, Republic of. *Sixth National Development Plan 1985/90*. Gaborone: Government of Botswana, 1985.

Bowen, Merle. 'Peasant Agriculture in Mozambique: The Case of Chokwe, Gaza Province,' mimeo, December 1987.

Bratton, Michael. 'Farmer Organizations in the Communal Areas of Zimbabwe,' *Working Paper 1/84*, Department of Land Management, University of Zimbabwe, 1984.

———'Financing Smallholder Production: A Comparison of Individual and Group Credit Schemes in Zimbabwe.' *Public Administraton and Development* 6:2 (1986).

Brown, B. 'The Impact of Male Labour Migration on Women in Botswana,' *African Affairs* 82:328 (July 1983): 367–88.

Bundy, Colin. *The Rise and Fall of the South African Peasantry*. Berkeley: University of California Press, 1979.

Burbach, Roger and Flynn, Patricia. *Agribusiness in the Americas*. New York: Monthly Review Press and North American Congress on Latin America (NACLA), 1980.

Burdette, Marcia. *Zambia – Between Two Worlds*. Boulder: Westview, 1988.

——— 'The Zimbabwean Fertilizer Industry: A Success Story for African Economic Development?' paper presented at African Studies Association Annual meeting, October 1988.

Buttel, Frederick H. 'Biotechnology and Agricultural Development in the Third World.' *The Food Question – Profits versus People?* Henry Bernstein *et al*., eds. New York: Monthly Review Press, 1990: 163–80.

Cawthra, Gavin. 'South Africa at War.' *South Africa in Question*. John Lonsdale, ed. Cambridge: University of Cambridge African Studies Centre and London: James Currey, 1988.

Centro de Estudos Africanos, Universidade Eduardo Mondlane. 'Re-Structuring the Southern African Region: Research Support for the SADCC Strategy,' paper presented at conference on Priorities in Southern Africa, Roma, Lesotho, November 23–27, 1981.

Chapin, Jim. 'The US in the Third World.' *Food Monitor* no. 36 (Spring 1987): 35.

Cheru, Fantu. 'Debt and Famine in Africa,' *Africa and the World* 1:1 (October 1987): 1–9.

———'Development, Debt and Dependency,' *Multinational Monitor* (July–August 1988): 15–18.

Chomsky, Noam. 'The Tasks Ahead I,' *Zeta* (May 1989): 24–32.

Clarke, Duncan G. *Agricultural and Plantation Workers in Rhodesia*. Gwelo: Mambo Press, 1977.

——— *Foreign Companies and International Investment in Zimbabwe*. London: Catholic Institute for International Relations, March 1980.

———'Economic Linkages in Southern Africa,' mimeo, Geneva, April 1982.

Clarkson, Fred. 'Privatizing the War,' *CovertAction*, no. 22 (1984): 31–3.

Cliffe, Lionel. 'Zimbabwe's Agricultural "Success" and Food Security in Southern Africa.' *Review of African Political Economy*. no. 43 (1988): 4–25.

Cock, Jacklyn and Nathan, Laurie, eds. *War and Society: The Militarization of South Africa*. Cape Town: David Phillip, 1989.

Cohcrane, E.D.D.; Ndlela, Dan and Riddell, Roger. *Study of the Manufacturing Sector in Zimbabwe*, Main Report, Vol. II, DP/ZIM/84/018, prepared for the Zimbabwe Government by UNIDO, September 12, 1985.

Cohen, Robin. *The New Helots: Migrants in the International Division of Labour*. Aldershot: Gower Publishing Co., Ltd., 1987.

Congressional Quarterly. *Farm Policy: The Politics of Soil, Surpluses, and Subsidies*. Washington, DC: Congressional Quarterly, 1984.

Crush, Jonathan S. 'The Colonial Division of Space: The Significance of the Swaziland Land Partition.' *International Journal of African Historical Studies* 13:1 (1980): 71–86.

————— 'Landlords, Tenants and Colonial Social Engineers: the Farm Labour Question in early Colonial Swaziland.' *Journal Of Southern African Studies* 11:2 (April 1985): 235–57.

Danaher, Kevin. 'Can the Free Market Solve Africa's Food Crisis?' *TransAfrica Forum* 4, (Summer 1987): 3–16.

—————, Berryman, Phillip and Benjamin, Medea. *Help or Hindrance? United States Economic Aid in Central America*. San Francisco: Institute for Food and Development, 1987.

Daniel, John. 'The Political Economy of Colonial and Post-Colonial Swaziland.' *South African Labour Bulletin* 7:6 (April 1982): 90–113.

—————.'South Africa and a BLS State: The Case of Swaziland,' paper presented at seminar on Dependency Relations and Development Assistance for Economic Independence in Southern Africa, Odelgarden, Sweden, April 1985.

————— and Vilane, Johnson. 'The Crisis of Political Legitimacy in Swaziland,' *Review of African Political Economy*, no. 35 (May 1986): 54–67.

Darch, Colin. 'Are There Warlords in Provinical Mozambique? Questions of the Social Base of MNR Banditry,' *Review of African Political Economy* 45/46 (1989): 34–49.

Davids, C.W. 'The Impact of Economic Sanctions Against South Africa on the SADCC States,' paper written for the Government of Canada, February 17, 1986.

Davies, Rob and Moyo, Nelson. 'Dimensions of Africa's Economic Crisis,' *Zimbabwe Journal of Economics* (1987): 62–80.

Davies, Robert. *South African Strategy Towards Mozambique in the Post-Nkomati Period: A Critical Analysis of Effects and Implications*. Quebec: Centre d'Information et de Documentation sur le Mozambique et l'Afrique Australe (CIDMAΛ), 1985.

————— 'South Africa Regional Policy in the Emerging Conjuncture: An Analysis of the Trend Toward Regional Militarism,' paper presented at conference on 'Security and Development in Southern Africa,' Paris, February 1986.

————— and O'Meara, Dan. 'The State of Analysis of the Southern African Region: Issues Raised by South African Strategy,' *Review of African Political Economy*. no. 29 (July 1984).

—————, O'Meara, Dan and Dlamini, Sipho. *The Kingdom of Swaziland*. London: Zed Press, 1985.

Debt Crisis Network. *From Debt to Development*. Washington, D.C. Institute for Policy Studies, 1985.

Dinham, Barbara and Hines, Colin. *Agribusiness in Africa*. London: Earth Resources, Ltd., 1983.

Dunman, Jack. *Agriculture: Capitalist and Socialist*. London: Lawrence and Wishart, 1975.

Dzarasov, Soltan S. 'Socio-Political Aspects of the Rise of Different Types of Integration,' in *Economic Integration: Concepts, Theories and Problems*, Mihaly Simai and Katalin Garam, eds. Budapest: Akademiai Kisado, 1977.

Egero, Bertil. *Mozambique: A Dream Undone – The Political Economy of Democracy, 1975–84*. Uppsala: Scandinavian Institute of African Studies, 1987.

Eicher, Carl. 'Agricultural Research for African Development: Problems and Priorities for 1985–2000,' paper presented at World Bank Conference on Research Priorities for Sub-Saharan Africa, Bellagio, February 25 – March 1, 1985.

————— and Rukuni, Mandivamba, eds. *Food Security for Southern Africa*. Harare: University of Zimbabwe/Michigan State University, February 1987.

Emmerich, Dirk and Hans-Ulrich, Walter. 'Subregional Cooperation in Southern Africa. Formation, Evolution and Prospects of SADCC,' mimeo, Karl Marx University, Leipzig, February 1985.

Evans, M. 'The Front-Line States, South Africa and Southern African Security: Military Prospects and Perspectives,' *Zambezia* (The University of Zimbabwe) 12 (1984–85).

Ezeani, Eboh C. 'An Appraisal of the African Debt Burden,' *Africa and the World* 1:2 (January 1988): 24–34.

Faulwetter, Helmut. 'The Concept of Increased Economic Relations among Developing Countries.' *Marxist Views on the Transformation of the International Economic Order. Asia, Africa, Latin America*, special issue 11. Helmut Faulwetter and Peter Stier, eds. Berlin: Akademie-Verlag, 1983.

Fauvet, Paul. 'The Roots of Counter-Revolution: The Mozambique National Resistance,' *Review of African Political Economy*, 29 (July 1984): 108–21.

Food and Agriculture Organization, United Nations. *SADCC Agriculture Toward 2000*. Rome: FAO, 1984.

————*The State of Food and Agriculture 1984*. Rome: FAO, 1985.

————'Policy Options Paper for Agrarian Reform in Zimbabwe,' 1985.

————Committee on World Food Security. 'Transnational Corporations in Food and Agriculture, Forestry and Fishery Sectors in Developing Countries,' CFS: 87/6, February 1987.

Frankel, Philip H. *Pretoria's Praetorians*. Cambridge: Cambridge University Press, 1984.

Frobel, Folker; Heinrichs, Jurgen, and Kreye, Otto. 'Changing Patterns of World Market Integration in Third World Countries,' paper presented at Conference on Economic Policies under Crisis Conditions, University of Zimbabwe, 2–5 September 1985.

Gakou, Mohamed Lamine. *The Crisis in African Agriculture*. London: Zed Books, 1987.

Geldenhuys, Deon. 'Some Strategic Implications of Regional Economic Relations for RSA,' *ISSUP Strategic Review*, University of Pretoria (January 1981).

————'Destabilization Controversy in Southern Africa,' *South Africa Forum Position Paper*. 5: 18 (1982).

————'South Africa's Regional Policy,' paper presented at conference on Regional Cooperation The Record and Outlook, South African Institute of International Affairs, 6–7 March 1984.

————*The Diplomacy of Isolation: South African Foreign Policy Making*. Johannesburg: Macmillan South Africa, 1984.

George, Susan. *Ill Fares the Land*. Washington, DC: Institute for Policy Studies, 1984.

Gersony, Robert. 'Summary of Mozambican Refugee Accounts of Principally Conflict-Related Experience in Mozambique: Report submitted to Ambassador Jonathan Moore and Dr. Chester A. Crocker.' Washington: Department of State Bureau for Refugee Programs, April 1988.

Gervasi, Sean. 'U.S. and South Africa Foment Terrorist Wars,' *CovertAction*, no. 22 (Fall 1984): 36–40.

Gifford, Tony. *South Africa's Record of International Terrorism*. London: Anti-Apartheid Movement, 1981.

Granberg, Per *et al*. 'SADCC Intra-Regional Trade Study,' Bergen: Chr. Michelsen Institute, January 1986.

Green, Reginold Herbold. 'Consolidation and Accelerated Development of African Agriculture: What Agenda for Action?' *African Studies Review* 27:4 (December 1984): 17–34.

————— and Thompson, Carol B. 'Political Economies in Conflict: SADCC, South Africa and Sanctions.' *Destructive Engagement*. David Martin and Phyllis Johnson, eds. Harare: Zimbabwe Publishing House, 1986.

————— *et al*. 'Children in Southern Africa,' *Children on the Front Line*. New York: UNICEF, 1987 and 1989.

Gruhn, Isebill V. 'The Recolonization of Africa: International Organizations on the March,' *Africa Today* (4th quarter, 1983): 37–48.

Grundy, Kenneth W. *The Militarization of South African Politics.* 2nd edition. Oxford: Oxford University Press, 1988.

Gutman, Roy. 'Nicaragua: America's Diplomatic Charade,' *Foreign Policy*, no. 56 (1984).

Haarlov, Jens. *Regional Cooperation in Southern Africa: Central Elements of the SADCC Venture.* CDR Research Report No. 14. Copenhagen: Centre for Development Research, 1988.

Hackel, Joy and Siegel, Daniel. *In Contempt of Congress – The Reagan Record on Central America.* Washington, DC: Institute for Policy Studies, 1985 and 1987.

Hamilton, Martha. *The Great Grain Robbery and Other Stories.*Washington, DC: Agribusiness Accountability Project, 1972.

Hanlon, Joseph. *Mozambique: The Revolution Under Fire.* London: Zed Books, 1984.

————. *SADDC: Progress, Projects and Prospects.* London: Economist Intelligence Unit, 1984.

————. *Beggar Your Neighbors: Apartheid Power in Southern Africa.* Bloomington: Indiana University Press, 1986.

————. *SADCC and Sanctions.* Brussels: International Coaltion for Development Action, January 1989.

————. *SADCC in the 1990s – Development on the Frontline.* Special Report, No. 1158. London: The Economist Intelligence Unit, September 1989.

Harsch, Ernest. *Apartheid's Great Land Theft: The Struggle for the Right to Farm in South Africa.* New York: Pathfinder Press, 1986.

Hayter, Teresa and Watson, Catharine. *AID: Rhetoric and Reality.* London: Pluto Press, 1985.

Heller, Peter S. *et al.* 'The Implications of Fund-Supported Adjustment Programs for Poverty,' Occasional Paper 58. Washington, DC: International Monetary Fund, 1988.

Henderson, Robert. 'The Food Weapon in Southern Africa,' paper presented at the Congress on Development and Destabilization in Southern Africa, National University of Lesotho, 17–20 October 1983.

Herwig, Rudolph. 'SADCC, Mozambique, RSA: A Trilateral Formula for the Future?' *Bulletin* (African Institute of South Africa) 24:2 (1984): 13–17.

Hightower, Jim. *Eat Your Heart Out: How Food Profiteers Victimize the Consumer.* New York: Crown, 1975.

Hill, Christopher. 'Regional Cooperation in Southern Africa,' *African Affairs* 32:327 (1983).

Hippler, Jochen. 'Low-Intensity Warfare: Key Strategy for the Third World Theater,' *Middle East Report* (January–February, 1987): 32–8.

Hoogvelt, Ankie. 'The Crime of Conditionality: Open Letter to the Managing Director of the International Monetary Fund,' *Review of African Political Economy*, no. 38 (April 1987): 80–5.

Houser, George. *No One Can Stop the Rain: Glimpses of Africa's Liberation Struggle.* New York: Pilgrim Press, 1989.

Hunter, Jane. *Israeli Foreign Policy: South Africa and Central America.* Boston: South End Press, 1987.

Hussain, Athar and Tribe, Keith. *Marxism and the Agrarian Question.* London: Macmillan, 1983.

Hveem, Helge. 'If Not Global, then (Inter-)Regional: The Mini-NIEO Alternative.' Mimeo, March 1988.

'Inside the Shadow Government,' Declaration of Plaintiffs' Counsel, filed by the Christic Institute, US District Court, Miami, 31 March 1988.

International Development Research Centre. 'Reports and Recommendations on SADCC Regional Food Security Projects 6 and 7,' Ottawa, Canada, January 1982.

Isaacman, Allen. 'Chiefs, Rural Differentiation and Peasant Protest: The Mozambican Forced Cotton Regime 1938–1961,' *African Economic History* 14 (1985): 16–56.

————and Michael Stephen *et al.*, ' "Cotton is the Mother of Poverty": Peasant Resistance to Forced Cotton Production in Mozambique, 1938–1961,' *International Journal of African Historical Studies* 13:4 (1980): 581–615.

———— and Isaacman, Barbara. 'Mozambique: In Pursuit of Nonalignment.' *Africa Report* 28:3 (May–June 1983): 47–54.

————. *Mozambique: From Colonialism to Revolution* (Harare: Zimbabwe Publishing House, 1985).

Ivon, David. 'Touting for South Africa: International Freedom Foundation,' *Covert Action*, no. 31 (Winter 1989): 62–4.

Jackson, J.C.; Collier, P. and Conti, A. 'Rural Development Policies and Food Security in Zimbabwe, Part II,' Geneva: Employment and Development Department, International Labour Office, 1987.

Jafee, Georgina. 'The Southern African Development Coordination Conference (SADCC),' *South Africa Review I*. Johannesburg: Raven Press, 1983, pp. 23–32.

Jaster, Robert S. *A Regional Security Role for Africa's Front-Line States: Experience and Prospects*. London: International Institute for Strategic Studies, Spring 1983.

————. *South Africa and its Neighbours: the Dynamics of Regional Conflict*. London: Institute for Strategic Studies, Summer 1986.

Johnson, Williard R. 'Optimists and Pessimists: Reflections on Africa's Economic Plight,' *TransAfrica* 5:2 (Winter 1988): 55–67.

Jolly, Richard and Giovanni, Andrea Cornia. *The Impact of World Recession on Children*. Oxford: Pergamon Press, 1984.

Jourdan, Paul. 'The Minerals Industry of Mozambique,' *Raw Materials Report*, University of Zimbabwe, 1986.

————'The Effects of South African Destabilization on Mining in the States of SADCC.' *Raw Materials Report* 5:1 (1987): 42–53.

Kalyalya, Denny *et al*, eds. *Aid and Development in Southern Africa*. Trenton, NJ: Africa World Press, 1988.

Karmiloff, Igor. 'Zambia,' in Roger Riddell, ed. *Manufacturing Africa*. London: James Currey, 1990: 297–336.

Kaunga, Ephraim and Rose, Tore. 'Case Study on SADCC Project 3.7.1. Development of Navigation on Lake Niassa/Nyasa/Malawi.' OECD Development Centre/SADCC Secretariat Joint Research Report (20 March 1987).

Kiljunen, Kimmo. 'Nordic-SADCC Cooperation.' *Cooperation and Conflict* 22 (1987).

Kingsbury, David S. 'Potential Incentive Effects of Pricing Policy on Agricultural Trade in Several SADCC Countries: Preliminary Results,' paper presented for conference on Food Security Research in Southern Africa, Harare, 31 October – 3 November 1988.

Knudsen, Odin; Nash, John *et al*. *Redefining the Role of Government in Agriculture for the 1990s*. World Bank Discussion Papers 105. Washington, DC: The World Bank, 1990.

Koester, Ulrich. 'Regional Cooperation to Improve Food Security in Southern and Eastern African Countries,' Research Report no. 53, International Food Policy Research Institute (IFPRI), July 1986.

Kumar, Andrej; Fischinger, Zdenka Ban; and Nemanic, Milojka. *Primary Commodities, Countertrade and Cooperation among Developing Countries*. Ljubljana, Yugoslavia: Research Centre for Cooperation with Developing Countries, 1984.

Kwarteng, Charles. 'Difficulties in Regional Economic Integration: The Case of ECOWAS,' *TranAfrica* 5:2 (Winter 1988): 17–25.

Lappé, Frances Moore and Beccar-Varela, Adele. *Mozambique and Tanzania: Asking the Big Questions*. San Francisco: Institute for Food and Development Policy, 1980.

————, Collins, Joseph and Kinley, David. *Aid As Obstacle*. San Francisco: Institute for Food and Development, 1980.

Lebayle, Henri. 'Continuité et Ambiguités d'une Cooperation Economique regionale en Afrique Australe,' *Année Africaine* (1982): 273–307.

Lee, Margaret C. *SADCC: The Political Economy of Development in Southern Africa*. Nashville: Winston-Derek Publishers, Inc., 1989.

Leo, Christopher. *Land and Class in Kenya*. Toronto: University of Toronto Press, 1984.

Lewis, Stephen R. *The Economics of Apartheid*. New York: Council on Foreign Relations Press, 1989.

Livingstone, Ian. 'Agricultural Development Strategy and Agricultural Pricing Policy in Malawi.' *Marketing Boards in Tropical Africa*. Kwame Arhin *et al*, eds. London: KPI, 1985.

Lockwood, Edgar. *South Africa's Moment of Truth*. New York: Friendship Press, 1988.

Low, Allan. *Agricultural Development in Southern Africa: Farm-Household Economics and the Food Crisis*. London: James Currey, 1986.

Maasdorp, Gavin. *SADCC – A Post-Nkomati Evaluation*. Graamfontein: South Africa Institute of International Affairs, August 1984.

Mafeje, Archie. 'Food Production and Agrarian Systems in Southern Africa,' paper presented at conference, Another Development for Africa, Maseru, 18–22 November 1985.

Magaia, Lina. *Dumba Nengue: Run for Your Life – Peasant Tales of Tragedy in Mozambique*. Trenton, New Jersey: Africa World Press, 1988.

Maharaj, Mac. 'Internal Determinants of Pretoria's Present Foreign Policy,' paper given at seminar in memory of Aquino de Bragança and Ruth First, Universidade Eduardo Mondlane, Maputo, 21–22 January 1988.

Mahjoub, Azzam, ed. *Adjustment or De-Linking? The African Experience*. London: ZED, 1990.

Makgetla, Neva Seidman. 'Theoretical and Practical Implications of IMF Conditionality in Zambia,' *Journal of Modern African Studies* 24:2 (1986).

Mandaza, Ibbo, ed. *Zimbabwe: The Political Economy of Transition 1980–1986*. Dakar: Codesria, 1986.

Marshall, Johnathan; Dale, Peter Scott and Hunter, Jane. *The Iran Contra Connection-Secret Teams and Covert Operations in the Reagan Era*. Boston: South End Press, 1987.

Martin, David and Johnson, Phyllis, eds. *Destructive Engagement*. Harare: Zimbabwe Publishing House, 1986.

Martin, Roger. 'Regional Security in Southern Africa,' *Survival* 29:5 (September/October 1987): 387–402.

Martin, Willian G. and Wallerstein, Immanuel. 'Southern Africa in the World-Economy 1870–2000: Strategic Problems in World-Historic Perspective,' in *Breaking the Links*, Robert E. Mazur, ed. Trenton, New Jersey: Africa World Press, 1990, pp. 99–108.

Mason, Edward and Asher, Robert E. *The World Bank Since Bretton Woods*. Washington, D.C.: The Brookings Institution, 1973.

Matthews, Jacqueline. 'Economic Integration in Southern Africa: Progress or Decline?' *South African Journal of Economics* 52:3 (September 1984): 256–65.

Mazur, Robert E., ed. *Breaking the Links: Development Theory and Practice in Southern Africa*. Trenton, New Jersey: Africa World Press, 1990.

Mbilinyi, Marjorie. 'Agribusiness and Casual Labour in Tanzania,' *African Economic History* 16 (1986).

————.'Structural Adjustment, Agribusiness and Rural Women in Tanzania,' *The Food Question – Profits versus People?* Henry Bernstein *et al.*, eds. New York: Monthly Review Press, 1990: 111–24.

McFadden, Patricia. 'Women and Wage Labour in Swaziland: A Focus on Agriculture.' *South African Labour Bulletin* 7:6 (April 1982): 140–66.

————.'The State and Agri-business in Swazi Economy,' *The State and Agriculture in Africa*. Thandika Mkandawire and Naceur Bourenane, eds. Dakar: Codesria, 1987, pp. 87–116.

Mellor, John. M. 'The Changing World Food Situation – A CGIAR Perspective,' *Annual Report 1984*. Washington: IFPRI, pp. 7–14.

Mengisteab, Kidane. 'Food Shortages in Africa: A Critique of Existing Agricultural Strategies,' *Africa Today* 32:4 (1985): 39–54.

Metz, Steven. 'Pretoria's "Total Strategy" and Low-Intensity Warfare in Southern Africa.' *Comparative Strategy* 6:4 (1987): 437–69.

Mhina, A.K. and Munishi, G.K. 'The Social Impact of Food Policies in Tanzania and Mozambique,' African Centre for Applied Research and Training in Social Development (ACARTSOD). *Understanding Africa's Food Problems: Social Policy Perspectives*. London: Hans Zell, 1990: 123–72.

Mhone, Guy C.Z. 'Agriculture and Food Policy in Malawi: A Review,' *The State and Agriculture in Africa*. Thandika Mkandawire and Naceur Bourenane, eds. Dakar: Codesria, 1987, pp. 59–86.

Minter, William. *King Solomon's Mines Revisited: Western Interests and the Burdened*

*History of Southern Africa.* New York: Basic Books, 1986.
————ed. *Operation Timber: Pages from the Savimbi Dossier.* Trenton, NJ: Africa World Press, 1988.
————'The Mozambique National Resistance as described by ex-participants,' mimeo (March 1989).
Mittelman, James H. *Out from Underdevelopment – Prospects for the Third World.* New York: St. Martin's Press, 1988.
Mkandawire, Thandika and Bourenane, Naceur, eds. *The State and Agriculture in Africa.* Dakar: Codesria, 1987.
Mondlane, Eduardo. *The Struggle for Mozambique.* London: Zed Books, reprinted 1983.
Montsi, Sam and van Arkadie, Brian. 'Case Study on SADCC Project 3.0.2 – The Sorghum-Millet Improvement Programme,' OECD Development Centre/SADCC Secretariat Joint Research Study, March 1987.
Morgan, Dan. *Merchants of Grain.* New York: Viking, 1979.
Mosha, A.C. 'Sorghum and Sorghum Products for Better Food Security and Income,' *SADCC Post Production Systems Newsletter,* no. 10 (October 1988):16–23.
Mota Lopez, José. 'The MNR: Opponents or Bandits?' *Africa Report* (January–February 1986).
Moyana, H. V. *The Political Economy of Land in Zimbabwe.* Harare: Mambo Press, 1984.
Moyo, Sam; Moyo, Nelson and Lowenson, Rene. 'The Root Causes of Hunger in Zimbabwe,' paper presented to conference on Churches' Drought Action in Africa, Geneva, September 1985.
Mozambique, People's Republic of. *Economic Report.* Maputo, January 1984.
————Comissão Nacional do Plano. *Informação Estatistica, 1975–1984.* May 1985.
————Ministry of Health. 'The Impact on Health in Mozambique of South African Destabilization,' March 1987.
————*Mid-Term Evaluation of the 1988–1989 Emergency Appeal, 30 April – 31 October 1988.*
MPLA-PT of Angola. *Pela Paz é Segurança Internacional.* Luanda: Imprensa Nacional, 1986.
Msambichaka, L.A. 'State Policies and Food Production in Tanzania,' *The State and Agriculture in Africa.* Thandika Mkandawire and Naceur Bourenane, eds. Dakar: Codesria, 1987, pp. 117–143.
Mumbengegwi, Clever. 'The Political Economy of a Small Farmer Agricultural Strategy in SADCC,' paper presented at conference of Overseas Development Council, Washington, D.C., 24–26 September 1986.
————'Food And Agricultural Cooperation in the SADCC: Progress, Problems and Prospects.' *SADCC: Prospects for Disengagement and Development in Southern Africa.* Samir Amin *et al.,* eds. London: Zed Books, 1987.
Munslow, Barry, *et al.* 'Effects of World Recession and Crisis on SADCC,' Review of Africa Political Economy Conference, University of Keele, September 1984.
Murray, Colin. 'Explaining Migration: the Tradition in Eastern and Southern Africa,' unpublished paper, University of London, Institute of Commonwealth Studies, 1979.
————*Families Divided: The Impact of Migrant Labour in Lesotho.* New York: Cambridge University Press, 1981.
Musoke, I.K.S. 'Capitalist Penetration and the Underdevelopment of African Peasant Agriculture: Swaziland, Southern Rhodesia, Nyasaland,' in African Centre for Applied Research and Training in Social Development (ACARTSOD). *Understanding Africa's Food Problems: Social Policy Perspectives,* London: Hans Zell, 1990: 22–60.
Mwakasungula, A.K. *The Rural Economy of Malawi: A Critical Analysis.* Bergen: The Chr. Michelsen Institute, 1984.
NACLA Report. *Debt: Latin America Hangs in the Balance* 19:2 (1985).
Naik, D.M. 'Production and Research on Grain Legumes in SADCC Countries,' paper presented at conference on Food Security Research in Southern Africa, Harare, 31 October – 3 November 1988.
National Security Archive, *The Chronology – The Documented Day-by-Day Account of*

the Secret Military Assistance to Iran and the Contras. New York: Warner Books, 1987.

Nesbitt, Prexy. 'Terminators, Crusaders and Gladiators: Western (private and public) Support for Renamo and Unita,' *Review of African Political Economy*, no. 43 (1988): 111–23.

Non-Aligned Countries. 'The African Economic Crisis: An Agenda for Action,' New Delhi: Research and Information System for the Non-Aligned Countries, 1986.

North American Congress on Latin America (NACLA). 'U.S. Grain Arsenal,' *Latin America and Empire Report* 9:7 (October 1975).

————'Bitter Fruits,' *Latin America and Empire Report* (September 1976).

Obasanjo, Olusegun. 'Southern Africa: the Security of the Front-Line States,' Report of a Special Mission, Commonwealth Secretariat, June 1988.

Oden, Bertil and Othman, Haroub, eds. *Regional Cooperation in Southern Africa: A Post-apartheid Persepective*. Uppsala: Scandinavian Institute of African Studies, 1989.

O'Keefe, Phil, ed. *Regional Restructuring under Advanced Capitalism*. London: Croom Helm, 1984.

————and Munslow, Barry. eds. *Energy and Development in Southern Africa – SADCC Country Studies*. Uppsala: Scandinavian Institute of African Studies, 1984.

O'Meara, Dan. 'Pretoria's Strategy in South and Southern Africa,' paper presented at conference on Peace and Security in Southern Africa, Mohonk Mountain House, New York, 7–9 December 1984.

————'Destabilization of the Frontline States of Southern Africa, 1980–1987,' Background Paper, no. 20, Canadian Institute for International Peace and Security (July 1988).

Onwuka, R. I. and Sesay, A. *The Future of Regionalism in Africa*. London: Macmillan, 1984.

Opie, John. *The Law of the Land: Two Hundred Years of American Farmland Policy*. Omaha: University of Nebraska Press, 1988.

Organization for Economic Co-operation and Development (OECD) Development Centre and the Southern African Development Coordination Conference (SADCC) Secretariat. 'Joint Study of Structures and Procedures in Development Co-operation,' March 1987.

Ostendorf, David L. 'Who Will Control Rural America?' *Christianity and Crisis* (May 2, 1988): 156–159.

Ostergaard, Tom. 'Aiming Beyond Conventional Development Assistance: An Analysis of Nordic Aid to the SADCC Region.' CDR Working Paper 88.1. Copenhagen: Centre for Development Research, July 1988.

————'Industrial Development in Southern Africa and the Role of SADCC.' CDR Working Paper 89.4. Copenhagen: Centre for Development Research, November 1989.

Ottaway, David and Marina. *Afrocommunism*. New York: Holmes and Meier, 1981.

Palmer, Robin. *Land and Racial Discrimination in Rhodesia*. London: Heinemann, 1977.

————and Parsons, Neil. *The Roots of Rural Poverty in Central and Southern Africa*. London: Heinemann, 1977.

Parkinson, J.R. ed. *Poverty and Aid*. London: Basil Blackwell, 1983.

Parson, Jack. 'The Potential for South African Sanctions Busting in Southern Africa: The Case of Botswana,' paper presented at the annual meeting of the African Studies Association, 19–22 November 1987.

Payer, Cheryl. 'Repudiating the Past' *NACLA Report* 19:2 (1985): 14–24.

Peet, Richard. *Manufacturing Industry and Economic Development in the SADCC Countries*. New York: Holmes and Meier, 1984.

Penaherrera, Germanico Salgado. 'Viable Integration and the Economic Co-operation Problems of the Developing World,' *Journal of Common Market Studies* 19:1 (September 1980): 65–76.

Phinister, Ian. 'Peasant Production and Underdevelopment in Southern Rhodesia, 1890–1914, with particular reference to Victoria District.' *African Affairs* 73:291 (April 1974): 217–28.

————'Commodity Relations and Class Formation in the Zimbabwean Countryside, 1891–1920,' *The Journal of Peasant Studies* 13:4 (July 1986): 240–57.

————'Industrialization and Sub-Imperialism: Southern Rhodesia and South African

Trade Relations between the Wars,' paper presented at conference on Alternative Development Strategies in Africa, Oxford, September 1987.

Price, Robert M. 'Pax or Pox Pretoria?' *World Policy Journal* (Summer 1985): 534–54.

Quan, Julian. *Mozambique: A Cry for Peace*. Oxford: Oxfam, 1987.

Ratilal, Prakash. 'Mozambique – Overview of the Economy in the Last Ten Years,' November 1988.

Relief and Development Institute (London). 'A Study of Triangular Transactions and Local Purchases in Food Aid,' *World Food Programme Occasional Papers*, no. 11 (July 1987).

*Report of the Congressional Committees Investigating the Iran-Contra Affair*, abridged edition, New York: Times Books, 1988.

Riddell, Roger C. *The Land Problem in Rhodesia: Alternatives for the Future*. Harare: Mambo, 1978.

————*Foreign Aid Reconsidered*. Baltimore: Johns Hopkins Press, 1987.

————'The Regional Crisis,' *South Africa in Question*. John Lonsdale, ed. Cambridge: University of Cambridge African Studies Centre and London: James Currey, 1988.

————'Zimbabwe in the Frontline,' in Robert Edgar, ed. *Sanctioning Apartheid*. Trenton, NJ: Africa World Press, 1990.

————'Zimbabwe,' in Roger Riddell, ed. *Manufacturing Africa*. London: James Currey, 1990: 337–411.

Robertson, Ian. 'Biotechnology: Its Potential Impact on Food Security in Southern Africa,' paper presented at conference on Food Security Research in Southern Africa, Harare, 31 October – 3 November 1988.

Rohatyn, Felix. 'On the Brink,' *The New York Review*, June 11, 1987, pp. 2–5.

RONCO Consulting Corporation. 'Study of Trilateral Food Aid Transactions,' Report to USAID, April 28, 1987.

Rotberg, Robert I.; Bienen, Henry S.; Legvold, Robert and Maasdorp, Gavin G. *South Africa and Its Neighbors: Regional Security and Self-Interest*. Lexington, MA: Lexington Books, 1985.

Rukuni, Mandivamba. 'Irrigation Research Priorities for Southern Africa,' paper presented at conference on Food Security Research in Southern Africa, Harare, 31 October – 3 November 1988.

————and Eicher, Carl. 'The Food Security Equation in Southern Africa,' MSU International Development Papers, reprint no. 5, 1987.

Sanders, Jerry. 'Terminators,' *Mother Jones* (August–September 1983): 36–41.

————and Schwenninger, Sherle L. 'A New Grand Strategy: U.S. Policy toward the Third World,' *Post-Reagan America*. Archibald L. Gillies *et al.* eds. New York: World Policy Institute, 1987.

Saul, John. 'Socialist Transition and External Intervention: Mozambique and South Africa's War,' *Labour, Capital and Society* 18:1 (April 1985): 153–170.

Schmidt, Elizabeth. 'Ideology, Economics, and the Role of Shona Women in Southern Rhodesia, 1850–1939.' Ph.D. dissertation, University of Wisconsin, 1987.

Schultheis, Michael J. 'The World Bank and Accelerated Development: The Internationalization of Supply-Side Economics,' *African Studies Review* 27:4 (December 1984): 9–16.

Sefali, M. and van Rensburg, Patrick, with Davies, Robert. 'Applicability of Another Development to SADCC,' paper presented to seminar on Another Development for SADCC, 18–22 November 1985.

Selassie, Bereket Habte. 'The World Bank: Power and Responsibility in Historical Perspective,' *African Studies Review* 27:4 (December 1984): 35–46.

Sellstrom, Tor. 'Some Factors behind Nordic Relations with Southern Africa,' in Bertil Oden and Haroub Othman, eds. *Regional Cooperation in Southern Africa: A Post-apartheid Perspective*. Uppsala: Scandinavian Institute of African Studies, 1989: 13–46.

Shapiro, Kenneth H. 'The Limits of Policy Reform in African Agricultural Development: A Comment on the World Bank's Agenda,' *Rural Africana* nos. 19–20 (Spring–Fall 1984): 63–8.

Shivji, Issa G. 'Introduction: The Transformation of the State and the Working People.' *The*

*State and the Working People in Tanzania.* Issa G. Shivji, ed. Dakar: Codesria, 1985.

————*Law, State and the Working Class in Tanzania.* London: James Currey and Dar es Salaam: Tanzania Publishing House, 1986.

'South Africa Imposes Sanctions Against Neighbours,' pamphlet prepared for the Eighth Summit of the Non-Aligned Movement (NAM), Zimbabwe, 1986. Harare: Southern African Research and Documentation Centre, September 1986.

Southall, Roger. 'Post-Apartheid South Africa. Constraints on Socialism,' *Journal of Modern African Studies* 25:2 (1987): 354–74.

Seidman, A.; Ndoro, H.; Zwizwai, B.; Austin, G. and Oforma, J. 'Transnational Corporations and the Sugar Trade: The Zimbabwe Case,' mimeo, University of Zimbabwe, November 1982.

Simbi, Iddi and Wells, Francis. *Development Cooperation in Southern Africa – Structures and Procedures.* Paris: OECD, 1984.

Sketchley, Peter and Lappé, Frances Moore. *Casting New Molds.* San Francisco: Institute for Food and Development, 1980.

Smith, Wayne. 'A Trap in Angola,' *Foreign Policy* 62 (Spring 1986): 61–74.

Southern African Development Coordination Conference (SADCC). *From Dependence and Poverty Toward Economic Liberation,* Blantyre: SADCC, 1981.

————'Report and Recommendations on SADCC Regional Food Security. Projects 6 and 7 [Post Harvest Loss and Food Processing].' International Development Research Centre, Ottawa, consultant. January 1982.

————*Agricultural Research Resource Assessment in the SADCC Countries,* I and II. Gaborone: Consultative Technical Committee for Agricultural Research, SADCC, 1985.

————'SADCC in the Context of the Lagos Plan of Action,' paper presented to the Organization of African Unity, Addis Ababa, 18–19 July 1985.

————*Macro-Economic Survey.* Gaborone: SADCC, September 1985.

————*Annual Progress Report, July 1985–August 1986.*

————*Food and Agriculture,* sector report presented at annual conference, Harare, Zimbabwe, 30–31 January 1986.

————*Industry,* sector report presented at annual conference, Harare, Zimbabwe, 30–31 January 1986.

————*Macro-Economic Survey.* Report on the Lilongwe Workshop, 25–27 August 1986.

————*Investment Policies and Mechanism of SADCC Countries.* Dar es Salaam: SADCC Industry and Trade Coordination Division, December 1986.

————*Annual Progress Report, July 1986–August 1987* and *1988–89.*

————*Food, Agriculture, and Natural Resources,* sector report presented at annual conference, Gaborone, Botswana, 5–6 February 1987.

————*SADCC: Investment in Production,* report presented at annual conference, Gaborone, Botswana, 5–6 February 1987.

————'SADCC 1987: Gaborone,' Report of the Seminar for Businessmen held in Gaborone, Botswana, 4 February 1987.

————*Industry and Trade, Mining, Tourism,* sector report for the annual conference, Arusha, Tanzania, 28–29 January 1988.

————*Workshop on Rehabilitation and Upgradation of Priority Industries in the SADCC Region – Objectives, Rationale, Approach.* Arusha, Tanzania, 27–29 August 1988.

————*Food, Agriculture, and Natural Resources,* sector report for annual conference, Luanda, People's Republic of Angola, 1–3 February 1989.

————Council of Ministers Meeting, Lusaka, Zambia, 29–30 January 1990.

————*Food, Agriculture, and Natural Resources,* sector report for annual conference, Lusaka, Zambia, 1–2 February 1990.

Stanning, Jayne L. 'Contribution of Smallholder Agriculture to Marketed Output in Zimbabwe 1970–85; Recent Experience and Some Future Research,' Working Paper 5, Department of Land Management, University of Zimbabwe, 1985.

Starnberger Institute for Research into Global Structures, Development and Crises

(Munich). 'Economic Implications of Sanctions Against South Africa,' paper commissioned by the Evangelical Church in Germany (FRG), July 1987.

Stevens, Richard P. and Elmessiri, Abdelwahab M. *Israel and South Africa: The Progression of a Relationship.* New Jersey: North American, 1977.

Stoneman, Colin. 'An Indicative Regional Plan for the Industrial Development of SADCC, 1987–2000,' Preliminary Report, Commonwealth, January 1987.

————, ed. *Zimbabwe's Prospects.* London: Macmillan, 1988.

———— and Cliffe, Lionel. *Zimbabwe: Politics, Economics and Society.* London: Printer Publishers, 1989.

Strange, Susan. 'Protectionism and World Politics,' *Internatioinal Organization* 39:2 (Spring 1985): 233–59.

Suckling, John and White, Landeg, eds. *After Apartheid: Renewal of the South African Economy.* London: James Currey, 1988.

Sweta, W. *et al.* 'The Minerals Sector of the States of SADCC: Possibilities for a Regional Minerals Policy,' mimeo, Lusaka: SADCC Mining Sector Coordination Unit, 1988.

*Third World Quarterly* 9:2 (1987). Special 'After Apartheid' Issue.

Thompson, Carol B. *Challenge to Imperialism: The Frontline States in the Liberation of Zimbabwe.* Harare: Zimbabwe Publishing House, 1985 and Boulder: Westview Press, 1986.

————'Regional Economic Policy under Crisis Conditions: the case of Agriculture within SADCC,' *Journal of Southern African Studies,* 13:1 (October 1986): 82–100.

————'Cooperation for Survival: Western Interests vs. SADCC,' *Issue* 26:1 (1987): 30–36.

————'Zimbabwe in SADCC: A Question of Dominance?' *Zimbabwe's Prospects.* Colin Stoneman, ed. London: Macmillan, 1988.

————'War by Another Name: Destabilization in Nicaragua and Mozambique.' *Race and Class* 29:4 (1988): 21–44.

Tibaijuka, A. 'Planning for Agriculture,' *Macro-Economic Survey,* Report on the Lilongwe Workshop, SADCC, 25–27 August 1986, pp. 35–60.

Torrie, Jill, ed. *Banking on Poverty: The Global Impact of the IMF and World Bank.* Toronto: Between the Lines, 1983.

Tostensen, Arne. *Dependence and Collective Self-Reliance in Southern Africa.* Research Report No. 62. Uppsala: The Scandinavian Institute for African Studies, 1982.

Turner, Barry. *The Other European Community – Integration and Cooperation in Nordic Europe.* London: Weidenfeld and Nicolson, 1982.

Turok, Ben, ed. *Witness from the Frontline: Aggression and Resistance in Southern Africa.* London: Institute for African Alternatives, 1990.

UNICEF. *State of the World's Children 1986.* Oxford: Oxford University Press, 1985.

United Nations Industrial Development Organization (UNIDO). *Regional Co-operation: Experience and Perspective of ASEAN and the Andean Pact.* Vienna: UNIDO, 1986.

————'Industrial Cooperation Through SADCC,' 15 October 1985. United Nations General Assembly. Report of Secretary General. *Special Assistance to Front-Line States and Bordering States.* A/42/422/Add.1, 17 September 1987.

————42nd Session. Report of the Secretary-General. 'United Nations Programme of Action for African Economic Recovery and Development 1986–1990,' A/42/560, 1 October 1987.

United Nations Economic Commission for Africa. 'African Alternative Framework to Structural Adjustment Programmes for Socio-Economic Recovery and Transformation,' E/ECA/CM.15/6/Rev.3, 21 June 1989.

United Nations General Assembly, Report of the Secretary–General, 'Special Assistance to front-line States and bordering States,' Addendum, A/42/422/add.1, 17 September 1987.

United States Department of Agriculture. *A Time to Choose: Summary Report on the Structure of Agriculture.* Washington, D.C.: USDA, January 1981.

United States Department of State, 'An Initiative for Economic Progress in Southern Africa,' 29 January 1987.

————Bureau for Refugee Programs (Robert Gersony, consultant), 'Summary of Mozambican Refugee Accounts of Principally Conflict-Related Experience in Mozambique,' April 1988.

United States General Accounting Office. Briefing Report to Congress. 'Agriculture Overview: U.S. Food/Agriculture in a Volatile World,' GAO/RCED-86-3BR, November 1985.

United States House of Representatives, Select Committee on Hunger. 'Humanitarian Needs in Angola – An Overview of Findings of Staff Delegation to Angola,' 14–21 January 1988.

Urdang, Stephanie. *And Still They Dance: Women, War, and the Struggle for Change in Mozambique.* New York: Monthly Review, 1989.

Vaitsos, Constantine. 'Crisis in Regional Economic Cooperation (Integration) among Developing Countries: A Survey,' *World Development* 6: 6 (June 1978). Reprinted in *Recent Issues In World Development: A Collection of Survey Articles.* Paul Streeten and Richard Jolly, eds. pp. 279–329. New York: Pergamon Press, 1981.

Vakakis and Assocs. 'Overview of Food Reserve and Food Aid Policies in SADCC Member States,' consultant interim report on Regional Food Reserve/Food Aid to SADCC Food Security Administrative Unit, June 1986.

Vale, Peter. 'Pretoria and Southern Africa: From Manipulation to Intervention,' *South African Review I.* Johannesburg Raven Press (1983): 6–22.

van Onselen, Charles. *Chibaro: African Mine Labour in Southern Rhodesia, 1900–1933.* London: Pluto Press, 1976.

Wagao, Jumanne. 'Trade Relations Among SADCC Countries,' Paper presented to SADCC Research Network on The Future of Africa, January 1986.

Wangwe, S. M. 'A Comparative Analysis of the PTA and SADCC Approaches to Regional Economic Integration,' *The Long-Term Perspective Study of Sub-Sahara Africa.* Volume 4: *Proceedings of a Workshop on Regional Integration and Cooperation.* Washington, DC: The World Bank, 1990.

Weiner, Daniel. 'Land and Agricultural Development.' *Zimbabwe's Prospects: Issues of Race, Class, State and Capital in Southern Africa.* Colin Stoneman, ed. London: Macmillan, 1988.

Whitsun Foundation, 'A Strategy for Rural Development and Data Bank No. 2: The Peasant Sector,' Harare, 1978.

Wheatcroft, Geoffrey. *The Randlords.* New York: Atheneum, 1986.

Wilson, Francis and Ramphele, Mamphela. *Uprooting Poverty: The South African Challenge.* New York: W.W. Norton and Company, 1989.

Winter, Roger. 'Refugees and Displaced Persons in Southern Africa,' Testimony before the U.S. Senate Subcommittee on Immigration and Refugee Affairs, 5 February 1987.

Wionczek, Miguel. 'Can Humpty-Dumpty Be Put Together Again and By Whom? Comments on the Vaitsos Survey,' *World Development* 6: 6 (June 1978): 779–82.

Wolpe, Harold. *Race, Class and the Apartheid State.* Paris: UNESCO Press, 1988.

Wood, Adrian P. and Shula, E.C.W. 'The State and Agriculture in Zambia: A Review of the Evolution and Consequences of Food and Agricultural Policies in a Mining Economy,' *The State and Agriculture in Africa.* Thandika Mkandawire and Naceur Bourenane, eds. Dakar: Codesria, 1987, pp. 272–316.

World Bank. *Ensuring Food Security in the Developing World: Issues and Options.* Washington, D.C.: World Bank, 1985.

————*World Development Report 1987.* New York: Oxford University Press, 1987.

————*Sub-Sahara Africa: From Crisis to Sustainable Growth.* Washington, DC: The World Bank, 1989.

————*World Development Report 1990: Poverty.* New York Oxford University Press, 1990.

————*The Long-Term Perspective Study of Sub-Sahara Africa.* Volume 4: *Proceedings of a Workshop on Regional Integration and Cooperation.* Washington, DC: The World Bank, 1990.

Wright, George V. 'US Foreign Policy and Destabilisation in Southern Africa,' *Review of African Political Economy*, nos. 45/46 (1989): 159–68.

Yates, Lawrence A. 'From Small Wars to Counterinsurgency: US Military Intervention in Latin America,' *Military Review* (February 1989): 74–86.

# Index

169

## 170 *Index*

Cabinda, 42
Cabo Delgado, 9, 13-17
Cahora Bassa dam, 30n, 42
Cairns, 91
Cambodia, 36
Camdessus, Michel, 105
Canada, 86, 96, 108, 126, 145
Cape Verde, 36
capitalism, 59, 65, 66, 76, 95, 105, 115, 128, 138, 139, 147, 149
CAPS Pharmaceuticals, 21
CARE, 40
Carter, Jimmy, 43, 52n
Casey, William, 36, 47
cassava, 7, 14, 88
cashews, 17, 62, 63, 103, 107
cattle, 7, 9, 10, 11, 12, 13, 17, 57, 60, 62, 68
Cattle Levy Act (1934), 12, 17
Central African Federation, 76, 97n
Central America, 27n, 31, 34, 45, 46 *see also* Latin America
Central American Common Market (CACM), 95
Central Intelligence Agency (CIA), 33, 34, 36, 42, 45, 46, 47, 48, 93
Chalimbana Research Station, 88
Chamber of Mines, 11
Chamorro, Edgar, 34
Chemical Bank, 115
Chemplex, 21, 147
Chicago Board of Trade, 126
children, 1, 8, 12, 13, 39, 45, 66, 67, 68, 69, 98n, 108, 116, 130n, 137 *see also* UNICEF
Chimoio, 84
Chobe, 62
Christianity, 35
Chrysler, 95
Citibank, 115
Citizens for America, 34
Clark Amendment, 36, 37
Clarke, Duncan, 92
Clarridge, Duane, 42, 46, 53n
coal, 19, 23, 56
coffee, 17, 18, 62, 64, 77, 83, 88, 104, 106, 107, 112, 122, 141
Cohen, Herman, 33
colonialism, 2, 3, 5, 7, 8, 9, 12, 13, 15, 16, 17, 18, 21, 23, 42, 51, 56, 59, 60, 61, 62, 63, 64, 69, 71, 76, 84, 85, 86, 90, 94, 97n, 103, 109, 133, 139, 140, 141
Colorado, 89
Commercial Farmers Union, 67
communism, 31, 32, 33, 34, 35, 37, 45, 47
Comoros, 36
Constellation of Southern African States (CONSAS), 5, 32, 41, 133
consultative technical committees (CTCs), 86
consumer goods, 22

contras, 35, 36, 37, 42, 45, 46, 48, 49
Co-op Lesotho, 66
Cooperative Federation, 65
cooperatives, 63, 65, 67, 79, 80, 103, 142
copper, 17, 20, 56, 57, 64, 107, 137
corruption, 45, 109, 141
Costa Rica, 45, 46
cotton, 14, 15, 16, 17, 22, 62, 63, 64, 77, 80, 84, 103, 104
Council for Inter-American Studies (CIS), 34
Council for Mutual Economic Assistance (CMEA), 65
counter-revolutions, 35, 36
Crane, Philip M., 34
Crocker, Chester, 40
Cuba, 6, 33, 34, 37, 38
Cuito Cuanavale, 37, 38

Dallara, Charles, 115
Dar es Salaam, 20, 146
Dar es Salaam corridor, 146
Dawkins, Maurice, 33
De Beers, 19, 72n
death squads, 46
debt, 44, 45, 104, 105, 107, 108, 113, 114, 115, 145
deforestation, 13, 16
Delta, 21, 91
Demery, Thomas, 53n
Denmark, 146, 148, 149; *see also* Scandinavia
destabilisation, 23, 25, 26, 27, 30n, 31-7, 39, 44, 56, 108, 147
development, 2, 3, 5, 7, 21, 23, 40, 44, 51, 61, 85-9, 92-6, 104, 115, 116, 119, 135, 136, 137, 139, 140, 144, 147, 149; African model for, 5
Dhilwayo, John, 126
diamonds, 18, 19, 56, 62
Directorate of Military Intelligence (DMI), 50
Dole, Robert, 40
Domoina cyclone, 24
Dondolo-Mndonzo, 79, 80
donor agencies, 2, 5, 69, 102, 103, 106, 109, 110, 115, 116, 117, 142
donor governments, 1, 3, 59, 93, 108, 117, 126, 127, 128, 136, 145
Dornan, Robert, 34
Dorowa Minerals, 147
drought, 5, 8, 9, 39, 43, 45, 57, 59, 61, 62, 64, 68, 69, 79, 90, 102, 106, 116, 121, 148
Durban, 20, 96
Dutton, Richard, 48

E B National Transformer, 147
Earl, Robert, 48
East Africa, 6, 145

**Zed Books Ltd**

is a publisher whose international and Third World lists span:

- **Women's Studies**
- **Development**
- **Environment**
- **Current Affairs**
- **International Relations**
- **Children's Studies**
- **Labour Studies**
- **Cultural Studies**
- **Human Rights**
- **Indigenous Peoples**
- **Health**

We also specialize in Area Studies where we have extensive lists in African Studies, Asian Studies, Caribbean and Latin American Studies, Middle East Studies, and Pacific Studies.

For further information about books available from Zed Books, please write to: Catalogue Enquiries, Zed Books Ltd, 57 Caledonian Road, London N1 9BU. Our books are available from distributors in many countries (for full details, see our catalogues), including:

**In the USA**
Humanities Press International, Inc., 165 First Avenue,
Atlantic Highlands, New Jersey 07716.
Tel: (201) 872 1441;
Fax: (201) 872 0717.

**In Canada**
DEC, 229 College Street, Toronto, Ontario M5T 1R4.
Tel: (416) 971 7051.

**In Australia**
Wild and Woolley Ltd, 16 Darghan Street, Glebe, NSW 2037.

**In India**
Bibliomania, C-236 Defence Colony, New Delhi 110 024.

**In Southern Africa**
David Philip Publisher (Pty) Ltd, PO Box 408, Claremont 7735,
South Africa.